Larbi Batma, Nass el-Ghiwane and Postcolonial Music in Morocco

Larbi Batma, Nass el-Ghiwane and Postcolonial Music in Morocco

LHOUSSAIN SIMOUR

Foreword by ALESSANDRA CIUCCI

McFarland & Company, Inc., Publishers
Jefferson, North Carolina

Library of Congress Cataloguing-in-Publication Data

Names: Simour, Lhoussain.
Title: Larbi Batma, Nass el-Ghiwane and postcolonial music in Morocco / Lhoussain Simour ; foreword by Alessandra Ciucci.
Description: Jefferson, North Carolina : McFarland & Company, 2016 | Includes bibliographical references and index.
Identifiers: LCCN 2016041853 | ISBN 9781476664149 (softcover : acid free paper) ♾
Subjects: LCSH: Popular music—Morocco—History and criticism. | Nass el Ghiwan (Musical group) | Bāṭmā, al-ʻArabī, 1948–1997.
Classification: LCC ML3503.M87 S56 2016 | DDC 781.630964—dc23
LC record available at https://lccn.loc.gov/2016041853

British Library cataloguing data are available

ISBN (print) 978-1-4766-6414-9
ISBN (ebook) 978-1-4766-2581-2

Front cover image of Nass el-Ghiwane by kind permission of Rachid Batma and Omar Sayed

Printed in the United States of America

McFarland & Company, Inc., Publishers
Box 611, Jefferson, North Carolina 28640
www.mcfarlandpub.com

Acknowledgments

I owe a debt of gratitude to all those who contributed in bringing this work to light. I am particularly indebted to Si Mohamed Hariba and his daughter Fatima Zahra, a student of mine whom I have taught for a couple of years and whose sister is currently engaged to one of Larbi Batma's brothers, for initiating the contact with Batma's family, namely with Rachid. I have been very fortunate to have the opportunity to meet Fatima Zahra in my class. She kindly offered to help when I once mentioned that I was working on Nass el-Ghiwane. In fact, she made the first contact with Batma's family easier than I would have ever managed to do alone. I would like to thank her and her father for their generous help and support in the last phases of the completion of this work.

I am grateful to Rachid Batma and Omar Sayed, from Nass el-Ghiwane, for their invaluable help. They both showed great interest in this project and encouraged me a lot. I would like to thank them so much, as they generously provided me with permissions to use the pictures of the members of the group in my book. I am deeply appreciative that they took time to meet with me on various occasions.

Professor Khalid Bekkaoui and Professor Sadik Rddad have always been a source of inspiration to me during my MA and PhD classes at the Moroccan Cultural Studies Center affiliated to Sidi Mohamd Abdellah University, Fez. Hassan Nejmi has also kindly motivated me to complete this work and offered constant encouragements and enthusiastic support.

I would also like to thank my family, particularly my parents, for their past and present enormous sacrifices, far greater than words could express. My intimate gratitude goes to my wife Assya, my kids, Lina, Walid and Anass for their warm support in the long course of the completion of this book. Their understanding and companionship helped me to achieve more than I would have believed possible.

My deep gratitude is extended to Professor Alessadra Ciucci for her pertinent remarks and feedback on the first draft of this work and for kindly accepting to write a foreword. I met Alessadra in Casablanca while she was doing fieldwork on a troupe of *'bidāt a-rmā* from Khouribga. Her reading and advice helped me clear up some confusion in the use of concepts pertaining to music. I would also like to thank her for initiating the contact with the International Council for Traditional Music and for supporting my membership as Liaison Officer for Morocco.

Finally, yet importantly, this book is dedicated to all those whom I have unintentionally overlooked to mention here.

Table of Contents

Acknowledgments v

Foreword by Alessandra Ciucci 1

Preface 3

Introduction 7

I. Disturbing the Canon: Non-Canonical Voices in Postcolonial Moroccan Writing 21

II. Narrating Marginality and Reinventing the Periphery: Larbi Batma's *Al-raḥīl* (The Departure) between Self-Narration, Individual Agony and National Allegory 35

III. Euphonious Voice(s) from the Margin: Nass el-Ghiwane and the Making of Alternative Popular Music 93

Conclusion 177

Discography 185

Chapter Notes 191

Bibliography 201

Index 209

Foreword
by Alessandra Ciucci

Mal kassi hzin mabin al-kissan?
(Why is my glass saddened among the other glasses?)

Anyone who has spent time in Morocco or who is interested in Morocco and its culture from afar, sooner or later will inevitably be exposed to the music of Nass el-Ghiwane. Although there is no dearth of information and writing on the influential role that Nass el-Ghiwane has played and continues to play in Morocco, this is the first monograph in the English language dedicated to a group whose sound reflected the intellectual, political, and artistic life of the time; a sound that revolutionized the Moroccan music scene and more.

Influenced by left-wing intellectuals and artists calling for the rediscovery and re-habilitation of a traditional culture based on orality and the vernacular, Nass el-Ghiwane experimented with Moroccan musical traditions ranging from a genre of sung poetry from the plains and plateaus (*'aiṭa*), to a genre of urban song traditionally performed in the all-male urban working-class milieus of craftsmen's guilds (*malḥūn*), to the music of the Atlas mountains, to that of religious fraternities such as the Gnawa, the 'Aissawa, and the Jilāla. Nass el-Ghiwane—along with hundreds of groups that followed its lead in the 1970s, including Jil Jilala, Lem Chaheb and Tagadda—embodied a Moroccan sound divested of any influence from 20th-century Egyptian music. By drawing upon the richness of Moroccan music, the group successfully synthesized the traditional and the popular, in what came to be referred to as the *phenomenon* of Nass el-Ghiwane. Also marked by European and American counter-culture and by the music associated with the youth movement of the time, Nass el-Ghiwane's infusion of the traditional into the contemporary scene was in conversation—albeit not necessarily a direct one—with similar musical experiments taking place throughout the

Mediterranean region, in those non–Anglophone countries that wished to shape their own popular music.

If Nass el-Ghiwane, as a group, changed the Moroccan music scene forever, the writings of its most charismatic member, Larbi Batma, may have been just as influential decades after the band's debut. In his "Ar-Raḥīl" (The Departure), a best seller since it was first published in 1995, Batma recounts his itinerary and that of Nass el-Ghiwane using a language that weaves the everyday Moroccan vernacular into the more formal standard Arabic, a writing style meant to recall Batma's own voice and that of his generation. "Ar-Rahīl," which depicts the life of Batma and of a thriving artistic scene in Casablanca where music, poetry, visual arts, and theater were inseparable, cemented the idea of Nass el-Ghiwane as a cultural phenomenon that went beyond sound. By depicting his life and that of a group of young men living in one of the marginalized working-class neighborhoods built by the French colonial authority for rural migrants who moved to Casablanca, Batma's "Ar-Rahīl," just as Nass el-Ghiwane had done decades before, expressed the spirit of a young generation that became a major force in Morocco during the 1970s and beyond.

In this book Lhoussain Simour allows us to understand the impact of Nass el-Ghiwane through Batma's "Ar-Rahīl" and through his own experience with the group, as a Moroccan who was brought up with the words and sounds of Nass el-Ghiwane and as a scholar of Moroccan culture. By weaving the personal and the academic together, this book gives us a rare insight into what Nass el-Ghiwane meant and continues to mean for Moroccans.

Alessandra Ciucci is an assistant professor of music at Columbia University (and a Mellon post-doctoral fellow in the Music Department, 2008–2010). Her research interests include the music of Morocco, North Africa and the Mediterranean, music and gender, sung poetry, and popular music of the Arab world.

Preface

Nass el-Ghiwane, transliterated in Arabic as "Nāss al-Ghīwān," is a Moroccan musical group that emerged in the 1970s as an exceptional musical adventure in Ḥay Moḥammādi, Casablanca, where the experience took place for the first time. The group started initially with a lineup of five musicians and artists who had already begun their career as professional theatrical performers. Larbi Batma, Omar Sayed, Boujemaa Ahagour (known as Boujemia), Allal Yaala and Moulay Abdeaziz Tahiri, who was later replaced by Abderrahman Paco, initiated an unprecedented and a remarkable musical experience in contemporary Morocco that has influenced the artistic landscape for years now. These artists were inspired by various existing Moroccan musical genres and created an alternative music that articulates and combines both traditional rhythms and musical genres with social and political concerns such as corruption, discrimination, humiliation, frustration and contempt in the post-independence era. These concerns inform the poetic diction of the group and remain at the genesis of the social, political, cultural and social inequalities that have plagued postcolonial Morocco for decades.

The group's musical repertoire expresses a great deal of social engagement with Morocco's socio-political and economic situation in the neocolonial era. It has revolutionized postcolonial Moroccan and North African music and left an indelible mark on the country's cultural landscape through the group's committed music. This musical orientation has been fueled by influences from the country's rich musical styles, through the powerful rhythms played with Moroccan traditional instruments, and through the poetic lyrics that reflect the discomfort of young Moroccans of the time. As Hassan Nejmi once said, Nass el-Ghiwane cannot be viewed as just a musical phenomenon in Morocco, but it is the "testing center that came out of the womb of history in order to reconstruct history."[1] Unfortunately, the group has not received the recognition it deserves from academic circles and has largely been overlooked by university scholars writing in foreign languages. This degree of historical denial is what has first and foremost incited me to look back at the experience of the group. This humble contribution attempts to rethink the position of Nass el-Ghiwane and its members in Moroccan literary, musical and cultural canon.

Martin Scorsese, the Hollywood film director, has once referred to the group as the "Rolling Stones of Morocco," an appellation that I am not comfortable with, though Scorsese might have meant to consider Nass el-Ghiwane's legacy equivalent in status and influence to that of the Rolling Stones in rock music. The epithet needs consideration. Defining the group through a western musical referential minimizes and freezes Nass el-Ghiwane's subjectivity and cultural identity. Such appellation which identifies the group not by its own cultural distinctiveness but from the Self's perspective, as defined in Edward Said's paradigm, (mis)represents, if not displaces and excludes any promising potentials to build up the Other's genuine musical identity and belonging. Why would not the epithet be inversed and turned upon itself to become something like "Nass el-Ghiwane of England," or "Nass el-Ghiwane of America"? This issue would certainly call for an insightful discussion on how the Western mindset in the ideological construction of Otherness perpetuates discourses that attempt to domesticate difference and assimilate histories, developments, cultures and identities.

On a cold winter, two years ago, while driving across Zerktouni Boulevard in Casablanca for a quick family errand, I turned right to avoid a traffic jam and found myself in *Rue Oran* Street (Zanqat Wahrān) where Larbi Batma used to live. I parked few blocks away and came back walking in the rain and stood in front of his former home. I forgot about the errand as a chain of memories cropped up in my mind. The first was when I first met Batma at Moulay Abdellah hospital in Rabat early 1994. I still remember the few words we exchanged while he was lying in bed with a syrum hanged to his left hand. I went back to my car, took my bag and headed towards a nearby coffee shop. I opened my laptop and started to write few sentences on his *Al-raḥīl*. Everyday, when time allows, I go to the same coffee shop and write, sometimes for more than six hours a day. It has been two years now and I am still in the same coffee shop, not far from where Batma lived, completing this book.

Fortunately, Batma has left an autobiographical account in two volumes—they offer rich background on both postcolonial Morocco and postcolonial Moroccan subjectivities that have sprung from the underground arenas of oblivion and denial. I have tried to read his *Al-raḥīl* and *Al-Alam* from a cultural studies standpoint. Both works came out with *Toubkal* Publishing in Casablanca and took me into a wonderful journey of investigation while trying to read them.

While completing this book, I received an unexpected phone call from Professor Hassan Nejmi, a Moroccan scholar who has written extensively on

Moroccan popular music over the past few years. Nejmi was planning to start an Association of Moroccan scholars working on Moroccan traditional music, and kindly asked if I would join. This made me feel confident about the level of academic interest in Moroccan music. Yet what struck me about Nejmi's conversation was the fact that Moroccan universities, unlike others around the world, have little in the way of established departmental study of music or ethnomusicology. This needs to be implemented as one of the best ways of preserving and promoting the cultural heritage of music across the country for generations to come. In that spirit, this book will serve as a reference for researchers interested in Moroccan popular music in general and in Nass el-Ghiwane's music in particular.

In the course of this endeavor, I met with Omar Sayed and Rachid Batma to get permissions to use the group's pictures. Rachid is an extraordinary artist who incarnates the Ghiwani spirit. I had to travel to Ḥay Moḥammādi on a hot sunny September day to meet with him. He lives with his family in Ain Sebaa, a neighboring quarter, but spends most of his evenings with neighborhood friends in Ḥay Moḥammādi. Rachid, to my surprise, looks exactly like his late brother Larbi—a humble man of medium build with curly thick hair, thick moustache and radiant smile. We talked for a while but we would often be interrupted by greetings from passers-by. He suggested moving to his car, in the presence of his friend Mr. Belkaid, where we sat for a while. I talked to him about the project and he was so excited about it. He suggested that his brother's books should also be translated into English and other foreign languages. He talked about the years he spent with him in hospital. I handed in the permissions that he kindly signed and we left each other.

Omar Sayed is an exceptional artist and "philosopher." When I met him, he seemed to have grown older than I really imagined he was. We planned to meet in a coffee shop downtown, but he soon suggested meeting him at home. Omar came to meet me—an old man with grey hair, holding a cane and moving slowly across Mustapha el-Maani Street. On the way home, he said that sadness about the death of his daughter, Siham, is still looming around his home. He always wears a shirt with picture of her whenever Nass el-Ghiwane plays on concert. We went in and he showed me the portraits hanging around his small apartment overlooking the main street—Nass el-Ghiwane, Boujemaa, Michael Jackson (his daughter's favorite singer) and many of Siham's, of course. We sat together and started our discussion. He first mentioned that he is working on a documentary film about his daughter; he then talked about Martin Scorcese, about *al-hāl* and about many technical issues in music, about Allal's skills and Paco's unsurpassed "*Tagnāwit*." When I mentioned Larbi Batma, he sighed and said that Larbi was really an exception in the group. Omar, like many fans of the group, seemed enthralled by Larbi's voice: "Whenever Larbi talks, you would simply feel that he is singing …

there is music in his voice. I always said to him that your voice is not attuned with your body; your voice is quite stronger than your body.... Larbi always sang what he felt." We both then evoked the urgent need to archive the whole repertoire of Nass el-Ghiwane, to which Omar showed great interest. In discussing a small section of *Ṣiniya*, he suggests translating the poem as "le plaisir de partager" (the pleasure to share), and not "the tray." Here of course, I became aware that the man is conscious about the transformations that literal translations could bring to Nass el-Ghiwane's songs. We both agreed on meeting again, but next time with students at the University to talk about his forthcoming documentary film *Sihām, aw al-ḥuzn al-jamīl* [Siham, or the Wonderful Sadness].

Introduction

Culture, as a set of meanings and as a human subjective construct, is an intricate and varied concept encompassing various discursive terrains of individual interactions and practices that shape a particular identity and perpetuate a sense of belonging. In his essay on culture and development, Mbakogu describes the multifaceted concept of culture as embracing

> all the material and nonmaterial expressions of a people as well as the processes with which the expressions are communicated. It has to do with all the social, ethical, intellectual, scientific, artistic, and technological expressions and processes of a people usually ethically and/or nationally or supra-nationally related, and usually living in a geographically contiguous area.[1]

This, preliminary discussion, broad as it seems, does not aim at delimiting or marking out the historical and the sociological implications of the intricacies of Moroccan popular culture; for this endeavor is demanding and would entail years of painstaking research. What I am mainly concerned with here is mapping out, in a general way, some challenging issues that Moroccan popular culture strives to raise. My intention is to bring forward some defining features of the Moroccan cultural landscape. Yet, before moving further it's important to draw a distinction between the use of the word "popular" in English and the meanings it conveys in Moroccan vernacular (*Dārija*).

In Moroccan *Dārija*, a "popular" person does not necessarily have to be widely known or "successful" to be popular; it can simply refer to someone who is thought of as belonging to or being from and for the people. In the Moroccan sense of the word, the "popular" connotes meanings of belongingness, modesty and humbleness. Popular culture is a social and cultural phenomenon that represents a community's shared roots and modes of expression.

Popular culture, accordingly, is about collective representations of ways of living, a community's desires, beliefs and vision of itself. The popular can be defined as relating to or indicative of a community's understanding and taste about widely accepted practices within a social system, whereby meanings and pleasures are generated and circulated actively. Hence, my use of "popular" in this discussion differs from its Anglophone meanings. I associate it with the specific social processes that are generated from the frequently encountered and widespread cultural practices in multiple expressive registers that are commonly known all over the country as "*Sha'bīya*," that is to mean "popular," and which contribute to the definition of the notion of Moroccaness and Moroccan identity.

In the Anglophone tradition, Stuart Hall has provided the most continuing legacy in theorizing the popular. He has argued that we cannot understand what "the popular" stands for at any given historical moment except by placing it in its broader cultural context; that is to say, in relation to those categories with which it is in opposition, in parallel, or in accordance. Hall conceives of the popular as a huge battlefield that integrates complex dialectics of resistance and acceptance, refusal and retreat. Hence, popular culture is in a state of constant transformation, its elements moving incessantly between resistance and appropriation. For him, popular culture is defined as the "ground on which the transformations are worked."[2] In fact, the notion of the popular cannot be understood independently of the political and social meanings it inscribes. As opposed to unpopular culture, or elite culture, popular culture usually implies the existence of an otherness that grapples with and challenges asymmetrical relations of power within a given culture.

Morocco is a country of profound diversity wherein cultural transformations remain powerful enough to turn the country's culture into varied but not divided entity. Intricate and complex physical and social features govern Moroccan life where the traditional and the modern are intertwined. In describing cultural patterns in the country, John Entelis states that "the historically determined, traditionally rooted and colonially encouraged axes crosscutting Moroccan society are no longer salient [...] urban-rural, sedentary-nomadic, secular-religious, and Arab-Berber differences remain as socioanthropological categories relevant to daily existence."[3]

Rather than being viewed as conflicting components, these axes are best understood as complementary parts of a single cultural tradition. Differences based on distinctive ethnic and cultural identities in the country have very narrow implications for the integrity of national identity and nation-state. In fact, from the outset, one can notice that Moroccan culture falls within three outstanding categories or constituents that have complemented and fed one another for centuries now. The Amazīgh (Berber) cultural legacy that had started years before Islam was introduced in Morocco by the Idrissid dynasty in the seventh century. The Arabs who arrived in Morocco took political power and started a process of Arabization that contributed in changing the ethnic makeup of the population, the language and the culture. Abbas al-Jirari, a renowned academic scholar, has stated that *Tamazīght* as a crucial constituent of Moroccan culture "still beats in the hearts and flows in them with liveliness."[4] The Arab cultural heritage with its Eastern features, Andalucian Moriscos culture, *Ṭarab al-Ḥassāni* from Moroccan Sahara, and the African roots altogether became one of the most influential and prominent sources that has enriched, strengthened and opened new perspectives for the Amazīgh heritage as well. Finally, foreign influences from colonial empires, namely European ones, added to the cultural landscape of the country, had both positive and negative effects on Moroccan culture.[5] According to Tarik Sabry,

> Al-Jirari excludes Moroccan Jewish heritage and its contribution to Moroccan popular culture. Jews, although a small minority in Moroccan society, have lived in Morocco for more than two thousand years—before the coming of Arabs or Islam. Their contribution to Moroccan culture, especially music and artisan craftsmanship was invaluable and must be neither ignored nor excluded. A thorough understanding of the make up of Moroccan popular culture is only possible through a critical historico-structural analysis that explores the structure of each *constituent* element, then studies that part of the whole that is the product of these very different elements' interaction, interference and coexistence.[6]

In fact talking about Moroccan culture is also taking into consideration all the constituents already mentioned and which constitute the cultural mosaic of the country as a whole, including the Jewish legacy and contribution, the Mediterranean tradition and its influences. The cultural heterogeneity of the Moroccan cultural fabric would not be endorsed and recognized "were it to exclude, alienate or suppress any constituent or contributing element, for whatever ideological reasons, for this would defeat the whole point of this intellectual exercise."[7] Actually, this intellectual exercise needs to be undertaken cautiously in reflecting about Moroccan popular culture since Moroccan culture is textured with overlapping convergences of various inclinations, fashions and styles representing different official, non-official, dominant, and subordinate voices within the country. Hence, to speak of Moroccan popular culture as one single homogeneous entity, without highlighting the ramifications of identity slippages inherent in the discursive and cultural construction of the nation, is to mask the particularities of the very voices heard or unheard that make up Moroccan popular culture, and conceal thereafter the dialectics of power relations at work within Moroccan society. As Abdassamad Belkbir observed in his article "on the meaning of popular culture,"

> What is considered popular culture in the *Rif* [northern part of Morocco] has no relation with popular culture in *Sous* [south Berber Morocco], *Jbāla* [mountainous area in the north of Morocco], Fez or in the East of Morocco.... What unites us nationally is not popular culture but religion, the modern state and institutions linked to it such us political parties, trade unions ... etc.[8]

Thus, it is inconceivable to think of a single and unique popular culture in the Moroccan context. Moroccan society is made up of various streams and diverse orientations that turn it into an amalgam of popular cultures. This assortment of different popular cultures that grapple with one another, most of the times in asymmetrical relations of power within one unified discourse over the nation, is what makes it exceptionally diverse in its construction. There is, for example, the popular culture of the *'aroubi*, pejoratively referring to people of Arab descent, depreciative of the peasantry's mode of life. The *'aroubi* is mostly associated with a popular music genre called *Sha'bi*. The *Fāssi* culture is also another component of the popular in Morocco that cannot pass unnoticed. The *Fāssi*, basically from Fez, but which can refer to anybody adopting a high and elitist culture in taste, esthetics and behavior. People from Fez or people aspiring to become *Fāssi* appreciate Andalucian music and *Malḥūn*, unlike the *'aroubi* who only finds ample delight in the vibrating rhythms connected with the countryside. On the other hand, there is the Amazīgh or *Shelḥ*, who appreciates *Amazīgh* music; the Riffian, or *Jebli* from *Jbāla*, the Northern parts of Morocco who is commonly known for musical inclination towards *Taqṭuqa* and its derivatives. There is the *Saḥrāwi* from Southern Morocco who is famous for *Ṭarab al-Ḥassāni* with its highly sophisticated poetry. As Sabry has mentioned,

> The stratification of tastes in Moroccan popular culture into those of the *'aroubi*, *Shelḥ*, *Fāssi* reflects power relations within Moroccan society. The *'aroubi* and the *Shelḥ*'s 'popular' tastes are seen as inferior to those of the *Fāssi* who appreciates Andalusian music and the 'modern' who reads Balzac, speaks with a Parisian accent, maybe listens to jazz and tunes to TV5 for a round of News.[9]

These systematic categories are challengingly complex as they go beyond any fixties; they overlap and can even be contradictory. Such overlapping terrains of esthetics have produced a kaleidoscopic and a heterogeneous popular music covering different parts of the country called *al-Sha'bī*, or "the popular" as would be translated. It is, in fact, the most popular musical orientation appreciated and widely listened to over the country since it is transmitted through a common linguistic medium, which is *Dārija* (Moroccan vernacular), and also since its rhythms and musical standards are based on local and traditional instruments.

Within this broader field of research, my interest revolves around questions about the dynamics of popular culture, the politics of music and literary esthetics that inform the study of popular culture, and which emerged from underground arenas of creativity and artistic taste in post-colonial Morocco. The study of popular cultural production entails studying popular music as well. While this would appear to be an incontrovertible claim, and following the lead of Roy Shuker in his *Understanding Popular Music*,[10] much writing on popular music tends to treat music in isolation from the literature on the general field within which it is historicized and contextualized. The main concern here is with popular culture as a social phenomenon in contemporary Moroccan society and with music as one of its main aesthetic facets.

In the past few years of the twenty-first century, the scholars' concern about the dynamic interaction of the politics of the local and the global, its involvement in the production, dissemination and reception of popular culture, has developed various ways of looking at culture. One consequence of this new orientation claims that conceptualizations of national narratives and nationalist ideologies have been relegated to a second-hand position in a world increasingly dominated by the processes of globalization, deterritorialization, and other forms of cultural hybridity. Yet, the importance of national popular culture remains a crucial component for understanding how cultural texts and practices operate in forging personal and collective identities and memories.

This book deals with Nass el-Ghiwane as a legendary musical group in Moroccan culture, and with Larbi Batma, the founding member of the group, through his autobiographical work *Al-raḥīl* (the Departure). It attempts to investigate how conceptions of music, as an intricate form of human expression and understanding, have informed popular cultural expressions and practices in post-independence Morocco. It also tries to look at how both the making and appreciation of music are critically bound up with musical practices that partake of, and help in the formation and construction of, identity distinctiveness and belonging, and also at how representations of class in Moroccan popular music are deployed to articulate signifiers of authenticity.

The understanding of musical genres and of musical expression by listeners and performers fosters affiliation with national belonging and provides clues as to how crucial cultural identity and discourses about musical practices are understood and mediated. In light of popular and cultural discourses delineating the expressive potentials of music in forging the lives of human beings, their sensibilities and belongingness, the issues undertaken in this work raise concerns, among others, about the importance of music in the construction of individual, national and pan-national ideologies and identities. It also attempts to understand the intriguing relationships and connections between the social processes that defined post-independence Morocco in the reconstruction of national identity that witnessed disintegration because of colonial encroachments and conflict over power and wealth in the postcolony. It also attempts to offer a reading of the artistic experience ensued by Nass el-Ghiwane through their individual efforts, artistic creativity, and collective performance.

This research endeavor starts from the premise that considers Nass el-Ghiwane's poetic text, lyrics, melodies, rhythms and subject matters an esthetic objective correlative to the notion of Moroccanness wherein integrated Arabo-Amazīgh, Islamic, individual and national identities are musically defined and expressed. The significance of Moroccan music and musical practices, as is the case with other music(s) of the world, lies in its cultural prowess in transmitting communal and national beliefs and in shaping spaces, places and selves. Musical practices construct, deconstruct and reconstruct cultural imaginaries by negotiating and inventing identities, social margins and epistemological boundaries to promote imaginative and "infinite horizons"[11] wherein individuals and communities orient and disorient their identities within the contradictory sites of cultural practices. Being musically Moroccan means looking at musical practices in their totality as a homogeneous entity that incorporates oral-based musical and cultural expressions and practices as well. These are powerful enough in the Moroccan context as they denote plurality that empowers identity for national unity. Hence, being musically Moroccan is also articulating identity within cultural junctures that serve in constructing narratives of community and in promoting collective memory formation whereby the individual's sense of being and belonging is defined, negotiated and challenged.

Earlier in the twentieth century, Morocco was exposed to a variety of mass media outlets and to immediate contact with musical cultures from global colonial powers, namely Spain and France, which affected and unsettled local musical esthetics and musical performances in the country. In addition, audiences were exposed to new forms of musical genres from neighboring countries, especially European and Middle Eastern ones. The aesthetic knowledge of both the musician and the audience was thus enriched with more musical tastes that were strange to Moroccan culture, but very enriching and empowering as well. Yet, few years later, and after independence from the French, changes in Moroccan musical landscape occurred as new artistic alternatives emerged and new genres established themselves as vehicles that disseminated discourses about identity construction and cultural belonging.

This book looks closely at the emergence of an alternative genre of Moroccan popular music pioneered by Nass el-Ghiwane during the 1970s and early 1980s, at a time when traditional Moroccan music that impacted profoundly on Moroccans received little artistic recognition. Nass el-Ghiwane and their *Ghiwanian* music in Morocco was at the forefront of the Maghreb's musical landscape of late twentieth century, and has played an important role in the construction of Moroccan national culture. Their music refers to a wide range of associations for Moroccan low and middle classes, such as connections to roots, unspoiled pasts, social and political confusions, and in some cases a distinct identity filiation. Through the blending of a variety of Moroccan musical forms and practices, Nass el-Ghiwane, as popular musicians, created a new musical style that was simultaneously novel yet deeply rooted in Moroccan folk music and which was also geared towards asserting claims to authenticity and roots. From this perspective, the group reshaped and re-drew the boundaries of Moroccan popular music, and offered a new disruptive esthetic style of expression that enthralled Moroccans for long. Hence, what do the analysis of the experience and a re-reading of the history of Nass el-Ghiwane tell us about changes in postcolonial Moroccan society, including the social, cultural and political topographies? Building upon scholarship on Moroccan popular music that has considered Nass el-Ghiwane's artistic experience, this work examines the emergence of "the Ghiwanian song," or *al-Ūghniya al-Ghīwāniya*, as a distinct and alternative musical genre. It deals with the complex cultural ramifications from which it emerged, the social conditions that fostered its growth as a musical movement, its musical characteristics, and the visionary lyrical esthetics that drove it to become an established musical legacy for over forty years now.

Looking at the experience of Nass el-Ghiwane from a cultural studies perspective also entails looking at the group's members and their artistic and literary achievements. This work also attempts to read *Al-raḥīl*, a narrative about the life experience of one of the charismatic leaders of the group. Larbi Batma (1948–1997), the founding member of Nass el-Ghiwane, who devotedly investigated Moroccan folklore and brought substantial amounts of obscure poetry and music to mainstream awareness, documented his life story in two volumes, both of which were written when he was diagnosed with lung cancer in 1993 before he passed away in 1997. Through the workings of memory, Batma revisits his past and blurs the boundaries between fact and fiction, text and image, imagination and reality to (re)construct a narrative that sheds lights on cultural and social issues that plagued post-independent Morocco. Interestingly enough, his autobiographical account offers ample grounds for the discussion of Morocco's underground spaces peopled by marginalized voices that sought redemption and retreat in artistic forms in order to lay bare the ordeals and anguishes of a postcolony in disillusionment. Batma's text is a rich narrative that documents not only a life story and experience but also a particular historical juncture in contemporary Morocco.

The idea of this book developed because of personal and scholarly motives. Writing about the experience of Nass el-Ghiwane is a project that I had in mind years ago when I first came in real contact with their music in a boarding house as a Higher School student and while living on-campus as a university student in the last decade of the 1980s. In fact, as is certainly the case with Moroccans of my generation living away from the glamors of city life, I first discovered Nass el-Ghiwane's music earlier in my life when I was a seven or eight year-old school boy in a rural part of Morocco, a mountainous Berber village with hardly any means of entertainment except the after-school football matches or the moving cinema, "wall cinema" as we used to call it since the films were always projected at night or late afternoons in the open against a smooth wall of a *Cantina* (bar) left by the French. This flat wall, painted white, served as a projection screen. The moving cinema came from time to time to the village to show American western films, Asian Kung-Fu movies or Indian romances. In my boyhood, the delight I derived was not only from those movies that I seldom paid for because it was difficult for me to save few coins to watch the films, but it was also, and to a greatest level, from the amplified music played before the projection of the films. In the afternoons, the announcement of the movie was often done through a shabby car touring the small village. After each announcement, music was played loudly. That very music was little bit strange to me, but very powerful in the effect it had on me at that time. I later discovered that it was Nass el-Ghiwane's. The rhythms echoed in that music were beating deep within the memory of the Amazīgh native I am, and who, in that period, was still learning the Moroccan *Dārija*. Language made no difference after all because in those melodies and musical rhythms that came from the amplified devices there was something more commanding and very impressive than words could ever express. No matter what one's ethnic background in Morocco is, Nass el-Ghiwane's music, though not fully understood, is appreciated. In my case, the first contact with this music was in the small village where I grew up, and it would always remind me of the stiffness and roughness of the countryside where I spent most of my childhood. Later on, when I fully became immersed in the Ghiwani rhythms, and under such wonderful spell of the band's music, connections with my past would come up spontaneously whenever I engaged in a ritual of listening; I mean there is something in this music that triggers feelings about connectedness and roots.

Nass el-Ghiwane's music takes me back home, to the countryside, to the essence of rural life in Morocco. It reminds me of the river I used to cross to get to a Koranic school; of the evening gatherings with my grandmother lulling me to sleep with her never-ending stories; of my family's sheep at sunset; of my mother milking goats and cows late in the afternoon; of the late-afternoon smoke and bread smell coming out of the kitchen; of the soil's smell; of the birds singing; of the cocks and hens in the barn; of the Autumn ploughing time and the harvest in summer; of my mother taking me to a nearby shrine to get the *Baraka* (blessings) and be cured of sturdy fevers I used to have. Nass el-Ghiwane's music reminds me of everything that embodies rurality in its uncontaminated and unaffected state.

The appreciation of Nass el-Ghiwane's music has grown and matured over the years and has had a tremendous impact not only on me but on my generation as well. Delusion kept inscribing my thoughts but the Ghiwani reverberations remained through such wonderful songs as *ṣiniya* (the tray), wherein the Ghiwani poet offers symbolic imageries and strong metaphorical visualization and representation of the tray as an icon of Moroccan cultural identity. Such representations highlight the collective imagination about communal beliefs and shared histories:

fin li jam'ū 'lik hal niya ?
dūk li wansūk, fin hal al-jūd o-rdā ...
wāldiya ntrajākūm la tlomūni f al-blya
bahr al-ghīwane madkhaltū bl'ani[12]

Where are those who gathered around you?
Those who kept you company, men of good faith
Generous and blessed as they are [...]
O my parents do not blame me for the passion
The Giwani spirit is not mere pretense.

To go further into the motivation behind this work, it is also worth emphasizing the scarcity of research on Nass el-Ghiwane's experience by Moroccans in Moroccan Departments of English. Research in Moroccan academic circles on the music and songs of this band often deals with few aspects that overlap with more general issues about popular music or folk songs without taking Nass el-Ghiwane as a separate component or exclusive focus for research and investigation. This academic shortage and research scarcity have contributed to some extent in the choice of the topic for my book. Likewise, and as the songs of the band were not documented by researchers before, the publication of *Klām al-Ghīwan* (The Ghiwani Lyrics), a collection of Ghiwanian poems by Omar Sayed and the appearance of Larbi Batma's autobiography *Al-raḥīl*, which both give insights into this rich and worthy artistic experience, have been at the heart of my motivation. Hassan Nejmi reflects on *Klām al-Ghīwan* and states that undoubtedly the book about the lyrical poems

> is a new venue to research studies that have not successfully been able to delineate the powerful meanings and singularity of the Ghiwanian songs. Perhaps this was due to the inaccessibility of researchers to the texts and poems in uncompromised and undistorted ways. This lyrical text will certainly help in completing studies about Nass el-Ghiwane.[13]

In fact, this collection of poems has largely contributed in clearing up some linguistic confusion about the lexicon and the lyrical jargon used in the Ghiwanian songs, and will certainly give future generations the possibility of understanding and appreciating the experience of Nass el-Ghiwane as a cultural and artistic Moroccan phenomenon. On the other hand, it will also enable academic researchers interested in folk music of the 1970s and early 80s-Morocco to clearly identify the poetic, the musical and the performative elements and images that permeate the band's art, lyrics and music, and which are in turn prompted by an oral tradition. Actually, Orality is an outstanding constituent of Moroccan culture. It is a valuable outlet of knowledge that constitutes a strong vehicle of cultural values. Oral poems and tales, for example, symbolically embody traditional standards, principles and understanding that have carefully been well-maintained and passed over to generations of Moroccans for centuries. Besides being a medium of expression, orality in the Moroccan context is powerful enough in the construction of identity and authenticity. Languages in Morocco, Arabic vernacular and Amazīgh, function as a central source for constructing and reconstructing Moroccan identity, a process in which orality still plays a pivotal role. As Fatima Sadiqi has clearly pointed out,

> The unique place of orality in Morocco is largely due to the fact that the two mother tongues used in this country (that is, Moroccan Arabic and Berber) are mainly oral. The tight link between non-written mother tongues and orality positions the latter at the center of the Moroccan speech community's sensory experience. As such, orality becomes a powerful system of communication that deeply shapes the way visual and non-visual representations of cultural roles [...] are constructed, maintained and perpetuated.[14]

Thus, *Klām al-Ghīwan* as a text has managed to transfer the inherited tradition of orality characteristic of Nass el-Ghiwane's language into a textual transcript that will help easily and accurately to get access to the myriad significances of a purely Moroccan colloquial jargon as used by the band. Nass el-Ghiwane's movement as a purely Moroccan singular musical experience appeared within ambiguous contexts, both locally and globally, flared up by the predicaments of a post-colonial order and by protests in a rapidly changing world. It was time of revolutionary and expressive movements around the world that gave rise to the Beatles, the Rolling Stones, Jim Morrison, Elvis Presley, Bob Marley ... etc., wherein ambivalence and ambiguity of meanings and hierarchies became forceful questions that found ample expression in music and arts. In the Moroccan context, as Hanoun Mbarek states, it was "a laden condition that concurrently needed a blasting music" and which brought the music of Nass el-Ghiwane from the margins to turn it into a chemical recipe about post-independent Morocco. For Salah Cherki, Nass el-Ghiwane "have come to attract the masses' attention and to shift attention away from other occidental musical genres," acknowledging that "we must pay tribute to them for the very simple reason that they have definitely refused the foreign influence."[15]

So, from the ember-tattooed memory of the local, and from marginal sites often relegated to oblivion, emerged the Ghiwanian experience to sculpt the groans inherent in Moroccan traditional music. Nass el-Ghiwane deployed wounded-like rhetoric and a diction of frustration to write about the despair, doubt and uncertainties, the sorrows of the everyday life in post-colonial Morocco. Their distinctive Ghiwani mode, as the name of the band has borne for decades now, suggests a state of esteem and adulation, a ceremonial mode of being and becoming, a condition of the wanderer's spirit and of the possessed bodies by mystical powers.

Nass el-Ghiwane's movement and rhythms became widely spread in various parts of Morocco and beyond borders as well during the seventies of the last century. Every neighborhood in the country had its own band inspired by and constructed through a Ghiwani-fashion. These bands also addressed the social issues plaguing Moroccan society such as corruption, poverty, hypocrisy, rural migration, exploitation and abuse of power. The Ghiwani rhythms and tunes are collective. They are conveyed through musical instruments that bear and voice out symbolic meanings of identity filiation. Their voice, in its literal and metaphorical ramifications, is a complex mixture of intricate melodies tuned up to capture the rhetoric of *Al-'ayṭa* (Moroccan popular music) in its authentic and most spontaneous implications. The lyrics are simple but express a profundity of thought that echoes marginality and destitution. They also echo identity and belonging, authenticity and roots nurtured by a musical repertoire about the "self." They are free of stereotypes and destructive descriptions but they are loaded with vivid Sufi and spiritual significances that resonate with the wisdoms of everyday-life inherent in Moroccan oral tradition.

Nass el-Ghiwane as members of the band and as avant-garde artists who have been battling against social injustice have never been involved in revolutionary struggles or demonstrations as such. Their struggle has been practiced through art; a visionary struggle for self-affirmation and self-definition best epitomized by their *Wāsh ḥna-homā ḥna?* (Are we these we are?).

> *wāsh ḥna-homā ḥna, ya galbī ūlla mūḥāl*
> *wash denyā hakdā, ya galbī ūlla mūḥāl*
> *manwīt zmān yaghdār wi-tbadāl al-ḥāl*
> *manwīt nās tbī' 'āzhā b-al māl*[16]
>
> are we those we are, or maybe not
> is this how life is, maybe not
> never did I know about time's betrayal, nor did I know about the change
> never did I know people would sell their pride

This song, among many others, articulates individual identities in complex overlappings; a quest for the self at a specific Moroccan historical juncture tyrannized by cultural and socio-political concussions and vibrations felt both through the colonial experience and the postcolonial condition. The metaphor comes full circle when we understand that the Ghiwanian songs and experience do not compromise esthetics for social and political causes, neither do alleged meanings get dissipated for the sake of art in their repertoires. The esthetic expression in Nass el-Ghiwane's musical and artistic movement has always been mobilized to serve meanings so that these meanings contribute to the construction of the overall esthetics of their texts. In fact, the esthetic fabric of the Ghiwanian text allows readers and listeners to grasp a distinctive style that moves beyond musical boundaries to represent spatial and contextual fragments of Moroccan society weighed down by post-colonial anxieties and frustrations.

At the artistic level, Nass el-Ghiwane's songs aspire to construct an artistic space overwhelmed by allusive images, symbols and metaphors that endow the lyrical texture with powerful implications. The text, hence, becomes open to various interpretations whereby images become bestowed with motion and speak of themselves in clearer terms. The in-built dialogical constructions in the Ghiwanian song move across various popular rhythms of the country and never fail their destinations. They are meant to pile up issues that need to be understood, grasped and reflected upon by the listener. The song in its structure in the Ghiwanian tradition features various ontological, existential and psychological facets that build up into an accumulative set of issues wherein remorse, melancholy, despair and depression find ample expression.

The book is divided into three parts. The first part reflects on issues pertaining to Moroccan popular culture, especially in arts and literature. It is a prolegomena to the study of Moroccan culture and revolves around literary and artistic production in post-colonial Morocco. In fact, just few decades after independence, the 1970s witnessed an intensification of social and political conflicts in Morocco and it was evident that the ideological and political discourses about nation-building failed to resist the accelerated transformations of Moroccan society. Inspired by an overheated reality, artistic production and narrative writing developed thematic concerns that revolved around the questioning of the social and political condition of the country. Most literary writings and artistic innovations were geared towards the quest for liberated horizons free of readily made conceptual classifications that characterized the country's esthetics for long.

The social and political conditions of the country after independence furnished ample grounds for marginal voices to emerge. Their writings resonated with provocative and foreclosed issues that raise existential, moral, political, religious, ideological, and esthetic questions through the capturing of details of mundane life. In fact, post-independence Moroccan writers that wrote from the margin brought new intriguing questions as immediate outcome of the inability of national elites to translate reality in clearer meanings. Failure to interrogate reality by the big narratives of nation-building project created a generation of writers whose writings were committed to literature as truth and worries, as facts and doubtful concerns. They addressed issues fraught with anxiety about subjectivity within a neocolonial locale of shattered dreams and false promises where characters, though not characters as such because they are almost real, endure imposed experience of agonizing alienation and painful dislocation while struggling for survival.

In the second part, I offer a reading of Larbi Batma's autobiographical text that documents the life-experience of one of the members of the group.

I start from the premise that self-narration is part and parcel of a narrative of individuation; or as Philipe Lejeune put it, a backward-looking prose narrative which "is written by a real person concerning his existence, where the focus is his individual life, in particular the story of his personality."[17] Batma is one of the founding members of Nass el-Ghiwane. His narrative moves across various textual spaces to document the human postcolonial condition of a subject in total distress and dissolution. The text is replete with situations, experiences and facts that give insights into the real underground world of Casablanca where most events take place. The city in Batma's text turns into a spiritual wasteland; a site of alienation, fragmentation, and conflict associated with modernization and capitalist urbanization. The city in the narrator's view is not only a site of community, social cohesion, and resistance; but a site of instability and disillusion with unfulfilled promises and dreams as well. In Batma's narrative, the fabric of the postcolony has started to dwindle as hopes and promises started to crumble down too. The author takes us into the real and concrete life of shantytowns that are scattered throughout Casablanca to give an idea about how the city fabric has failed the dreams and aspirations of many of its inhabitants. The underground sites in Batma's text however become empowering and revealing when we discover that they give rise to experiences that can defy the unilateral constructions of identity through musical renewal, artistic creation and esthetic renovation.

The third part sketches the experience of Nass el-Ghiwane in the Moroccan musical landscape. It attempts to shed light on various aspects pertaining to the emergence of the "new song" in Morocco as a cultural movement that bore new forms of self-recognition, self-definition, and which promoted novel possibilities in engaging with the country's collective and older expressive artistic forms. The desire to forge a new postcolonial subjectivity and the quest to develop a cultural realm of expression through novel artistic forms detached from the colonial past as part of a wider struggle for control over the representation of the nation is at the genesis of the rise of Nass el-Ghiwane. The new song in the Ghiwanian distinctive mode bridges the gap between text (Ghiwanian poems) and ideology; it has opened up a propitious ground for a new decolonized subjectivity to emerge, and also for discursive modalities that redefine the means through which the Moroccan postcolonial subject sees himself/herself in seeking to acquire authority and establish legitimacy of identity in the new socio-political condition of late Sixties and early Seventies of the past century.

The "new song" in Morocco pioneered by musical bands such as Nass el-Ghiwane provides a fascinating example on the use of poetic strategies to connect ideological versions of politics with the daily practices and customs through which selves are constructed and imagined. It does so through a creative and balanced intermingling of genres, harmonies, instruments, performance modalities associated with popular folk music styles and rhythms, melodies, and texts drawn from the rich traditional repertoires of Moroccan culture. Traditional performance genres in postcolonial condition powerfully invoke, as Fanon puts it, "the existence of a new type of man,"[18] that seeks out new patterns to help "the native rebuild… his perceptions"[19] and produce a new consciousness about the new realities of postcolonial society as defined by the new hegemonic imperative. In its reconfiguration of older stories, songs, and poems to theorize new modes of thinking, of being, of becoming and acting, the new Ghiwanian song is surely among those genres to which Fanon would call attention, and which to some extent point to the emergence of new subject positions, and eventually, to the production of a new social imaginary.

This part also attempts to shed light on the early beginnings of the group's members. This endeavor is singularly concerned with few aspects of the members' life stories as told and narrated by themselves or retold by their friends. The life experiences and stories of the members of Nass el-Ghiwane offer suitable terrains to engage with the complexities of the postcolony, and raise fascinating questions about issues pertaining to nation, culture, history and music. The last section tries to offer a succinct discussion on the impact of the Ghiwani movement on Moroccan generation of young artists and musicians who started an alternative musical genre in the early 1990s. In a context of democratic transition in Morocco, the *Nāyḍa* movement in music emerged to take over protest issues to deal with the country's social and political unrest. This movement was initially started by young artists, and developed a new musical style that advocates the enlargement of the scope of freedoms in society than before. This alternative music soon became an interesting cultural phenomenon that articulates discourses on the influence of traditional and transnational music in shaping new musical identities and subjectivities. This section also attempts to read this new movement in its local and global contexts and tries to look at the possible connections between the Ghiwani tradition and this new musical genre.

◆◆ I ◆◆

Disturbing the Canon

Non-Canonical Voices in Postcolonial Moroccan Writing

In an intensely blistering social and political context, post-independence Morocco has produced prose writers such as Mohamed Choukri, Driss el-Khoury, Mohamed Khair-Eddine, Mohamed Zafzaf, to name but a few, who wrote for and about truth and for the real Moroccan daily life. Subversive, as they were, sometimes provocative, these postcolonial writers were always inspired by the socio-political condition to talk of a country stuck-up by its elites. Often referred to as a cursed generation of writers, these dipped their pens in the sweats of mundane life and wrote about the afflictions that plagued the country and its people. This generation of writers, whose scandalous break with the previously dominant esthetics reconciled novel writing with society, wrote in Arabic and few of them in French; and were all looking for an identity that has not yet been documented by the official history; a history of society and its expanding changes which can be retrieved and rethought by writers and artists.

Critics assume that the birth of Moroccan literature of Arabic expression dates back to the first centuries after Islam was introduced in the country by the Idrisid dynasty that ruled in the Berber areas of Morocco from 789 until 921. Yet, the real development of Moroccan literature is often associated with the reign of the Almoravids under Youssuf Ibn Tachafine whose empire stretched to include the Andalusian enclaves of the Iberian Peninsula. The succession of other dynasties over Morocco in various historical junctures, particularly the Almohads, the Merinids, the Sadiyins and the 'Alawites, enhanced a strong preservation of classical Arabic in literature that marked the canonized esthetics of the *Mashriq* (Orient) and which remained prevalent until the end of the Nineteenth Century.[1] Unlike other countries in the *Mashriq*, and due to political instability, Morocco would witness its literary renaissance belatedly. The shift towards modernization and modernity in

Moroccan literary writings was bound up with the historical and social contexts that brought changes to the esthetic trajectories of narrative development and writing. Two historical events were influential in the development of Moroccan literary esthetics and production.

Studies about Moroccan history focus on nineteenth century, especially the period between 1844 and 1860, as a turning point and a new historical juncture in Moroccan modern society. Franco-Moroccan relations from 1830 to 1843 were characterized by the Sultan's continuous efforts to eliminate the dangerous French presence in Algeria. The profound mutual resentment between France and Morocco during the first half of 1844 resulted in a bloodshed war historically known as the *Isly* battle wherein Sultan Moulay Abderrahman's troupes came to help remove the French from Algeria by providing massive aid to the Algerian resistance leader Emir Abd al-Qader. The defeat in the Isly battle would soon reveal the fragility of the Moroccan state and the urgent need to update the country's military structures through a series of urgent reforms. The year 1860, on the other hand, records the occupation of Tetouan, a Northern Moroccan coastal city, by the Spanish forces. This occupation stood as a blatant manifestation of the State's crisis and of the Moroccan community of the nineteenth century. This war and the previous one triggered the beginnings of the renaissance of modern Morocco with the need for renewal. These events prompted the State to renovate both military and intellectual spheres by sending scholars to Europe for education and training.

In the second phase, Morocco will witness a critical process of modernization that impacted clearly on national sovereignty and territorial unity. On March 30, 1912, France would force Sultan Moulay Hfid to sign a treaty of protection. The protectorate would enable France to military occupy the country and to embark on administrative and economic reforms deemed appropriate to the colonizer's colonial objectives through a purgative endeavor to establish security systems and "modern" reforms in administration, education, economy, finance and the military. No doubt, the efforts deployed by the colonizer were designed primarily to serve the interests of the colonial metropolis. The French occupation was a decisive factor in the intellectual awakening of the elites who struggled to justify their existence and ensure cultural promotion and expression. In fact, this awakening movement was reinforced by the return of an enthusiastic intelligentsia that was part of the delegations sent for training after the *Isly* defeat; yet their influence was not noticeable as they were appropriated by the French colonial system.

Later on, gradual awareness about colonial reality will be developed in an attempt to overcome the state of disqualification and deal with the factors that led to the demise of national sovereignty initiated by the colonizer. In the Moroccan context, as was the case in the African continent and in the

Arab world as well, the Moroccan novel of the first half of the 20th century devoted its aesthetic crafting to the promotion of nation-oriented ideologies and to the spread of a culture of resistance and struggle, in order to free the country from foreign occupation. A great deal of these nationalistic thoughts was initiated and empowered by *Salafist* ideologies. These called for a return to the Arabo-Islamic teachings and heritage in order to fuel up social, cultural and political awareness and rescue national and Islamic identity from French cultural occupation. Hence, the *Neo-Salafist* ideological doctrine as a social and political movement for religious reform and national action against foreign encroachment will be adopted. This movement targeted the development of popular awareness about the national cause and aimed at framing the country's national unity and integrity. It led to the blending of both religion and nationalism as mutually indispensible components for national integrity. Also, the movement had an undeniable impact on all means of esthetic expression geared towards the national cause. Literary production was one of these means that was marked by an ethical reformist discourse of national dimension that will become in fact the ideology implicit in Moroccan literature, and which in turn will express the collective consciousness of a whole society in transition.

Thus, Moroccan literature flourished in conjunction with the country's socio-political conditions. The organic relationship between national awakening and esthetic development is a fact that cannot be overlooked by any means. Literature of the time was committed to the national cause, to nation building and to the reconstruction of a homogeneous national identity. Literary texts enhanced the new context generated by the asymmetries of two distinct worlds, the colonizer and the colonized. The spirit of national awakening and struggle against colonialism were at the heart of literary production at that period. Political concerns in Morocco were disseminated and expressed through militant and nationalist writings to castigate colonial presence and glorify ambitions for independence. In the meantime, the classical literary esthetics and rhetoric informed by the *Neo-Salafist* conservatism started to be questioned bringing a larger shift in intellectual epistemological orientations paving the way to novel forms of expression that reconsidered the renewal of individual identity within a broader concept of a collective socio-cultural identity. With the heyday of independence, the cultural and political landscapes unveiled two basic ideologies. The already existing one expressed the concerns and choices of the national bourgeoisie, and the second one whose intellectual vision was inherent in the first one, imperceptibly developed out of the need and out of awareness to represent the aspirations of the middle and working classes. Such was the case with the literary and intellectual circles in Morocco.

During the 1950s up to the 1960s and 1970s, after independence, the country would experience a movement of literary revitalization influenced by the esthetic genres of the *Mashriq* and inspired by Western literary trends as well. During its history, the Moroccan novel was largely influenced by and depended on the esthetics of Eastern literary writing. Its thematic imbrications imitated, and to a larger extent, the Eastern ones and impacted on various Moroccan forms of expression. Abdellah Guennoun argues that in late 19th century and early 20th-Morocco "intellectual and literary activities remained stagnant, imitative as they were of classical works in themes, form and style. Writers wrote their books in the same way as their ancestors did, and deployed the same archaic techniques."[2] Within the same vein, Guennoun also argues that these works had no literary value for they lacked the spirit of creation and innovation as literary production did not differ at all from those written three centuries ago.

Poetry was the most permeable genre to both orient and Occident influences in Morocco. The social and cultural changes that the country had experienced from 1912 until independence in 1956, as well as the post-colonial social and political vicissitudes of the early decades that followed, is a rich background to consider in appreciating Moroccan literary production and its evolution. The various literary genres and forms that appeared during this period were deeply rooted in the authors' and poets' reactionary discourses towards the political and ideological situations before and after independence. Resentment and disillusion about the postcolonial socio-political conditions were also of vital importance, not only in Morocco but also in the neighboring Maghrebi countries. In the post-independence era, literary activities were geared towards discussing and revealing immediate political and national issues. In this context, Marxist and leftist thoughts prospered and became a viable and inspiring medium through which social injustices and political corruption were exposed. Literature, according to this perspective, needs ultimately to be oriented towards envisioning social and political conflicts and unearthing the negative factors that grind down the post-colonial era in order to respond to the demands of the middle and lower classes.

So, it becomes clear that the 1960s onwards was a turning point in the history of the Moroccan novel, and witnessed the birth of the modern Moroccan fiction. Moroccan narrative writing experienced significant revitalization and growth that have led to the coming on of well-written and socially devoted narratives that reflected on individual and collective concerns. The 1960s prose writers initiated a tradition of dealing with social issues in complex ways. They struggled to represent real social concerns that intrigued Moroccan society and politics. When the regime in mid–1970s aborted the revolutionary spirit of the leftist intellectuals inherent in literary production, Moroccan writers, as well as the rest of the population, felt deeply disappointed by the narrative of independence and deceived by their own patriots who proved to perpetuate the cultural politics of the French colonizer. To avoid censorship or trouble with official authorities, Moroccan novelists chose to alienate themselves from society and politics and sought refuge in the vast realm of imagination. The writer's *Self* became the chief theme of the novels written in the 70s and the early 80s.[3] In fact, the first outstanding characteristic of the early Moroccan fiction is the presence of the writer's autobiographical elements in literary works.

Recent critical approaches to writing about life experiences focus on the ways in which autobiographies are being inscribed and used, and highlight the transformations that are developed though the inscription of self-representation. Significantly enough, autobiographical texts are sources about individual lives but they are also historiographical narratives that discern the processes that delineate the articulation of collective histories and memories. Historical contexts are conditioned by personal experiences and stories that the author has lived in the course of their lives. The notion of the subject and the ways in which it is constructed and reconstructed within cultural and historical contexts are of course central to the strategies employed in any autobiographical discourse. Of critical importance in the Maghreb, prose writers, including Moroccans, have literary tendencies to storytelling as a predominant cultural mode of narrating individual and national histories and stories. They show a strong inclination to produce autobiographical works.[4] Teetze Rooke argues that "the seemingly self-centered and individualistic subject of 'my life' dominates many works, regardless if they are written in French or Arabic."[5] However, the self-centered narration in these works does not solely and exclusively focus on the author's (hi)story in the course of the development of events and experiences. The close individual focus of this literary genre in many cases tends to shift to a wider scale of representation to encompass the social, cultural, and political upheavals of the society as a whole.

This growth in the meanings of the autobiographical narrative becomes textually interwoven with chronotopes of symbolic and metaphorical interpretations that give the text in its entireness analogical and complex knots of ambivalences and contradictions. These ambivalences and contradictions where the individual and the nation become textually one single entity in the act of narration emphasize on the one hand the singularity of the narrating self while picturing its "otherness," and on the other hand its dissimilarity and difference from the surrounding group and its norms. One of the ways adopted in autobiographical writings to come to terms with the ambivalences and contradictory sites of representation in the narrativization of modes of being and becoming is through the selective processes of shared crises and events to suit the overall texture of the story.

In autobiographical writings in Morocco, the first person narrator is endowed with significant representative functions. Often caught within the cleavages of endless journeys into the quest for the self which often culminate in a struggle to release the self from the constraints and limitations of a given social order or historical situation, the author needs to be read within the symbolic implications of the textual fabric. The narrative may include signifiers of symbolic twists and turns that help in fleshing out the discursive modalities, whether conscious or unconscious, deployed in the act of narration. These symbolic modalities may give ample meanings to the understanding of the author's intricate actions, reactions and interactions within a spiral set of attributes such as class, gender, generation, race and nation.

Hence, the construction of identity in Moroccan autobiographical texts does not solely allude to a single individual's experiences, but it is also a discourse on nation, and the narrative can be read as an allegorical text about national identity. Fredric Jameson insists on reading postcolonial writings within the conceptual framework of what he terms "national allegory."[6] Allegorical structures in autobiographical writings by Moroccans are pertinent to the understanding of the formation of Moroccan national identity in specific historical junctures and periods. Fredric Jameson's argument refers to the importance of the literary production from the so-called third world or postcolonial countries. It also triggers a debate on canonical and non-canonical aspects of literature as a whole. For him, critics should acknowledge the difference between both aspects and explain it. According to Jameson, in reading postcolonial literature, "We sense, between ourselves and the alien text, the presence of another reader, of the Other reader, for whom a narrative, which strikes us as conventional or naive, has a freshness of information and a social interest that we cannot share."[7] Reading a text adequately needs to take into consideration the historical, cultural and geographical circumstances within which it is entangled. Bound up with this idea is the notion of literature as an artistic expression of people and nations that has emerged with the rise of nationalisms around the world. As Frederic Jameson assumes,

> Third-world texts, even those which are seemingly private and invested with properly libidinal dynamic—necessarily project a political dimension in the form of national allegory: the story of the private individual destiny is always an allegory of the embattled situation of the public third-world culture and society.[8]

As a result, Jameson argues, the profound rupture between public and private that shapes the literary landscape in the West is blurred in the "third world," whose literary productions become far more political than they are ever about self-absorption. The construction of national identities, thus, becomes tightly connected in various degrees and through various configurations to national history. Such is the case with Moroccan literary productions in the twentieth century, namely in the autobiographical genre. The epistemological boundaries in narrating the personal and the national "Self" in autobiographies are blurred and easily drawn. In Moroccan autobiographical writings, metaphors about the nation are thematically explicit in the act of narration. The narrative turns concurrently into a story of the nation whereby individual experiences become part of a collective discourse about national identity and culture.

Benedict Anderson has reflected on the concept of nation as an imagined community[9] that goes through various phases of development, as is the case with the individual self. He argues that ideas that emanate from communities, be they local, national or global, are socially constructed through a range of discourses, beliefs and behaviors. Such social constructions, nevertheless, are contextualized by specific material conditions. Boundaries exist between nation states and these are frequently invoked when discursive parameters are demarcated and drawn. In addition, nations and people are narratives that are narrated through the circumspective forces of memory and amnesia. Individual amnesia creates a (hi)story about personal identity and about nation as well. Both need to be narrated since they cannot be remembered. Anderson reminds us that "as with modem persons, so it is with nations. Awareness of being imbedded in secular, serial time, with all its implications of continuity, yet of 'forgetting' the experience of this continuity [...] engenders the need for a narrative of 'identity.'"[10] Consequently, a text about an individual experience can be read in the light of national and cultural identity. In Morocco, nationalism and national struggle with its popular disillusionments, failures, joy and disappointments is reflected in autobiographical narratives. Most of these refer to the colonial experience and the struggles for national independence. They often relate events about the development of an independent, unified, personal identity entangled within endless struggles against authoritarian regimes and oppressive social and family codes. The allegorical dimension cannot be detached from the formation of the individual identity the autobiography purports to represent. The personal identity in the process of construction through textual weavings becomes concomitantly complicit with the metaphor of national identity in quest for the construction of a certain cultural specificity.

An important dimension in the formation of the individual self in Moroccan autobiography is also the construction of the national self. Narrating life experiences through the rhetoric of an autobiography is also the narration of a communal identity. The individual's story is a metaphorical extension into the collective imagination wherein social and historical conditions are shared by many, and whereby memory and oblivion as exigencies of autobiographical writings construct, deconstruct and reconstruct both individual and collective identities. This critical reflection on textual allegories of autobiographical texts about nation brings another discussion about the canonization of Moroccan literature.

In fact, the foundation of a literary canon in Morocco is certainly linked with national awakening as the first works to have appeared in modern Moroccan literature cannot be detached from the nationalist and anti-colonialist agendas. The French colonial encroachment in Morocco, with its imperial leitmotif of "divide and rule" targeted the fragmentation of national unity through the famous "Berber Dahir" of 1939. This symbolic event in the history of Morocco's colonialism blinked the nationalist movement. In 1938, Abdellah Guennoun published his *al-Nubūgh al-Maghribī fi al-Adab al-Arabi* (Moroccan Intellect in Arabic Literature), banished by the French colonial authorities for its controversial and subversive appeals. This work tackled the history of Arabic literature in Morocco for the first time. As Gonzalo Fernandez Parrilla states,

> It was the intention of this work to draw attention to the long and continued Arabic literary tradition of Morocco and to underline the contributions of its people to classical Arabic literature and Islamic heritage. This work contributed decisively to the creation of a first canon of national literature which in the prose Kannun traced back to the famous *Khutbah* by *Tarik Ibnu Ziyad*, conqueror of al-Andalus. Kannun's book might then be understood as a patriotic reaction against colonial practices within the field of literary studies. However, this was not the first venture of its kind. In 1929, Muhammad ibn al-Abbass al-Qabbaj had already published an anthology of Moroccan poets, *al-Adab al-Arabi fī al-Maghrib al-Aqsā* (Arabic Literature in Morocco), unanimously considered the pioneer contribution of modern literary criticism."[11]

In his *Taṭawur a-Naqd al-Adabī fī al-Maghrib* (the Development of literary Criticism in Morocco), the Moroccan critic Abdelhamid Aqqar points out that the main objective of *al-Adab al-Arabi fī al-Maghrib al-Aqsā* was to legitimate Arabic literature in Morocco and establish its identity within the canonical literature of Arabic expression that was then under construction as well.[12] Both Abdellah Guennoun's *al-Nubūgh al-Maghribī fī al-Adab al-Arabi* and Al-Qabbaj's anthology *al-Adab al-Arabi fī al-Maghrib al-Aqsā*, as foundational critical texts, also aimed at redefining Morocco's literary productions within the Arabic tradition of literature writings as a symbolic way of combatting colonialism. After independence, efforts started to be deployed to delineate literary genres within modern Moroccan literature. In 1964 Guennoun published *Ahādith ʿan al-Adab al-Maghribī al-Ḥadīth* (Reflections on Modern Moroccan Literature), the first critique to have been devoted to the cataloguing and classification of artistic modalities, genres and authors by drawing a line of demarcation between modern literature and classical Arabic literature. Later, Moroccan literary critics would proceed to theorize a canon for each genre based on the accumulated set of literary works. These works were decisive in shaping national identity through various historical junctures and became institutionally and officially established.

The efforts to construct a literary canon, pioneered by earlier attempts to define distinctive genres of Moroccan Literature, were deployed by Ahmed Al-Yabouri in the publication of a series of essays that endeavored to delimit artistic and literary genres through the study of texts available in the Moroccan groves of literature at that time. In his analysis titled *Fan al-qissah fī al-Maghrib 1914–1966* (Narrative Crafting in Morocco 1914–1966), Al-Yabouri paid considerable attention to the Moroccan novel and included works such as Abdelhadi Boutaleb's *Wazīr Gharnātah* (Granada's Minister, 1950), *Fi a-ttofūlah* (In my Childhood,1957) by Abdelmajid Ben Jelloun, *Sab'at Abwāb* (Seven Gates, 1965), and *Dafannā al-Mādī* (We Buried the Past, 1966) by Abdlkarim Ghallab, *Jīl Aẓama'* (Generation of Thirstiness, 1967) by Mohamed Aziz al-Hbabi. With the exception of al-Yabouri's critical research theorizations, and up to the last decades of the seventies, critical essays on Moroccan literature, particularly the novel, were published in newspapers and journals. One of the most influential of these articles was *al-Usus al-Naḍariyyah li'l-Riwāya al-Maghribiya al-Maktūbah bi-Logha al-Arabiya* (1969) (Theoretical Foundations of the Moroccan Arabic Novel), where Mohammed Berrada established *Fi a-ṭofūla* as a foundational text, along with the already mentioned *Dafannā al-Mādī* and *Jīl Aẓama.'* These works for Berrada were mainly motivated by a strong desire to set narrative standards for the practice of Moroccan novel writing. If there has been common consensus about the 1960s as a temporal juncture that laid down the foundation of the Moroccan literary canon, the beginnings, however, have been the focus of endless debates among Moroccan researchers today. Some of them, as did Berrada himself, considered the publication of *Fi a-ṭofūla*, "In Childhood," by Abdelmajid Benjelloun in 1957 to be the real foundational phase in the history of Moroccan novel. Some went back into history and traced the elements of Moroccan novel genre in literary works such *al-Zawiya* "The Shrine" (1942) by Thami al-Wazzani, and Ibn al-Mouakit's *al-Riḥla al-Morrākoshiya* "the Morrakoshi Journey" (1924).

Unlike al-Wazzani's "the shrine," which narrates the childhood of a Moroccan in a traditional school and his spiritual itineraries into a Sufi brotherhood as a disciple of Sheikh al-Harraq, *Fi a-ṭofūla* is an autobiographical narrative of a young Moroccan from a bourgeois family from Fez. Ben Jelloun (1919–1981) spent his early childhood in England where his father ran a business in Manchester. At the age of nine, he returned to Morocco with his family, finished primary school in Marrakech, and then attended the Qarawiyin University in Fez. He afterwards left for Egypt where he graduated from al-Azhar. While in Egypt, he established and managed the Office of the Arab Maghreb in Cairo until Moroccan independence in 1956. Upon his return to Morocco after independence, he served as ambassador to Pakistan from 1958 to 1962 and worked in the Moroccan Foreign Affairs Ministry until his death. Benjelloun's autobiography could be conceptualized within what Khatibi calls "the ethnographic novel"[13]; a phase in literary Moroccan production which is characterized by the writers' urgent need to revisit thematic concerns dealt with by Western travel writers to Morocco. Ahmed Sefrioui's *la Boite à Merveilles* (The Magic Box) (1954) falls also within this category, and it is another instance that enhances this ethnographic phase wherein the author moves on through different exotic places with meticulous details and reproduces the same patterns of representation symptomatic of colonial travelers.

Ben Jelloun's text, on the other hand, moves across various physical and epistemological boundaries and gives a detailed description of the narrator's childhood in Manchester. He narrates the emotional and spiritual ordeals in becoming accustomed to his "native" culture, then his gradual adjustment to that culture through narrative restoration of powerful moments of recollection and memory. The text pictures the events that marked the narrator's early childhood beyond borders. These events experienced in a very different cultural space oscillate between restraint, recklessness, fear and adventure. What is certainly of critical importance in Ben Jelloun's text is that it reflects the sites of enunciation of a post-colonial mindset, incarnated by the Moroccan national Bourgeois class that benefited from the colonial order in the country, and for whom nation-building simply meant the transfer of colonial advantages to serve their own economic, political and ideological interests. Hamid Lahmidani states that *Fi a-ṭofūla* is "an expression of the ambitions of the rising Moroccan bourgeoisie: we see in the writer's position something of an expression of the concern of the national bourgeoisie that benefitted from the West, within the framework of what conforms to its ideology and special interests."[14]

In fact, the rising of the Moroccan ruling middle-class maintained and adopted ideological strategies of colonial determinism that was not serving national unity by any means. After a long-held struggle for independence, writer activists from the bourgeois class who were supposed to defend the national cause and cultural awakening in Morocco soon seized governmental positions and moved away momentously from literary production and cultural activities in general. This bourgeois class stepped into the shoes of former colonial settlement, while deploying its class aggressiveness to secure the government positions previously held by the colonizer. Its mission as delineated by this narrative and later by the author's career as a diplomat was far from transforming the nation but consisted prosaically of mediating Western colonial capitalism in the country.[15] The identification of national bourgeoisie with the Western one, coupled with the reproduction and perpetuation of colonial attitudes and politics, created social, economic and political disparities and divisions that drained the country and its people in endless poverty and marginalization.

At the artistic and literary levels, the publications that appeared at that time, and as mentioned earlier, inaugurated a literary esthetics called "nationalist realism" pioneered by works such as Ghallab's *Dafannā al-Mādī.* This movement, as literary critics assume, is engulfed within a *Salafist* ideology that emerged in the first decades of the nineteenth century as intellectual and religious movement that stood against European colonial ideologies, and which was informed by a strong will to question modernity within Muslim civilization. The perpetuation of the national *salafist* ideology in post-independence Morocco allowed for the emergence of dissent voices among some intellectuals who tried to represent the frustrated and disenchanted aspirations of Moroccan society. These were influenced by the spread of Marxist ideology and started to read Moroccan literary texts in the light of national narratives to question and react against the prevailing ideas of the national "Salafists." This young generation of writers and intellectuals shifted literary focus from the "glorious" past of resistance against the colonizer into social reality. Moroccan literature, thus, became real intellectual, social and political battlefield between the prevailing cultural patterns of "nationalist realism" and the new wave of Marxist-oriented thinkers who engaged with various cultural issues in order to complicate and challenge the grand narratives of the nation, colonialism, modernity and postcoloniality as epistemological sites of disruption.

The agitated literary background, traversed by fresh ideological currents flared up new outlets of expression that gradually influenced the cultural realm. Literary periodicals and journals such as *Aqlām* (Pens) (1964) and *Anfās* (Breaths) (1966), along with the rise of the short story as a new genre suitable for the new aspirations of social change in Morocco, inaugurated a literary movement for the post-independence generation of writers, poets and filmmakers who sought to bring national issues of secular reform, postcolonial language politics and cultural production into dialogue with broader debates about humanism. The new literary turn, working against the grids of "official" narratives through the questioning of the imbricated ideologies of nationalist discourse advocated by nationalist elites, yearned for social and political transformations while laying out the foundations of a new liberated Moroccan culture able to engage with the social, political and historical challenges of that time.

Just few decades after independence, the 1970s witnessed an intensification of social and political conflicts in Morocco and it was evident that the ideological and political discourses about nation building failed to resist the accelerated transformations of Moroccan society. Inspired by an overheated reality as it was, narrative writing developed thematic concerns which revolved around the questioning of the social and political reality in quest for liberated horizons free of readily-made conceptual classifications. Amid the controversial ideological background of the Seventies, two novels would change the course of Moroccan novel writing. Abdellah Lroui's *al-Ghurba* (Alienation) (1971) and Mohamed Zafzaf's *al-mar'a wa al-warda* (The Woman and the Rose) (1972) developed new ways and insights into literary writing that sought to overcome the traditional narrative modes reflected in the act of narration, in character development and in the use of language. This period witnessed the appearance of realism as an outstanding literary orientation in Moroccan esthetics wherein much literary production attempted to consciously parody Moroccan reality. This tendency manifested a creative understanding of realism achieved through the capturing of real social topographies of shattered dreams and delayed desires with spontaneous brutality and ironic bitterness. Works that fall within this experimental realism, as I venture to call it, are Mohamed Zafzaf's *al-mar'a wa al-warda* (The Woman and the Rose) and *Qobūron fi-al-mā'* (Graves in Water); Abdelkader Smihi's *Ashyā-ūn lā-Tantahī* (1983) (Endless Things); Abdellah Laroui's *al-Yatīm* (The Orphan).

The social and political conditions of the country after independence furnished ample grounds for marginal voices to emerge. Their writings resonated with provocative and foreclosed issues that raise existential, moral, political, religious, ideological, and esthetic questions through the capturing of details of mundane life. In fact, post-independence Moroccan writers that wrote from the margin brought new intriguing questions as immediate outcome of the inability and national elites to translate reality in clearer meanings. Failure to interrogate reality by the big narratives of nation-building project created a generation of writers whose writings were committed to literature as truth and worries, as facts and doubtful concerns. They addressed issues fraught with anxiety about subjectivity within a neocolonial locale of shattered dreams and false promises where characters, though not characters as such because they are almost real, endure imposed experience of agonizing alienation and painful dislocation while struggling for survival.

In Morocco, texts from the periphery, the underground literature as it is often referred to, inscribe and register cultural discourses that could be deployed to redefine, relocate and illuminate history beyond elitist representations of Morocco and against such conventional diametric oppositions as canonical and non-canonical, or official and ordinary. Distanced from the canon building, these marginal voices have established a literary trend that problematizes canonical texts. Their narratives are authentic and revealing in the new subversive mode they purport. On the cultural level, the discourse on marginality is fraught with a strategic vision about morality through a revolutionary mode of writing that shakes the prevailing traditional concepts.

Narratives from the margin are replete with textual signifiers that disturb social mythologies such as the issue of sexuality, which is textually uncovered beyond its institutionalized practices. Hence, the poetics and politics of marginality purport to establish a new literary vision that reacts against social dogmas and beliefs. As practice in Moroccan writing, stories from the margin furnish the topographies of the marginal discourse that contrasts institutionalized practices in their manifestations and forms by rejecting the logics of dogmas, static codes and social stereotypes while foregrounding the little stories and dreams, the wrenches and anguishes of characters living on the margins of society.

Marginality is a cultural space that has much to reveal not only as a site of deprivation, but also as an enabling site of radical possibilities and opportunities. It is a space of resistance and a central location for the production and perpetuation of counterhegemonic discourses. It offers the possibility of radical perspectives from which to see, invent, create and imagine alternative new literary, artistic and cultural modes of expression. The margin, as a site of deprivation connotes shifting spatial boundaries that surround and enhance cultural practices that are significant in popular imagination and to collective memory. From the perspective of literary post-colonial consciousness, marginality, for Ashcroft et al. may be regarded as a "condition constructed by the posited relation to a privileged center, an 'Othering' directed by the imperial authority".[16] Bound up with this idea, marginality is not only a condition suggested by the complex ideological orientations of colonial discourse, but also perpetuated from within by post-colonial regimes wherein totalitarian power relations have created their otherness to rule and dominate.

In postcolonial texts, the concept of transforming the literary margins into enabling sites of enunciation for the production of meaning also transforms these peripheral locales into a space of possibility and power, the possibility to invent and articulate a voice, and the power to reinvent that voice in light of the ever-changing nature of reality lived and experienced by individuals and nations. In their insightful and comprehensive work, Bill Ashcroft and Helen Tiffin recognize that "post-colonial reading strategies acknowledge that readings and the formations that bring them into being are corrigible. They are not immutable 'truths' but changeable social and political constructions."[17] The social, political and cultural changes that post-colonial settings have experienced and witnessed give ample grounds to re-envision the concept of marginality as an inevitable process that emerged with the constricting grid of unbalanced power relations dictated by a neo-colonial order.

In Moroccan literature, it is often authors who locate themselves within the underground precincts of social margins that write about and through this space and grapple with marginality that they mobilize as a strategical authoritative voice. It has often been suggested that "autobiography is an art often practiced by marginalized groups to express their protest against their subordinate position in society."[18] Writing an autobiographical work in

Batma's case is an "act of empowerment that visualizes the self in order to expose the suppression and define a way out."[19] By reading Larbi Batma's autobiographical text in the context of post-colonial marginality as an empowering space of artistic and literary creation, I shall consider the fact that his text discloses an endowed marginal space that establishes a distinct individual and collective experience. Such experience is powerful enough in the production of identity and the production of meanings associated with selfhood, nationhood, and shared histories of experience and repression.

Marginality as inherently powerful and as an evolving radical ingenuousness for the construction of collective consciousness in Batma's case is a space marked by its own unique predicament and challenges whereby struggle for self-definition and assertion grapple with questions of national identity, inclusion and exclusion, despair and hope, allegiance to roots and cultural distinctiveness. Batma's text illustrates the author/narrator's struggle to survive under exceptionally difficult circumstances, namely extreme poverty and violence. It is also about a life lived and fought for within the confines of social, economic and political marginality; but also, and more specifically, it is a life story that manipulates margins in order to talk about and against contradictions in Moroccan society.

◆◆ II ◆◆

Narrating Marginality and Reinventing the Periphery

Larbi Batma's Al-raḥīl *(The Departure) between Self-Narration, Individual Agony and National Allegory*

Just around the *Mashra' ben Abbou* region, in one of those breathtaking slopes stretched over an enthralling plain from the unfathomable Morocco near *Oum Rabī'* River, precisely on the outskirts of *Dowār Shougga*, an oak-like tree is deeply implanted close to a cemetery and overextends its shadows on the Dome of a marabout named *al-Wāli Būḥamriya*, a descendant of *Oulād al-Masnawi* Saint. The tree is known in the region as *Labtam*. What is known about these species is that if the original tree dies, its roots spawn and yield other trees that might grow even in years of drought. What is also special about *labtam* in this part of the country is that it is myhthologically constructed in local collective imagination as being possessed by divine spirits and no one is allowed to cut it or use its wood for heating or for any other purposes whatsoever. From this mysterious and sheltering tree Batma's family derived, if not pulled out from the tree's roots their name. This filiative mode of being and existing which in a certain way conjures up images of connection and fascination with the natural world and shows profound compassion to the spiritual realm of saints and shrines would later turn Batma, the family name, into an icon of creativity, artistic flair and authenticity in Ḥay Moḥammādi neighborhood in Casablanca, and around the whole country.

Larbi Batma is the charismatic leading figure of a popular band of musicians that has been an influential and a visible component of the Moroccan cultural mosaic during the three last decades of the twentieth century. He was a singer and drummer within Nass el-Ghiwane since 1970 when the band first came into existence. His version of the band's success story is presented and represented in his autobiographical account, *Al-raḥīl*. It is the life story of an artist who takes readers into a journey of tears, sufferings, frustration and pain; a journey that started with a battle against poverty and ended up with a struggle against a deadly disease.

Batma was born in 1948 in "Dowār Oulād Bouziri," a small Moroccan village extending its shabby clay-made houses over the *Chaouiya* plains of *Maroc utile* (useful Morocco), and died in a 1997-cold winter in a clinic in Casablanca. The impulses and turbulences of an innocent childhood started in the "Dowār" where he grew up before moving to Casablanca. Larbi Batma is an artist who wrote vernacular poetry (*Zajal*), theatrical shows and scenarios for Moroccan television and cinema. In addition to his musical and theatrical productions, he was also interested in Moroccan literature. While stating repeatedly that he never claims to be a writer, his autobiography, shows a very powerful self-spirited individual who has a powerful, albeit simple, linguistic potential in capturing minute details about life in its complexities. He was also one of the main founders of the musical group, Nass el-Ghiwane.

Larbi Batma (left) and his brother Mohamed, member of Lamshāhab musical group during their childhood (courtesy Rachid Batma).

Batma has drawn his musical influences from the *moussems*, popular festivals, in his native region

"Oulād al-Messnawi." This region is known for its agrarian mode of life and for its rich musical styles that are often performed in festive gatherings by peasants and rural dwellers. Batma was also influenced and to a great extent by Al-ḥalqa theatrical performances. Al-ḥalqa is a traditional form of entertainment that is based on oral narratives for its festive underpinnings, and it literally means "Circle." Within this physical space which delimits movement and action, narration and subjectivities, the storyteller recounts, sings and performs amid a circular gathering of people.[1] Al-ḥalqa has been a dynamic source of artistic delight and entertainment, as well as a means of enacting cultural identity in Morocco for yeas. As a performance event fit for dramatization and celebration, and in addition to its esthetic forms and theatrical structures, it is a medium for the circulation of information about people's upheavals, social confusions and political energy. In other words, it is a social drama that has contributed over the past centuries to the representation of historical consciousness and cultural identity in Morocco through a systematic artistic expression.

Outside his musical group, Batma acted and composed songs; and during his artistic life, he was often viewed as introvert, reticent, secret, engulfed in sadness and melancholy. He talked little but wrote much. He conceived of writing as art about life, or life through art, or art for the sake of human values. Those who have kept him company for long and who have been acquainted with his writing rituals confirm that the only moment that provided Batma with a pleasant diversion to writing is the evening time. For him, longest nights were an appropriate moment to consider in the enduring appeal of writing, as some of his relatives have confirmed.[2]

Nights in Batma's writing process become a deeper sleep that absolves the everyday worries and sufferings. He was a "nocturnal creature" who observed life with meticulous and detailed imagination when everybody else was sleeping. Sailing through the night by the light of a candle on his dining table, threading his verses and pampering his imagination from sunset to sunrise, Batma perceived with distinctive intensity the images captured previously and inscribed them with accurate emotional density in his poems. This bohemian impulse visible enough in Batma's unconventional and disordered lifestyle that is fraught with dissatisfaction, disappointment and frustration, as Naima Benchrayta, a relative of his, would tell us, and which may viewed as an order in itself as she puts it, is mainly due to his real artistic involvement in people's everyday ordeals and concerns.[3] His nocturnal rituals in writing inspired him much to write about the blurred and depressing, yet chaotic and courteous world of the people he belonged to; the underworld life and poverty-stricken arenas in postcolonial Morocco.

According to the same source, Batma was sensitive to issues that beleaguered the Moroccan society. Once, as they were all in a family gathering talking about the educational system in Morocco, immediately and few months later, he came up with his *la'qal wa Ṣabūra* (brain and blackboard), a famous theatrical show that delves into the real problems of educational institutions in the country. Also, during his artistic visits to various European countries with a large proportion of North African immigrants, he noticed the desperate life and sordid conditions of his fellow Moroccans, and wrote his *Lahabāl fi-al-koshīna* (Madness in the Kitchen), another play about displacement, nomadism and self-affirmation in hostile locales of racial violence and hypocricy.[4] Batma was very committed to writing about social reality as caught by an artist's observant and attentive resourcefulness; an artist who lived and wrote in straightforwardness and uncomplicatedness. As Ahmed al-Maanouni, the director of *Al-ḥāl* tells us, Batma was an emblematic figure who lived in modesty:

> What struck me about this man was his faithfulness and steadiness; he was exactly the same man that I knew in Ḥay Moḥammādi, his neighborhood, or in Club Med, Agadir amid tourists, or even at the Cannes Film Festival in France where we were both talking about *Al-hāl*; Batma has always been the same."[5]

Batma has adopted an exceptional lifestyle and has charted himself a unique and singular mode of creativeness. The influence of the haunting rhythms of the village life and the impressive rural poetry of the roots that he learnt earlier in his life turned him into the charismatic figure of his musical group, and soon into stardom for years to come; a celebrity status that, nonetheless, foreshadowed simplicity, modesty and mystery as well. He has composed songs, acted for theater and cinema and performed with Nass el-Ghiwane without failing inadvertently to demonstrate loyalty, devotion and admiration to his roots that stretch deeper in the small village where he was born. Batma has led a harsh life and has undergone harsh experiences as well, but as is the case with honest and authentic artists, he was born to live for others. His affiliation with art has always been honest and respectful. He respected and estimated what he was doing. Othmane Benalila, who has become familiar with Batma through an un-regrettable friendship ever since 1974, tells us that

> The man [Larbi] was multifaceted; he composed, performed, and sang; he was a bundle of strange and wonderful contradictions; open and reserved at the same time, which made him procure strong presence and prominent personality.... Writing for Batma was a daily ritual. He had this undeniable power of staying home for days, facing himself over twenty-four hours, a week after a week. He lived large isolation imposed by his art. The man's personality was full of mysteries; when you think you have understood him, he would surprise you with something new and unexpected at any moment.[6]

Batma, also, left an undeniable repertoire of songs that he wrote and composed for his band, most of which are now available for readers in Omar Sayed's *Klām al-Ghīwān*. He also left a collection of poems titled *Hawd*

Ana'nā' (Field of Mint), and an ambitious epic poem he titled *Malḥamat al-Hūmam Ḥūsām* (the Epic of Chivalrous Houssam). *Chivalrous Houssam,* a *Zajal*-based work of a hundred and twenty thousand verses, is about human emotional states and spirits. Batma had planned to publish it in three parts, two of which had already been ready by the time the author started writing his autobiography wherein he declared, "if I still have time to live, I will finish the third part."[7] He knew he was condemned by the deadly disease, which in no way did ever distract his creative mind from writing as obsession. Batma describes his long poem sometimes as mystically incorporating mythical elements from the Moroccan culture, and at times, he describes it as an epic poem about the heroic achievements and endurance of a wandering protagonist. Yet, beyond any critical analysis of this literary genre, his text takes the readers into an amazing journey of sufferings, disillusionment, contradictions, agony and hopelessness; probably that very same journey into the self in which Larbi fought against all forms of social and historical discontentment witnessed and experienced in post-colonial Morocco. The Ghiwanian mode of writing which is closely linked to people's ordeals, to the oppressed and to the disposable populations remains one of the most striking feature that is largely dominant in this wonderful work.

Larbi Batma at home in his apartment at Gauthier neighborhood in the late 1990s (courtesy Rachid Batma).

Besides this exceptional literary work that needs to be read and appreciated within the historical and cultural circumspective forces and contexts that produced the post-colonial Moroccan nation, Batma also left an autobiographical narrative in Arabic that came out in two volumes, *Al-raḥīl* (the Departure) and *Al-Alam* (Pain). These autobiographical accounts, written when he was first diagnosed with cancer in early 1993, and later when he was fighting against his fatal disease in hospitals, are not only stories about an individual life wherein the human and the social experiences coalesce together. They are also intriguing narratives about postcolonial issues on national identity, cultural practices and the potentials of popular music in constructing individual and communal identities.

Al-raḥīl came out in 1995 and relates the experience of a prominent popular artist who was at the genesis of the rise of a famous artistic musical band that changed the Moroccan musical landscape in the 1970s of the twentieth century. *Al-raḥīl*, as will be discussed, is an audacious and daring, if not unflinching and blunt, representation of individual sufferings and pain inscribed with simple sentences and words that are in turn constructed in the streets and by the environment itself; a poignant autobiographical novel that captures in astute details, without fabrication or distortions, the unpolished reality of dispossession and deprivation of a whole post-independence Moroccan generation. It offers glimpses from the life of an artist from the margin who lived in poverty, misery and rejection. Batma's work is not about the postcolony's dreams and hopes but rather about the end of the dreams and expectations in a postcolonial locale of absolute destitution in its most degrading forms. Batma's narrative is not simply an addition to the new *écriture* genre in Moroccan literature that was previously established by prominent writers such as Mohamed Choukri and Mohamed Zafzaf, but also a historical document which unfolds the contradictions and disparities that have existed and still exist between two disparate worlds; disparate in terms of class, beliefs, wealth and yet present within the boundaries of the same nation.

This chapter is concerned with a reading of Larbi Batma's two-volumed narrative *Al-raḥīl* and *Al-Alam*; an effect-evoking and self-revealing voice from an autobiographical text on the author's feelings about his life—his fears, his angers, his sorrows, his guilt, his joys and his ordeals. This is an inspiring text from which the author has produced affect-lading journeys into other issues of intensely apprehensible meanings: the social, the cultural, the historical, and the artistic. In fact, Btma's text, regardless of its overall thematic effect that bears witness of a life story-oriented narration, deals with very emblematic issues of vital importance to post-colonial Morocco as well. It seeks to rewrite Morocco's personal and collective memory, by reinterpreting the nation's colonial history and the sensibilities of the post-independence era through an omniscient narrative voice. Offering imaginative challenges to the country's situation characterized by corruption, poverty, injustice, etc., *Al-raḥīl* attempts to put into question individual and collective histories of Moroccans. Crucial to Batma's *Al-raḥīl* is the reflection on the Moroccan contemporary life with its ordeals and tribulations. This autobiography's concerns with colonial history, political corruption, social injustice and the complex mechanisms of power relations put into question the plagued situation of post-colonial Morocco. Also essential to this text is that it provides memories of the past which closely investigate the past experiences of ordinary people, and offers its own vision of the traditional Moroccan society in transition, by creating conflicting discourses between authenticity and modernity. What readers of *Al-raḥīl* get while moving to flesh out the hidden transcripts of the text is an overall impression about the deception of the whole nation in living peaceful, dignified and prosperous life after independence.

However, before moving forward into the analysis, it is important to mention that Batma's narrative has not quite received the scholarly attention it deserves in Moroccan academic groves in comparison to other equally interesting and subversive works by Moroccan writers. Furthermore, and to my own understanding, it has not been translated into any foreign language so far. As far as the first issue is concerned, though Batma's narrative evokes pertinent aspects of post independence Moroccan culture and offers an absorbing discussion on postcolonial subjectivity in its impediments, it has not yet been studied carefully and thoroughly by academic scholars involved in postcolonial matters. Also, though the text hammers on structural constraints and opportunities associated with the social, economic and cultural situation in contemporary Morocco, it has been overlooked as a genuine work that documents the graphic and explicit reality of the country in a specific historical juncture.

Larbi Batma in late 1980s (courtesy Rachid Batma).

Just like Mohamed

Choukri, though in varying degrees in terms of explicitness and linguistic eloquence, Batma survived street life to thread an autobiographical tale of the underground urban and rural lives, a tale of obsolete denial, bewilderment and bitterness. His work, like Zafzaf's, albeit undeniably in varying terms of language mastery as well, is written in a straightforward and authentic style that recalls past events as experienced by a postcolonial subject in disillusion. However, Zafzaf's and Choukri's works have exhaustively received national and worldwide credit through academic studies or through translations. This would lead me to the second issue about the act of translation of Batma's account.

What certainly makes the act of translation demanding and incredible, if not almost impossible and unbearable, is the linguistic inequality between the Moroccan way of writing in Batma's case and the targeted language of translation. Batma uses a diction that is completely rooted in Moroccan life, though he himself finds it sometimes difficult to transfer Moroccan words into classical Arabic, let alone turning them into English or into another foreign language. The "inequality of languages,"[8] as Talal Asad puts it, is what turns Batma's narrative almost untranslatable. There are differences in the internal workings of the targeted languages that are more likely to convey compulsory transformations and aggressive deformations in the translation process of this book. The cultural imbalance between the source language, classical Arabic suffused with Moroccan vernacular in *Al-raḥīl*, and the target language, English for example, has obvious implications for lexical choices and stylistic effects adopted in translation. One word in Moroccan Arabic, for instance, may have a single meaning that can be expressed in English through different words and with various linguistic and structural nuances. Similarly, a word and expression in English may not perfectly fit and match the cultural meanings of the lexis used by the narrator in *Al-raḥīl*, or any other text that he had written. Furthermore, there are words in Moroccan vernacular that may often be used within an array of complex meanings that coexist in the source language and enrich its metaphorical imageries but are almost impossible to convey in the targeted language.

Hence, this untranslatability of words and their meanings in the case of *Al-raḥīl* would often result in pushing the text further to unexpected directions and in creating abortive language spaces wherein originally subtle and complex meanings get distorted, transformed and often deferred. As the French saying goes, "traduire c'est trahir" (to translate is to betray), it is important to state that translation of *Al-raḥīl* needs to be taken cautiously. The inaccessibility of Batma's autobiographical text lies in the very fact that any attempt at translation might lead to the recreation of the work and its reconstruction through another language, as it has been the case with other translated works of Moroccan writers. The question that impels itself is how to initially remain faithful to the author's simple but realistic ways of expressing his feelings and thoughts while narrating situations about his childhood and life experience in the village and in the city.

Larbi Batma's life could be read as a journey of tears, frustration and pain; it started with struggle against poverty and ended up with the battle against a fatal disease. Larbi, or *Ba-Arroub* as he is called by his fans and acquaintances, passed away in 1997. Though his body is no longer on stage where it has mostly been visible throughout his artistic career, his voice that has long sung and cried for the pains and sorrows of others is still eternal; a voice that has spoken with honesty and accuracy about dispossessed people and their sufferings. Batma's voice addresses all the senses and carries a message of sincerity; sincerity in expression and faithfulness to his roots and to the routes he has tracked by the force of circumstances.

Larbi grew up within a poor family with his six other brothers and a sister, and spent his early childhood in the countryside away from the city's restricted freedom and containment before moving to the city to lead thereafter a shanty life in Casablanca. Larbi Batma is the quintessential embodiment of misery and suffering; sufferings, as he himself declared on various occasions, that have turned into genuine companionship throughout his life. These sufferings that inform Batma's poems and texts are evident in the writings of Nass el-Ghiwane and could easily be felt while listening to Nass el-Ghiwane's lyrical archive or while reading their musical experience. Through his autobiography *Al-raḥīl* (the Departure), Batma has tried to open sad fragments and bifurcated chapters about a gloomy life he has led for years. His work is a diary of memories truncating an artist's itineraries in life and charting his artistic journey, his ideas and his philosophy in life.

Batma's simple yet moving autobiography about growing up in a Moroccan bidonville that grinds on with exclusion, sufferings and crudeness, as well as its reception in Morocco, is a story of success that negotiates meaning about an artist's lumping life. It is a narrative of personal fortitude and, ultimately, personal triumph that interprets an individual's past and present memories across significant temporal junctures; and it concomitantly backgrounds a miniature social and cultural history of cultural transformations in postcolonial Morocco. In *Al-raḥīl*, there is an extraordinary poignancy, intimacy, and richness of detail, reminiscent of autobiographical writing in Morocco. Not only does it chronicle in acute details the author's own personal tribulations and turbulences as the outstanding charismatic leader of a famous Moroccan troupe of musicians from a highly underprivileged and predominantly excluded Moroccan shanty town community in the bidonville of Casablanca, but it simultaneously charts a new and uncontested literary space for an emerging marginalized generation.

In this briefly written first-person account, a young Moroccan from the

Shāwiya highland slopes in Morocco who moves to an urban shantytown recounts a story of physical and socioeconomic misery, a condition of oppressive poverty from which an ensuing escape would appear almost impossible. Batma takes his readers through a journey of this world by examining his own humble yet spectacular development from a bidonville dweller to a famous artist in the country. Nevertheless, this is more than a genuine portrait of a young man growing up in extreme poverty. It is also an important statement about political and socioeconomic inequality and change as viewed from below, and a bitter complaint about the injustice and despair that overwhelm so much of postcolonial Morocco. Batma's work seeks to articulate a voice for the voiceless and lay bare the deepest feelings and grievances of the impoverished masses that are consumed on a daily basis by the struggle to survive. Morocco's supposed post-independence politics of social development seems barely to have impacted on the country's urban and rural peripheral sites. For those raised in such an environment of anguish and despair, political promises of a better future seem depressingly hollow and muffled. This sense of frustration and futility is captured in the author's own bitter account in a sobering confessional and unheroic tone.

Al-raḥīl by Larbi Batma is an authentic narrative of human experience during the last decades of the twentieth century of a Moroccan subject caught within the grid of unequal struggles between an authoritative regime and the people who aspire for freedom. It traces the life of an artist/writer struggling across vanished dreams and evaporated expectations for liberty at all levels. Batma's text is also about a knot of intricate discourses at work wherein the national and the personal coalesce to produce moments of revelation and anxiety about the postcolonial condition in Morocco. It offers powerful moments where the author narrates the hideousness of his life and the ugly memories from Morocco that was. He excels in demonstrating simple realistic writing skills in expressing his feelings while narrating his childhood and early life experiences, either at the village or in the city. What is also worth considering is the shifting temporal moment(s) that endow the text with complex knots of ambivalences. In fact, the complexity of this text which moves through unstable spaces of narration, and which twists events into intricate episodes where past and present become entirely blurred to express an individual's experience stems naturally from the fact that the entire story is governed and conditioned by an oral mode of narration. This becomes noticeable when we move with the author in flashbacked episodes through temporal and spatial narrative boundaries that create delirium and confusion, but which, nonetheless, convey the subject's feelings and predicament in meaningful terms.

Al-raḥīl explores the archeology of memory from the point of view of a postcolonial subject in agony and disenchantment and traces the tragic social transformations of the postcolonial Moroccan society in the seventies and eighties. The writer/narrator adopts polyphonic styles of narration and does not settle on a specific mode of narration. Such strategy creates a horizon of expectations and suspenseful events that construct an overall effect which excels in moving across various textual boundaries wherein memory and narration become complicit and complacent in inscribing the pains and abuses of the postcolony. Memory in *Al-raḥīl* becomes a resurgence site through which the past is literally constructed and inscribed. It is not a nostalgic detour into one's memory, as Ismail-El Outmani claims, "but a daring inquiry into the tormented self of a subject claiming dignity" through writing.[9]

The narrative investigates the bottom of Moroccan society; deeper even into the other Morocco peopled by marginal figures that are considerably crushed economically and socially. Batma's autobiographical text, explores issues of marginality as texture informed by social discrepancies, cultural disintegration and identity in crisis. It is set within various physical and epistemological precincts that adopt shantytowns and rural spaces to construct a narrative of struggle between two distinct worlds, urban and rural, center and periphery, the well-off and the trodden-upon. It is also a narrative about despair and agony, amnesia and memory, instability and estrangement wherein characters from real life struggle for survival and self-definition. In fact, struggle in the textual fabric of the narrative takes various dimensions that are shared by the characters; what unifies Batma's individualized characters is a struggle against poverty, subordination, exclusion, political ideologies and social anxiety; but above all a struggle against the erasure and metamorphosis of an authentic past of cultural roots and belongingness that bond collective identity together.

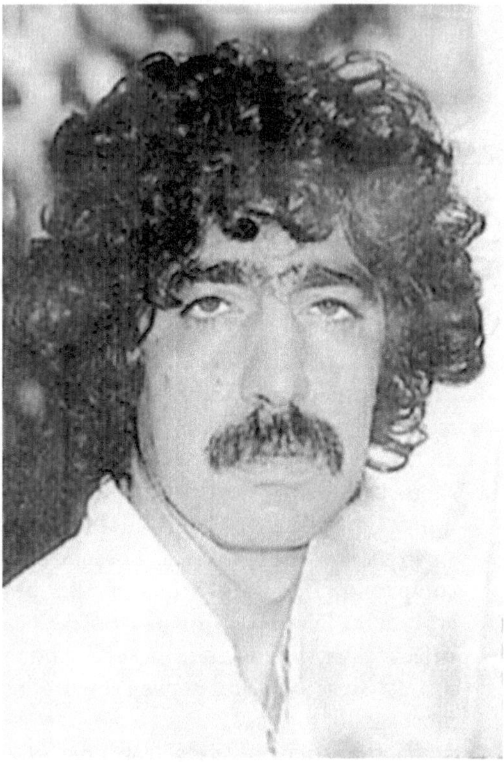

Larbi Batma in the early 1990s (courtesy Rachid Batma).

Larbi Batma's life was a

success story: a journey from rural poverty to urban shanty life, from the village mentality of simplicity, authenticity, ignorance, and superstition to the renowned musician and artist who challenged traditional thinking and thereby impacted on the whole generation of the 1970s and 1980s. The poverty, not particularly felt throughout the years he spent in his village, became a desperate affliction when the young Larbi moved to Casablanca to integrate another mysterious life full of tricks and traps in quest for survival. The bitterness of his memories seems to reveal more about the marginal spaces he and his family were relegated to. The decisive element in his autobiography is his experience of the marginal horizons of the city, and this was a torturous itinerary that he had to track as an individual when he first discovered the world of the shantytown.

The re-visioning and envisioning of self-individuation in marginal spaces is illustrated repeatedly in Batma's text through ironic manipulation of characters within specific temporal and spatial junctures. This process of self-individuation, pervasive in the text as it is supposed to be, is suffused with an auspicious hope for self-transformation that turns the discourse on margin and marginality into an implicit site of radical possibilities prescribed in a new socio political order of freedom, recognition and emancipation at all levels.

Batma's autobiography, narrated in a matter-of-fact style with bare and spontaneous language, and backgrounded in the direct experience and immediate concerns of everyday trepidations, describes a bleak childhood and youth in Morocco wherein the narrator and his characters survive the cramps of hunger, and the hazards of street life. This compelling and strikingly memorable account of marginal life in Morocco is textually interwoven with chronotopes of incessant displacement and estrangement to reveal moments of passion and hope, pains and joys, disease and poverty, ecstasy and pleasure. The retrospective forces of Batma's gaze into his past events and experiences reveal a very shocking life itinerary; the memories that surface the narrative are those of a traumatic childhood, repressed violence, frustrated desires, shattered dreams and abortive expectations. Earlier in his life, and in his wanderings, Batma is confronted with the world of the dispossessed in the shantytowns of Casablanca. These outcasts of the social system became his companions in misery throughout his journeys in a narrative that takes readers into the lives of craftsmen, workers, peasants, drunkards, thieves; marginal voices that are excluded from social and moral orders predetermined by conformist structures and conventional schemes and exposed to poverty in its most sordid forms.

Batma's narrative is a true story of extreme anxiety about human condition. His sites of creativity are inspired by the underground worlds. Following the lead of his predecessors who investigated the margin in their writings such as Mohamed Choukri and Mohamed Zafzaf, Mohamed Mrabet, Mohamed Khaierddine among others, Batma is trying in his own way to exorcise the ghost of poverty while striving to spurt social abscesses and reveal the ugliness and sordidness of a life lived and experienced in post-colonial Morocco. Like these Moroccan writers, Batma writes to expose the two-facedness of Moroccan society and its duplicitous attitude towards its citizens. Drinking heavily, stealing occasionally, café-wandering regularly are all enacted ways, if not forced pretexts, in which the protagonist of *Al-raḥīl* together with the other characters try to cope with and battle against power ad social injustice. As Salah Moukhlis argues in talking about Choukri's *For Bread Alone*, these ways "become articulations of a demystifying discourse that inevitably clears the smoke screen to expose the horrendous reality of large populations forgotten and left alone in their struggle against poverty, discrimination, and oppression."[10] Also, as it is the case with the previously mentioned writers who are involved in issues from the social life of Moroccans, these scenes are meant to surprise and even shock readers of various classes, namely the bourgeois ruling one, into a hidden reality that is meant to remain concealed and covered. It is mostly through the widely open eyes and through the workings of plain memory of the first-person narrator that we are allowed to probe into the world of the disposable populations to

Larbi Batma (right) and Ahmed Snoussi in the early 1990s at Batma's home (courtesy Rachid Batma).

witness the bleakness and austerity of the postcolony. It is through the spiny and thorny life led by the narrator and his characters that readers are forcibly taken into the miseries of the forgotten side of Morocco, and the pains of individualized subjects living in the gloomiest arenas of the city. As a matter of fact, and far from the syrupy embellished sentimental and compassionate discourses in autobiographical writing, the author is trying to denounce with shrewd details the social and political systems in post-independence Morocco that have robbed a collective childhood, and suppressed the dreams and desires of a whole generation tormented by the specter of poverty and social injustice. *Al-raḥīl* 's themes are ontologically entangled in Moroccan society, history and culture. As readers move through the precincts of this text, they are immediately confronted with types of characters as they are cast in endless journeys through self-definition, incarnating the labyrinthine experience of growing up in colonial and postcolonial Morocco. These characters and protagonists mercilessly usher readers into the heart of Moroccan society with its various incarnations and dilemmas. As Salah Moukhlis has pointed out, "we are constantly barraged with familial conflicts, images of ruthless patriarchs, a corrupt and hypocritical society, and an apparently perennial opposition between modernity and tradition. These wider conflicts are captured in microcosm within the family as the basic social unit."[11]

Rediscovering the Self and Reinventing the Postcolony: (In)visible Sites of Postcolonial Memory and Malaise performed in Batma's Al-raḥīl

Moroccan literature of the 1980s and the 1990s developed a literary trend known for its affinity for the marginal, and for the exilic condition of the individual within his or her own social milieu. Many writers themselves experienced marginalization in their lives and created narratives of unsettlement, homelessness, solitude and impoverished independence through immediate confrontation with the periphery. The peripheral sites of Casablanca, mostly troubled by complicated issues of class inconsistencies, offer intriguing stories from a postcolony in deep-seated malaise. The narratives that emerge from these underground locales narrate and reconstruct the ironies of everyday life, and are endowed with immense social significance as they voice out the voiceless and create promising possibilities for regeneration and revival.

Such is the case with Batma's *Al-raḥīl*. Larbi Batma reconfigures the space of the underground Casablanca and projects it as a productive zone where the other of the city is recognized. Indeed, this specific site in the writings and in the artistic career of Batma remains rhetorically powerful as it evokes "asymmetrical relations" of pleasure and ambivalences, of identities and voices in transitional moments of social and cultural exclusion. Such peripheral sites have inspired Batma's narrative tradition of subversion. The postcolonial malaise of Casablanca recorded and saved by Batma's particular experience of life and writing seems to be at the genesis of *Al-raḥīl's* significant preoccupation with the periphery.

The power of Batma's tradition comes from his site specific narrative images of exclusion that are associated with his ultimate focus on peripheries; a double-oriented strategy that is primarily meant to destabilize the totalizing ideologies of hegemonic discourses both locally and globally. Discourses on an otherness that is relegated to oblivion are temporarily reformulated to shift the focus on the socially negated others who live in total anguish. The focus on the peripheral sites of Casablanca performs the politics of resistance against esthetic figures of national power. I argue that Batma's narrative could be read as a performance act of social narration where local otherness emerges to disrupt national and global discourses on the city, an endeavor to save the stories of marginalized spaces and people. It is a form of gazing up to disorient official discourses on the city and a gaze back to dislocate discourses on otherness while shifting the focus into the socially excluded other. This otherness in exclusion is what gives Batma's narrative a powerful esthetic dimension worth reading and discussing. It is characterized by forthrightness, spontaneity and extreme sincerity where fiction and reality, death and life, past and present, despair and hope come together in mutual embrace. In fact, *Al-raḥīl* is an intriguing story of a striking account about what it means to live in the Moroccan underclass. It operates within a real world inhabited by a cast of characters living on the outer reaches of society, struggling for existence. Driven by the turmoil of abject poverty from the village, Batma's family moves to the city in search of better life. In the course of events, the author/narrator struggles to make sense of his physical and epistemological quests for survival in the periphery of Casablanca's economic and social life. He finds himself in the shantytown streets embracing neglect, hunger and abuse. Raised in desperate scarcity, he lives by doing menial jobs, stealing, and hanging around in cafés smoking and drinking.

Casablanca, as "an ideal location of marginality"[12] and as a territory ruled by time's flexibility and infinity, is a "site-event" whereby social, historical and textual forces overlap with each other, and whereby new spaces and subjects are continually decomposed and recomposed to produce new relations between the textual fabric in Batma's narrative and the dynamics of the city. Hence, the proper context in which to better understand Batma's uncompromising subversive stance is the underground arenas of Casablanca. These sites that are fueled with images, memories and stories, and which create borderless narratives that unsettle the existing ones, acquire ample appreciation and amplification once read against the postcolonial subversive background. They are easily recognized and identified as spaces of "imagined communities, little histories and little ironies of an inconceivable social malaise in postcolonial Morocco. As Khalid Amine argues, "when humans attach meaning to space, it becomes a practiced place with evident markers and idiosyncrasies."[13] In fact, Batma has understood well how to cede the painful experiences of everyday life to writing and how to violate the logics of associations to "invent the spatial ... coordinates within which history could occur"[14] and turn peripheral sites, lamented in being corrupt, into powerful narratives of Otherness in transitory moments of possibilities.

Batma's underground tale moves across peripheral boundaries of disposable postcolonial subjects caught within the cleavages of emptiness, estrangement and repression. It negotiates particular geographies within the city and restages human drama as a conspicuous performance through the evocative signs of memory and belongingness. The textual fabric of Batma's narrative is made up of "locations and settings, arenas and boundaries, perspectives and horizons." These miscellaneous places and spaces "are coordinated by various kinds of temporal knowledge and experience, from circumscribed routines to linear notions of progress or transformation."[15] I read these underground geographies of Casablanca as inherently unstable terrains of "paradoxes and contradictions where human subjectivity meets the forces of abstraction and objectification."[16] It is through these sites that have been excluded from the mainstream narratives of history that the voice of Batma and his characters becomes more visible.

Indeed, *Al-raḥīl* works on the reconfiguration of the sites of exclusion, while reshaping Casablanca to involve peripheral sites as significant forms of cultural expression. These peripheral sites are not mute in Batma's work; they are endowed with historical dynamism and produce multiple identities. If postmodern grand narratives have excluded indigeneity from the process of establishing a local identity, *Al-raḥīl* as a text reconsiders periphery as a contesting narrative that rethinks the process of re-indigenizing textual spaces through the celebration of the excluded other. It allows us "to inquire into and recover from history and literature those excluded voices of the marginalized or, in the term used by the Marxist intellectual, Antonio Gramsci, the subaltern."[17] Subalternity in Batma's text becomes a potential terrain which "disclose[s] that which is concealed"[18] and allows ample possibilities to go beyond the bracketed narratives of history into the subalterned ones, move from neo-colonial amnesia into the marginal's memory.

Underground Casablanca in *Al-raḥīl* remains an essentially symbolic site whereby the other is glorified and the official is ridiculed, mocked and over parodied. The underground sites are brought in a carnival-like celebration that remaps and reorders social contestations, and entails the possibility of filtering through the boundaries that demarcate the two entities and highlights their essential hierarchical ambiguities. In dealing with Rabelaisian carnivals, Bakhtinian undertaking brings a clear-cut distinction between the classical body, which corresponds to the official self, and the grotesque body, which refers to the low and the common. Central to carnival imagery, according to Bakhtin, is the "grotesque body" and "the material bodily lower stratum" where the emphasis is on indeterminacy and indecency, so that the body which is abandoned to exuberantly obscene excesses of a physical kind becomes a parodying form that undermines finality or purity. Bakhtin asserts, that "the grotesque liberates man from all the forms of inhuman necessity that direct the prevailing concept of the world. The official self is accordingly uncrowned by the grotesque and reduced to the relative and the limited."[19] Hence, the juxtaposition of both forms creates new meanings and allows for the emergence of the multiplicity of voices that question the hegemony of the "officialdom." The body in Bakhtinian undertaking becomes transgressive and subversive; the popular is allowed a voice to resist the hegemony of official discourses.

Al-raḥīl pends on Bakhtenian theoretical framework and offers an insightful discussion on the subversive potentials of the periphery. The neglected peripheral sites, the underworld of the unwanted and of the outcasts, as opposed to the "high and official space, where society mirrors itself in order to appease its own conscience"[20] is what renders Batma's text subversive. Another version of the ignored and the forgotten Moroccan history is being told through the incorporation of these critical symbolic sites in the text, thereby sharing the author's experiences about the sordid reality ignored by "official" literature. Readers of Batma's text discover in due course not only the identity of an individual (the subject), but also the history of a group of people marginalized by society, namely, thieves, delinquents, prostitutes, drug-addicts, and madmen who expose some of the officially so-called "non-existent" social phenomena, such as poverty, corruption, nepotism, theft, and prostitution.[21]

Hence, Casablanca in Batma's work is vividly depicted in dreadful deprivation as it symbolizes all that the characters try to escape from, "the net that society has flung them and from which they must escape in order not to be ravaged."[22] What is mostly significant about its characters is that they "act upon the fact of their displacement in a dynamic negotiation with place. Far from being lost or invisible, to representation, their identities as strategic individuals are made out of this interaction, and new identities emerge in praxis, in performance."[23] The performative aspect of identities in Batma's text trespasses boundaries that produce various realities in time and space and resonate with the peripheral as a force of subversion, that which is repressed, excluded and marginal.

Marginality in Batma's case "represents a challenge to the defining "center" ... the embrace of marginality is, above all, an oppositional discursive strategy that flies in the face of hierarchical social structures and hegemonic cultural codes."[24] Batma shows a defiant attitude towards authority once he becomes aware of the inherent wickedness of those in power; his rebellion will be more radical in its form, and his sufferings will be more physically intense. The world of underground Casablanca is best approached in Batma's text through a symbolic analysis that can cite as evidence the topography of the city. In such an important way, the reader sees how Batma writes a universe of marginal bodies that drift, narrates untold stories and builds topography of peripheral sites, giving it structure and architectural diction. His accurate description of the peripheral sites of Casablanca refers to the cultural divide that is instantaneously visible through the opposition of two zones, that are, in Fanonian terms, "not in the service of a higher unity"[25]; thus forming a binary partition that reproduces and perpetuates colonial attitudes and politics of division which deny the natives a coherent and homogeneous cultural identity. It uncovers inadequacies of post-independence institutions in Morocco and hints at the historical legacies of colonialism, which have produced both a rigid demarcation of spatial structures and a bureaucratic ruling mindset that replicate colonial strategies of power and domination.

The author never kept a diary that would theoretically turn later into a refined autobiography. He has relied much on the circumspective powers of self-reflection, self-agency, self-ownership and personal temporality in traveling back into time to relive events and inscribe what he could remember from a past that eventually belongs to his present self, and which he revisits with much honesty without trying to hide from it. His writing can be perceived throughout his autobiographical account as an instantaneous and spontaneous process without embellishments or vast exaggerations, that drew up on episodic memory retrieval in narrating life events and experiences. As he confirms in an epilogue that came in the back cover of his book, "This is what I remember.... I wrote it with honesty, love and tears. Now I am bidding farewell to everything I have seen ... the color of the days, the color of the nights, memories and things."[26]

Al-raḥīl is a candid and straight confessional autobiographical narrative wherein the act of narration and the circumspective powers of reminiscent memory interplay with each other in significant ways. The memories documented in Batma's book stand beyond romantic and tender-based narration that often characterizes autobiographies. They are immersed in reality and loaded with harshness and anger about an ambiguous world of incongruities and contradictions. Batma's narrative mode is uneven and does not celebrate ready-made classifications or inflated reality. It is a narrative mode that transforms disreputable attitudes and behaviors into rich creative literary material that carries limitless amount of meanings and interpretations. The dull underground world of loss and turmoil, of malice, scandals and bad habits, in Batma's case, makes the writing experience a possibility that associates individual experience with historical reality and with shared construction of the past. Batma has managed to free his underground world from being nominally negative and embarrassing, and to turn it into a text that exposes reality and revolts against all past and present forms of seclusion and exclusion.

Batma did not seem to have spent much time in writing his autobiography. The whole process took almost less than two years because his ideas were overwhelming his mind for a long time. They came out as an overflow of memories triggered by a strong desire to shed light on the neglected history of Morocco; the other version of the oppressed Moroccan. His recollections in his book evoke alien, marginalized and downtrodden Morocco troubled and devastated by memories of colonial violence, by a reality of social and political stagnation, and by a post-colonial legacy that preserves and promotes colonial power relations. The book opens with the veneration of and tribute to writing

> Good morning white paper and pen.... The night was caught between the mazes of loud screams.... 'How come that my life has been worthless than most unfavorable people? I see my cradle and grave. I followed the steps of girls on the loose singing, nothing is left except deals and I sold passion in the underworld and it was just a fancy trade. The most attractive ones are trivial ... with oblivious beauty.... Love is evidence ... and there is no evidence about what I said.' I heard these words from a pimp when I was in Agadir.[27]

The novel as an autobiography can roughly be categorized within the picaresque genre that narrates in episodic flashbacks and with realistic details the life story of the author from late 1940s to mid–1990s. The picaresque in my undertaking does not look at the narrator as an engagingly roguish hero, but as an honest and authentic character who is involved in a spontaneous act of narration of events and experiences that marked his physical itineraries in life. The picaresque in *Al-raḥīl* resonates with the popular wherein the ordeals of mundane life and the folk's way of life are described with astute details. Hence, in the case of Batma's picaresque autobiography, the picaresque "I"-eye of the narrator intersects with reality as dictated by a post-independence social and political order. In other words, the embodiment of the personal dimension in this narrative crisscrosses the objective mode of narration that plainly, if not bluntly, depicts the real Morocco; the underground Moroccan sites of marginalization and alienation, of existential anguish and loss produced and perpetuated by rotten systems and tyrannical regimes. Batma makes use of very simple language to launch a derisive critique of postcolonial Morocco; its social inequities, cultural alienation, and, most of all, the miserable state of the downtrodden that experience an exilic-like condition inside their own country.

Al-raḥīl, as mentioned before, falls within the tradition of picaresque writing in Morocco best epitomized by Mohamed Choukri's *al-Khubz al-Hāfi*, translated by Paul Bowles as *For Bread Alone.* At the esthetic level, Choukri's and Batma's narratives share creative affinities in their arranged ways of capturing details with an unpretentious, if not down-to-earth, language. If Choukri's work is blunt in the audaciousness and in the realistic frankness that the narrator espouses, Batma's, however, uses soft and tamed language in his narrative wherein frugal and prudent revelations coalesce with various levels of spiritual consciousness at work. In other words, obsession with death in Batma's case, since the writing of the book started when the author discovered his incurable disease, reveals much about how the picaresque manifests itself to thread social reality with mystical discourses that hinder the narrative discursive manifestations to become too blunt or too direct.

Batma's narrative could also be conceptualized within what Nirvana Tanoukhi calls, following Ferial Ghazoul's discussion of Mohamed Choukri's *For Bread Alone*, a "subaltern autobiography" which, in a sense, attempts to rewrite "the communal autobiography of an independent nation."[28] The national history written by *Al-raḥīl* envisions a community brought together as a nation not by race or religion, but by a shared cultural and social experience of colonial encroachment and postcolonial predicament. This community includes various social groups, the subalterned and excluded ones who have been hopelessly condemned to remain silent given the constricting grid of representation. Subalternity is crucial for understanding the narrative boundaries drawn in Batma's testimonial account. In fact, Batma's narrative is ultimately a "social document" that attempts to document the life of subalterned groups within Moroccan society and not merely a creative work of art in the form of an autobiography. In talking about his work, Mohamed Choukri identifies *Al-Khubz Al-Hāfi* as a communal autobiography. In an interview with the literary journal *Alif* in 1986, Choukri tried to position his writing style in relation to the existing literary genres:

> When I said that my autobiographical novel *Al-Khubz Al-Hāfi* is more of a social document than a work of art I meant that I actually attempted a semi-documentary endeavor about a social group that included myself and my family. A work of art, be it a novel, a short story, a play, or a poem is more condensed, symbolic, inspirational. In other words, it requires a writer to be detached from the events he is depicting. This does not mean an autobiography can never aspire to the realm of art. It would have been so had I written with an intellectual orientation where the philosophical and psychological levels were fused together[...]. In my autobiography, however, I did not overload my characters (including myself) with cultural dimensions except as befits their simple social status. Most literary works stem from a combination of social and political experiences that are

often closer to a documentary[....]. Arab writers, on the other hand, are still struggling to get rid of three swords dangling over their heads: politics, religion, morality[...].[29]

By describing *Al-Khubz Al-Hāfi* as a "semi-documentary endeavor about a social group," Choukri attempts to situate his literary orientation within a factual position that seeks to draw artistic lines of demarcation between both Western works and Arabic woks. For Choukri, Western works in their modern artistic inclinations, develop autobiographical narratives where a protagonist's psychological life is endowed with abstract philosophical (or high "cultural") dimensions. On the other hand, Arabic works, for him, are entangled in political, religious, and moral debates that lead nowhere except to the production of idealist knowledge that does not represent the various social, literary, artistic and esthetic fabrics of the country. Rejecting the autobiographical modes of both the individualistic Western artist and the idealistic Arab intellectual, Choukri adopts an alternative mode of writing through "works [that] stem from a combination of social and political experiences." Such works of "documentary" call for the creation of "lettered," authorial Arab national subjects through the democratization of authorship as well as authority, in the Benjaminian sense of cultivating "an increasing number of readers becom[ing] writers."[30]

Such mode of writing which calls for the inscription of communal autobiography of an independent nation in Moroccan literary production is also what characterizes Batma's *Al-raḥīl*. His autobiographical narrative can best be theorized within the alternative discourse of semi-documentary esthetics about Moroccan society whereby shared social and political experiences of the nation are realistically dismantled, aesthetically highlighted and discursively challenged. The discourse on the nation in Batma's account is defined primarily by the shared experience of colonial history which was based on the intensification of racial, ethnic and cultural hierarchies, and which undermined the political and social systems to create an impoverished community. Nation as narration in Batma's writing is an important aspect that is textually crafted to reconstruct the lives of his characters through memory and through the lenses of past events that characterized the country's history.

The re-visiting of the past and the reconstruction of "the turning-points at which history failed to turn"[31] is a potential endeavor in postcolonial studies. This discipline seeks to bring new perspectives on present moments by viewing them through the prism of their past. This view of the past is "arguably so much tied to present-day understandings of what it is to be in a post-colonial world...."[32] Within this intellectual critical position, the postcolonial stance is mainly based on the revisionist attitude of the forgotten histories and cultures that the national narrative of history has consistently subjected to various forms of domination and exclusion. It is important to note that esthetic approaches to literary representations often detach texts from their highly complex historical, political and cultural circumstances of power and exclusion. Once, texts and representations are viewed as contradictory discourses, those conventional oppositions between fact and fiction, reality and representation, history and imagination are blurred and transgressed. Postcolonial critics in Morocco and elsewhere have done much to deconstruct and disorient those diametric oppositions between history and imagination, fact and representation, esthetics and politics, knowledge and power in order to retrieve and revisit other histories and voices that could not be heard because of the continuous ramifications of political will to power over representation and history in colonial and national cultures.[33] Such conscious attempt is geared towards the possibility of re-orienting and redefining, or at least diversifying and expanding the postcolonial landscape of critical practice, that is to say, to create a new critical space that can help go beyond the conventionally paradigmatic critical and cultural practices of history writing from the perspective of the ex-colonized, and locally excluded Otherness.

Larbi Batma in his home village (courtesy Rachid Batma).

Batma's autobiographical account has attempted, following the lead of Mohamed Choukri and Mohamed Zafzaf, to challenge the construction of narratives about the nation by national historians who have excluded subaltern voices from the mainstream narratives of the nation. In this sense, Batma has successfully tried to offer an alternative reading to history by textually investigating memory from below and by including in the history of the nation the histories of the groups previously left out from it. Writing about social marginality with an unconstrained creativity has allowed the author to lay bare the lives of his characters and stage them as real agents of history. By contextualizing the little stories of his characters, Batma gives a rich account of how the sociopolitical order and institutions coalesce in forming individual subjectivities in the postcolony. He has successfully brought to the forefront the social processes that have plagued Moroccan society from within and have impacted on people's lives. He has also succeeded in narrating the psychological conditions that affected the physical being of his characters. He has steeped himself in their daily concerns, their ordeals and their dreams as well, and has come out with an authentic narrative of subaltern individuals aspiring for social equity and political justice. His autobiography provides greater insights into human experiences laden with oppression, neglect, and marginality. His first-person narration records direct experiences of individual characters that stand for a collective dilemma in postcolonial Morocco. This is an aspect that is obviously delineated not only in his account but also in his writings and poems for Nass el-Ghiwane. So, along these lines, Batma's autobiography is a valuable material for the understanding of significant episodes of the past about the lives of real people entangled within the cleavages of postcolonial social order in Morocco. His vividness in representing these categories is not incidental as he himself was one of these marginalized groups.

Al-raḥīl is an intriguing story that not only contains, as it does, powerful moments and impressions of a postcolonial subject in dissolution and in moments of confusion because of a fatal disease he was diagnosed with in early 1990s, but it is also an individual narrative about the sufferings and experiences of the author who is an archetypal representation of his whole generation that underwent tragic moments of despair, anxiety and shattered dreams in post-independence Morocco. In a powerful moment of revelation and in an authoritative squint of confession that lay bare the inner bewilderment of a subject in total dejection, Batma states: "I drank deeply from the cup of life till exaltation.... I drank from the cup of love, happiness and sex.... I experienced the ecstasy of laughter, licentiousness and promiscuity."[34] Through this extract, readers are given the chance to discover that very side of the artist they would ultimately miss to think of; or of that very aspect most of us would probably overlook when taken in a trance-like muse by the serene attitude and melancholic voice of Batma on stage during Nass el-Ghiwane's performances. He reminds us that he plumbed the depths of art and creativity, and lived torment in various ways, and that he was "brother of hope and son of peace, grandson of tolerance, of altruism and of compassion."[35] These revelations are meant to enhance the polyphony of voices at work in Batma's psyche while writing his autobiography.

These few enlightening sentences taken from Batma's autobiographical account show the hidden side of the artist within the author. These and many others to come give a clear idea about the rich experiences and events, albeit harsh and desperate, that the author had lived and witnessed in the course of his life till he discovered that he was dying of an incurable disease he never mentioned by name, but which was cancer. The book sketches these events and narrates the pains, ordeals and sufferings of a young Moroccan living on the fringes of society. It takes the readers in acrimonious journeys into the miserable life and world of a popular musical artist whose notoriety in Morocco became established within the band of Nass el-Ghiwane until his death on a Friday winter night in 1997. He narrates his sad story with dejected and melancholic quotes and verses from Moroccan sayings, proverbs and songs spoken in Moroccan vernacular Arabic. This variety of language structured in a traditional poetic model which is spicy—as a member of the band, Omar Sayed, would often assume *"dārija dyālna fiha al-'aṭriya"* (our Moroccan vernacular is full of spices) is also used spontaneously for most of the text. In the beginning the author feels inclined to give a translation of an utterance into standard/classical Arabic (*Fuṣḥā*), whereupon he writes that his father was once proud of him, and his pride, twisted in a metaphorical tone, became excessively noticeable through this translated sentence: "Larbi will become a real man … he can get money even when this is hidden under a fly's wing." Of course, the translation of this metaphorical image from the Moroccan vernacular (*dārija*) into English cannot be accurate, because, the meanings differ in varying linguistic degrees and become difficult to convey. As Larbi himself has put it, "It is so because it is a pearl hidden in the depth of the ocean."[36] Bound up with this idea is Spivak's notion of the problematic self wherein one's own subjectivity is not constrained by language as the experience of an autobiographer cannot be reduced to a state of signification since the experience felt and lived takes it over language.[37]

In this positive and over celebrated metaphorical construction of the Moroccan vernacular as a pearl in the ocean lies a new conception of national identity. *Al-raḥīl* anchors its vision of personal/national identity in folk-culture and popular traditions. Larbi Batma shows no complexity towards the use of the mother tongue; neither does he show any signs of inferiority as to his artistic career that has been built on and enhanced by a lowly device, the *Bendīr* (Moroccan drum). As he puts it in clearer terms, "the *Bendīr* became my pen; I made my life and got married out of it, I got things, bought clothes, a car, traveled around the whole world. It was my companion from childhood, and I am proud of its company and I do respect it. I think it is an honorable percussion device that rivals international ones."[38]

The book is a thought-provoking text in the history of the country's autobiographical writings in the twenty-first century. It is an additional benefit to the already existing Moroccan autobiographies such as Abdelkabir Khatibi's *Tattooed Memory*, Mohamed Choukri's *For Bread Alone* and Abdelghani Abu-al Azm's *The Shrine*. The narrative is chronologically ordered with a time-span from childhood to adulthood and onwards, concurrently fluctuating both between an unsettled rural life and urban spaces. It is divided into four themed parts, each part bears an intriguing title that comes as an Arabic idiom which literally means "within the ribs"—*ṭay al-ḍolū'*—but when translated into English it distorts the metaphorical meaning that originally stands for hunger. Whatever the meanings assigned to this idiom in the book, we nonetheless discover strong metaphorical images about poverty, blustered expectations, hunger, despair and disillusionment. The introduction titled "the years of Locust"[39] states the author's motivation to write his autobiography and his strong desire to write the longest epic poem in Moroccan dialect, *al-Hūmām Hūssām* "The Chivalrous Houssam" that he had started years before his health stroke.

The first part delves into the author's early childhood while narrating purely innocent memories in various spaces around an insignificant rural village named "Oulād Bouziri" where he grew up in a traditionally authentic tribal community. He led a free life as most children of the rural villages did, though harsh and nascent in many aspects as it was. The village as a powerful signifier and a metaphorical space of ordinariness invokes not only a sense of belonging to roots, but also pictures the Bedouin and humble lifestyle of the countryside dwellers in Morocco whereby hills, birds, rivers, tents, woods and market places furnish the dominant spatial tropes of the text. The spatial backdrop in Batma's text is enunciated through the movement of various characters such as the father, the mother, the grandfather, Sh-hība (the blonde), farmers, French soldiers. The interactions of these characters with textual spaces set up the narrative's events in the first part wherein moments of memory in the author's early beginnings are shared with readers. He says, "Childhood ... innocence. I shall start with pleasant memories ... let me call these beautiful ones, though the word is too much for my imagination. Those memories have had moments of sexual situations and strange behaviors since childhood up to adulthood and even to manhood."[40]

The readers of Batma's text are often amazed, if not shocked, by the type of characters and situations he presents and represents. Most situations and events in *Al-raḥīl* deal with people who go through hard times trying to survive in the respites of poverty, in filthy surroundings, or in the margins of society. Like Choukri, Zafzaf and other writers who have dealt with marginality in their writings and with the real social world of their characters, Batma also does not use misleading terms that dissimulate or downplay the condition of his characters. Euphemistical diction does not furnish his descriptions.

His language, laden with dense expressions, does not hide the shocking reality of his characters and their conditions, including his as well.

The author's characters furnish the narrative texture that takes readers into a marginalized world; the other side of Morocco where hunger, diseases and mundane life are described with vividness and acute intensification. In fact, in his *Al-raḥīl*, Batma is most closely associated with the depiction of the peripheral and disregarded landscape of the rural parts of the country. His work remains unsurpassed in its portrayal of the stark disparities that characterize rural Morocco, while providing crucial insight into the complexity of the country's pre-independence realities. He inscribes and transcribes the experiences of the village-life (Dowār) as did Zafzaf, for example, in writing about the alleys of Casablanca's bidonvilles in his novel *Muhāwalat 'aysh*—"Attempt to Live." Batma's work offers intensely vibrant sketches of the seldom-represented people in their inhabited spaces and through their downtrodden status. It uncovers the peasants' mode of life and their drifts in a perpetual struggle for survival. Being one of them, the author offers intense moments of revelation and powerful descriptions that takes readers into forceful journeys that give voice to marginal characters who are totally and temporarily disconnected from the rest. In Batma's text, these characters provide clear example of the postcolonial subject in quest for a stable identity and for a space where cultural diversity and historical plurality can be articulated. Through Batma's text, we discover the dialectical relationships and connections that bound up the characters with their village's historical and socio-economic life; but also we discover the unremitting violence imposed by a postcolony that has created displaced, alienated and ambivalent subjectivities. Through the spatial arrangement where these characters interact with the author, readers first and foremost recognize the rhetoric of the marginal moving across the narrative boundaries of the novel. Batma tries to bring the readers' focus back to those people that we get acquainted with outside but often choose not to notice. Through this first part of the narrative, the embellished life of superfluity that covers many of the country's public spaces is dissolved; the attention is primarily directed to a periphery that is inextricably unable to produce the country's coherence, unity and homogeneity. In here, *Al-raḥīl* aims at questioning and challenging the established official discourse by parodying it, historicizing it and contextualizing it.

The discourse on the marginal and marginality is reinvented in Batma's text to forge new spaces wherein the marginal is given voice against fixed oppressive hegemonic labels from within and from without the country. His text offers alternative routes for rethinking marginality and marginal identities that the official narratives have eclipsed. Through the telling of an individual life story, the author translates the malaise of a society weighed down by economic, social, political and cultural crises. His autobiographical narrative reflects the historical legacies of power relations that are reformulated through the politics of exclusion as imposed by the colonizer and by the ruling class of the time. There is an overall determination by the narrative to uncover the inherited legacies of exclusion transmitted by the colonizer and the oppressive forms of marginalization initiated from within by the colonial ruling bourgeois class.

What is very important about Batma's narrative is that it tries all the way through to create prototypes of proper Moroccan characters that have been relegated to oblivion whose individual stories are mostly tragic and missing in the archives of national history. Larbi recollects the story of his grandfather's shepherd, el-Makki, who would often carry the young Batma over his shoulders touring the sheep corral and humming his chants or telling him fragments of stories from the "Shepherd and the Wolf" fairy tale. El-Mekki was diagnosed with tuberculosis and had no relatives. When everybody knew about his tuberculosis, they got scared of being contaminated. His disease soon became serious and nobody was allowed to visit him in his shelter.... Batma says,

> I always tricked my mother and paid regular visits to him ... he very often called me yelling "O Larbi, the train is on a burn-out" ... I would soon understand that he needed water to drink, then I had to serve him ... as soon as he would finish the drink, he would keep coughing till he threw up blood.... One day, I did not hear him calling me as he usually did, I went to his cabin and found him dead....[41]

Batma moves on to talk about one of his brothers who has been ruined by the negligence of a medical staff. When he was still baby, the brother was diagnosed with the whooping cough, or *a'waya* as is collectively known in Morocco. His mother took him to a public hospital in the nearby town called *Settat*. The medical staff mistakenly gave him a shot in one of his nerves, and both his foot and arm were paralyzed. The parents did not notice anything abnormal about the baby; but after some time the grandmother found out that he would move neither his right arm nor his leg. The mother took him to the shrine of a venerated saint named "*Sidi Abdeslam al-Wāli Būḥamriya*," his hand started to move, but the leg remained handicapped forever. According to Larbi, nobody in the family knew at that time if the miraculous blessings of the saint made his hand move or something else happened in the body system. In talking about his handicapped brother, Larbi states that his brother had suffered a lot in his life due to his disability which was the main reason for his failure to complete his studies because his classmates would usually make fun of his handicap. When he left school, he started selling retailed cigarettes in front of the *Essaada* Movie Theater, then figs, candies, cartoonish stories, balloons and many more odd things. In 1970, when Nass el-Ghiwane was at its earlier stages of development, his brother was also a member of one of those musical groups that followed Nass el-Ghiwane's lead because he had a wonderful "sad voice." He had learnt to play the banjo, the guitar and the lute without instructors. He had also developed his writing skills to become a *Zajal* poet, and compose his songs. He used to learn by heart Indian songs he listened to while watching Hindi movies that *Essaada* Movie Theater used to show. He had an innate capacity of learning those Hindi songs in a spectacular way. Batma states that his brother "would hear the song once and then learn it by heart though the language was not understandable … 'Dosti,' 'Singham,' 'Teesri manzil,' and many more songs and films that made us cry when we watched them.… There were times when I heard him singing, I would immediately be taken into deep melancholy and I would often ask him to stop or I leave the place…."[42]

Batma has succeeded in capturing the pathos of a society undergoing deep and bitter change. Such change is set against the backdrop of extreme tension between the colonizer and the colonized in colonial Morocco: the distressing hostility, remnant of colonial legacy, that grew between the natives and the French settlers, and the suspicion and hatred felt for natives by the ruling class. Batma's use of varied stories and narrative voices is one of the most striking aspects of his autobiography, and this in turn enhances an attractively expository style, capable of disclosing the individual perspectives of both his characters and readers. As the author allows us into the minds of his characters, we see that they struggle with a sense of belonging to a land and to a culture they consider theirs. His style creates a direct bond between the geographical world and its human inhabitants. It is this connection to place, to the landscape and to the natural world of the village life that is mostly fundamental in the narrative.

Batma brings into the fore the story of "Khali Hammou," uncle Hammou, killed by "Kaznav," the French settler. The uncle was not biologically connected to the family as village dwellers in rural parts would often use the word uncle or cousin to call each other, even if there is no a family connection or ethnic linkage. Uncle Hammou was a skilled fisherman who lived close to the "Oum Rabiaa" river. He was exceptional for Larbi and strikingly impacted on the young boy's childhood. He was handsome, brown-complexioned, and slim with slender stature; he walked in a lofty way and his face bore an eternal smile. He told jokes and fairy tales that kept the family mesmerized all nights long. Men, women and children were often enthralled by his visits except the grandmother and grandfather whom he respected a lot, if he ever talked in their presence; it was with great respect and reverence.[43]

The author kept good and sad memories of him. For example, whenever uncle Hammou planned his visits to Batma's family or to the other families in the *Dowār*, and on his way, he would often pick oranges from Kaznav's farm to offer to children. One day, Kaznav, the French settler seized him with a rifle and shot him dead; and

> Women, men and kids from the nearby villages, or let's say from the "Rhamna" and "Oulād Bouziri" tribes, grieved for his death ... as late uncle had strong and worthy relationship with everybody, young and adult alike ... he died, and the protest was only through tears, since the country at the time was in the colonizer's hands.[44]

Uncle Hammou's story is a case in point that depicts in clearer terms the connection of the natives with the natural environment that is supposed to be theirs while in the hands of the colonizer. In moving closely into uncle Hammou's mind, as a pivotal character, we can immediately understand that orange picking from Kasnav's farm was not ultimately motivated by hatred or revenge against the colonizer, but it was an act of pristine behavior that every bedouin would engage in while visiting others. This humble gesture is not supposed to end up in murder if it had been from another farm owned by a native. For Batma, Kasnav, on the other hand, incarnates the spirit of the colonizing authority driven by the need to protect a confiscated land he takes for granted to be his. This incident in the narrative turns the colonizing machine into a symbol of brutality, cruelty, and sadism, with no humane contacts except relations of domination and submission that turn the colonizer into an army sergeant, and the indigenous other into an object to be subdued and civilized. Batma comments on this event: "I can't really understand why Europe is currently punishing the sordid inhuman Nazists and not the French colonizers ... perhaps the West and the Africans who were once colonized should punish those murderers.... But ... and in the word "but" there is a lot to be discussed...."[45]

Batma also takes his readers into the ambiguous space of an emblematic character in his autobiography. "Sh-hība," or the blondish, is of significant importance in the author's narration of his childhood's eventful development. Sh-hība thickens the novel's thematic imbrications and forces a discussion on the author's earlier sexual identity. She was blonde and beautiful; she took care of the author when he was a child. She was not a baby sitter in the modern term, as Larbi declares, but a relative of the family from the mother's side who has been brought in to care for family daily matters. What is clear is that Batma does not offer graphic depictions of sexuality in his book, as Mohamed Choukri, for example, did in his autobiography. In going through *Al-raḥīl*, we learn that the narrator often, and in various occasions, refers to "sexual situations" that he experienced in his life, but never do we get confronted with graphic scenes of uncovered and straightforward erotic diction of sexual connotations. Instead, what the narrative chooses for its textual imbrications to lay bare the sexual experiences of the narrator bears little resemblance to the timid protagonist who is aware of the social, religious constraints of openness towards a taboo issue in Moroccan society. It is through the storying and re-storying of the person's innermost and darkest secrets that he manages to make some sense of this seemingly perplexing experience in the book.

During the publication of *Al-raḥīl*, the information that circulated at that time was that in the process of re-reading and reviewing the book, Batma insisted on dropping out a whole chapter narrating his most intimate and sexual adventures. The chapter was titled "rib-hidden sexuality." Taking out a whole chapter remained somehow obscure, as Batma himself never talked about the omission during interviews or meetings for the promotion of his book. The tradition of writing about aspects of life that are inseparably intertwined with the private lives of autobiographers and memoirists had already been established in Morocco by the time Batma produced his text. Perhaps the author of *Al-raḥīl* was very much aware of the religious, social and cultural constraints on representing his sexual experiences. For fear of being stigmatized, he probably did not want to take the risk in order to keep a positive image with the public, but this is debatable as well. The nondisclosure of sexuality as a symbolic dimension for the development of the narrative is a serious omission in the book. After all, autobiographies are considered to be true, faithful, objective and sincere.

An early encounter with Sh-hība and another female relative, from the grandmother's side, is the only plain and straightforward situation in the book, wherein the narrator discovers the body of a lascivious fifteen-year old girl; a situation wherein both Sh-hība and the relative in turn try to come to terms with their sexual drive at an early age. Through these characters, we discover with Batma his childhood's trusting, fumbling and embarrassed physical encounters. One evening, when Batma was eight years old, he found himself face to face with both girls in the nearby fields. The relative untied her "Bedouin trousers" and forced the young boy "to blow" in her genitalia in order to stimulate her. The girl, in Larbi's descriptions, "engages in terrible enjoyment, squirming, and reeking like a snake."[46] This incident was unusual and traumatic for Larbi and marked his life ever after. During her stay with the family, the relative would force the narrator into the same scenes repeatedly, either at home or outside in the fields. When she left, Sh-hība engaged in the same sexual behavior. Sh-hība in Batma's imagination is a little weird but whose weirdness and eccentricity are compatible with his as well. The narrative joins up both of them and brings them together into mutually nourishing weirdness. The affair with Sh-hība lasted for a long time until the mother found out about the whole story.[47]

Batma offers an interesting fragment on Sh-hība as a real emblematic character in the narrative. In episodic scenes, the author relates the story of a countryside young girl who is torn between patriarchal dominance and sexual yearnings. In the course of events, "the blonde" left the house when the family discovered that she was raped by a shepherd from the neighboring Dowār whom she met "somewhere in the woods, [he] took advantage of her unwiseness, and raped her … then ran away … when she came back home, blood was noticed between her thighs...."[48] The news spread into the neighboring villages. The grandfather took his horse, followed by few shepherds, and went to look for the escapee. He was later caught and taken to the authorities. The girl's family came and took her away; "they tied her up with a rope and put her on a donkey back while cursing her using the most vulgar words I could hear ... whore ... bitch ... jennet, 'You dishonored us.'"[49] Batma depicts this character in the depths of repression, domination and sordid violence; his descriptive mode in narrating this episode takes readers into village traditions, into dreams about village life and family ethics and into reflections on unembellished, thought-provoking realities and truths of postcolonial Morocco. A "bloody curtain" was drawn on Sh-hība's story; an eternal character living on the margins of society and whose departure was unbearable to Batma. Yet, the question that forces itself is how this same story could be read if the girl had been given the chance to write it from her own perspective. This will certainly add an important dimension to the portrait of the Moroccan village woman. What is clear, though, is that through the interplay of fact and fiction, narrativization and reality, *Al-raḥīl* is interrupted by a progressively representational style, punctuated by extracts that reflect the plight and condition of women from the rural parts of the country; a text with multifaceted levels of consciousness that unveils conflicting discourses about society, religion, culture and tradition.

From Sh-hība's story that left undeniable imprints on the narrator's psychological and sexual lives and experiences, Batma relates other equally interesting sub-narratives that enrich the text's sexual and textual imbrications. These moments of self-definition in the text are redefined through the workings of memory as an itinerary for temporal traveling. Batma remembers specific events in the context of his life narrative and gives a reasonably coherent account of the past memories he retained over long durations of time. Batma seems to be engaging a conversation with past events as they accurately and faithfully occurred. With astute details of a crafted storyteller, he moves to talk about a temporally structured vivid event memory from childhood reminiscences about a personal loss that he never forgot.

The departure of "Zouhra bent al-moudir," the school headmaster's daughter, was a trauma-like event that still vibrated in Batma's recollections when he was writing his life story. The narrative unveils an abortive secret love story between the two wherein another schoolmate, Hassan, disturbs the templates crafted for a successful romance. The whole story started when Batma developed an incredible secret passion and intimacy with Zouhra. This intimate connection is not really uncovered in the text; but Batma recalls events that provide rich human narrative tapestry that is interwoven with personal meanings. Zouhra was an intrinsic part of Batma's early adolescence. In the narrator's eyes, she was another pure version of strong emotions, wild, passionate and ambiguous in their intensity, though the story ended up suddenly and cruelly in heartbreak. This story, according to Batma, was so powerful that it remained seared into his imagination with vividness and clarity and never faded away. However, as readers we never know about the beginnings of this love affair; what is eminently known, instead, is that "innocent love often leads to damaging departures" as he puts it. Batma takes us immediately and steadfastly, with intense emotional sensations, into the traumatic episode and puts us in the real picture and its aftermaths. In Batma's life, we only read about sudden failures, shocking lifetime disappointments, highly painful losses and uncompromised departures but never about arrivals. Through Zahra, we discover a decidedly more fluid sexual awakening of a child in quest for a sexual identity. The school headmaster's departure triggered this episode as, for unpredicted circumstances he had to leave to another school. Pupils and teachers were all standing in the school courtyard listening to the farewell speech; but only three were affected with tender and passionate emotions. As the narrator states, "Zouhra was crying because of Hassan, Hassan was crying for Zouhra, and I was crying my heart out for everything to the point that I came closer to Hassan whom I had hated a lot, we hugged each other and started to weep together."[50] The secret love, though unrequited, of both narrator and Zohra portrays a heartwarming love story that puzzled the narrator at such an early age and which represents the acting out of trauma and loss as well as offering moments of utopian hope. Zouhra is involved in a sexual relationship with Hassan, a fact we get to learn through a love letter that Batma picked from Hassan's pocket. Batma, on the other hand, holds a pure innocent love to Zouhra who, in turn, remains an unresolved enigma in the narrative. Within this complex intersecting moments of conflict over bodily desires and unspoiled emotional cravings, and being unable to adjust herself to and plot a route in such ambiguous situation, Zouhra has simply to disappear from the narrative in order to be resurrected more completely elsewhere.

Zouhra, Halima, Sh-hība and many others whose names he could not remember furnish the ideal setting for the narrator's boyhood wherein disappointment, resentment, failure, unfulfilled dreams, aborted ambitions and delayed aspirations are narrated in straightforward terms. In the course of events, Batma interrupts the first part of his *Al-raḥīl* to offer flashes about the early beginnings of his artistic flair that would later become imminent when he would join a theatrical company in Casablanca as actor, musician and drum player. He remembers with pride transcribed in humble meanings a fascinating episode that took place in the village school. This remarkable chapter in Batma's life was significant as to the curiosity and inquisitiveness it initiated in a schoolchild who discovered his early artistic impulses. The event started when Batma was taught by an artist teacher in the primary school. The teacher played the violon. At the end of each class, he would play for a couple of minutes before the students left. This impressed the young Larbi who enjoyed the teacher's class. One day, the teacher asked if any student had a singing potential so that they could perform together. Batma stood in front of the students singing *msāk msāk, ya-lī ʿaqlī maynsāk* "good night for the one in my thoughts," a popular song that was famous at that time, and which the young Larbi learnt when he visited Casablanca with his father during a national festivity. That was the beginning, as he said; "the pupils gave a round of applause and that was the first warm handclapping I got in my life."[51] Creativity for Batma is an innate flair that starts earlier in life. The village life as he insists was his real source of inspiration. He loved winter times and appreciated the smell of earth when it rained. From reed flutes that he made himself, he also developed a passion for violon that he created using empty oil metal boxes which he equipped and adjusted with strings from a horse's or a mule's hair tail for both the instrument and the bow. The artistic flair in Batma's case also found ample terrains in the weekly performances of two Moroccan troubadours, *Qashbāl o-Zarwāl*, he used to see in the marketplace whenever he had the chance to go with his father. These traveling artists performed in villages and *Souks* (marketplaces) and had, according to Batma, a powerful artistic flair for the improvisation of musical pieces that talked about colonial resistance and national awakening. The village life and the natural world of uncontaminated rurality, together with the incongruities of the city life have largely contributed in uplifting, inspiring and expanding Batma's artistic creativity and musical consciousness.

The second part of Batma's *Al-raḥīl* talks about the author's experiences and adventures in Casablanca after the family's migration from the village to a shantytown in the city. The city space becomes an important device that shapes the narrative structure as events unfold and experiences are revealed. The first encounter with the city in Batma's text was cruel. While he was alone in his family's shanty hut with his brother, who would later become a leading member of *Lamshāhb* musical group, he noticed a half-empty bottle of red wine that the father had left the night before. Out of a real desire to emulate their father, the two took the bottle and got drunk. From that time on, at the dinner table, the father would give them few drinks, thinking that red wine "fortifies blood." According to Batma, the most unpleasant and dreadful chapter of his life would open in the city—he calls it "rib-hidden hideousness." Besides wine, Batma tells us about his addiction to *Ḥashīsh* (cannabis). His father used to smoke it as well and the whole story started when Batma and his friend got home for lunch, but found nothing to eat. They stole the father's pipe and cannabis wallet and started to smoke. As he states, "we forgot about food … we got excited and started endless laughter … in few days we became among those who would always keep looking for cannabis dealers everywhere."[52]

Larbi Batma and Omar Sayed during their stay at Eden Hotel, Paris, for a recording session of their famous song *Mahmūma* (ca. early 1980s) (courtesy Rachid Batma).

Batma takes us into the realm of his characters in the neighborhood around *Essaada* movie theater, around *al-Azhar* school. Lahcen Charlot, a heavy drunkard, Bouchaib Tirlabar, Bouazza and many more archetypes living at the margin of society; characters that share moments of estrangement, disappointment and loneliness. We meet Batma as a student. He gets his primary school certificate, moves into middle school, sells cigarettes at retail and does odd jobs. The narrative stops at the 1965 strikes in Morocco, in which he took part and got arrested as member of the Students' National Union. From school into prison, Batma's life took another turn through what was known as "the events of '65," when the National Union of Moroccan Students incited high school teenagers to take part in some social protests against the government. The bruises he bore in his back, as he confirms, stand as witness to a particular political moment in Moroccan History. As a school dropout and a prisoner, Batma became an anti-institution artist, who has a special attitude towards politics. The category of politics that appeals to Batma is the politics of art, and not party politics, as some would think. For him, Art is a political space through which political positions get articulated. The artist, then, is expected to keep his autonomy and speak truth to power though artistically.

The author concludes this part with the unexpected diagnosis of cancer during the screening of a serial for Moroccan Television. He states that he had been leading a peaceful life before the medical staff found out about his health problem. This event changed the course of his life.

> The only illness complaints I had ever were flu, fever or intestinal cramps.... I mean illnesses that I managed to treat with medicine from the chemist's. I never knew that this disease was eating me up; I never realized that my destiny had already been certain ... and that my life would turn upside down.[53]

The uprooting from the village is delineated by the story as a "catastrophe" that the author wished it had never happened. How did this happen? His father was active member of the nationalist resistance movement during the time of the protectorate and a member of the *Istiqlāl party;* the independence party whose policy was to encourage parents to educate their children. Therefore, after independence, he decided that the family should move to the city in order to provide children with better educational opportunities. However, he writes that he failed in his secondary school and dropped out. The only things he learned inside and outside school walls was to fight and steal, smoke and hang around in the neighborhood cafés with sullen corner boys and prowling *kif* smokers.

> Our class was against anything that had to do with the law of the High School. My classmates were the most troublesome students there, known for skipping classes, fighting and stealing. They were against everything. Most of them were from Ḥay Moḥammādi ... the poor students were against education, politics and even civil society.[54]

Batma's father, though a member of the Independence Party, a bourgeois-oriented political party that mobilized the masses for independence, had to endure the affliction of poverty, misery and destitution. This miserable social reality was not a natural lot. It was rather an outcome of a political system that was created by colonial collaborators and mediators. Within such a destitute family environment, Batma grew up feeling that his family should have been rewarded for his father's committed resistance against French colonialism, and not thrown into the shabby slums of Ḥay Moḥammādi. Batma's forced migration from the village to the city brought individual memories about his father's involvement in resistance against the French colonizer:

> This man [his father] carried out martyrdom operations. The nationalists used to assign tasks to him like taking arms, bombs.... But he lived and died without a card that identified him as a nationalist. He used to refuse to talk about what he did and his achievements, especially when he knew that the card was given to some people who had no connections with the struggle.[55]

This memory of Batma's father, as a militant nationalist who was denied reward and recognition for the sacrifices he offered for the nation is not to be taken as a personal archive, but rather as a public political statement about the frustrating lot resistance fighters met once Morocco got its independence. Still, Batma was proud of his ancestral resistance legacy: "The blood of the traitor was the first blood I saw in my life. The first pride I felt was my father's. At that time, I felt creativity.... I felt like writing.... I wanted to narrate, to visualize ... to say and describe what I saw."[56]

For Batma, the blood of treason was not only a source of his pride and dignity, but also a source of his creativity: His creativity, his inclination towards narration and description. Such a denial of reward and recognition was the major source of his family's poverty: "My father had a wooden slum in Casablanca, amid many slums on a land which was owned by the railway company ... a village of slums ... where candles or carbon lamps gleam every night."[57]

Such circumstances made Batma a school dropout and trouble maker. The adult narrator blames the corruption of society in general and the authoritarian methods of instruction in particular for his own failure, but he also finds causes in his family's poverty and constant internal quarreling. His father in particular is accused of having been insensitive, and a bad example in terms of vices like drinking wine and smoking *kif*.

The third part gives insights into the author's artistic career that first started in neighborhood theater troupes such as *al-Ināra Dahabiya* (Golden Lights troupe) and *Rowād al-khashaba* (Stage-Goers troupe), and then shifts into his career as a professional actor with Taeib Seddki's theatrical company. In here, the author relates the sufferings forced by his father who refuted his theatrical and artistic ambitions. Batma states that he had spent three years within this troupe as amateur actor and that he suffered a lot at that time because of his constant expulsions from home and everlasting quarrels with his father "who used the most horrid epithets I could ever hear[...]. He, God's

Mercy on him, did not want me to become artist and he mostly feared that he would be hassled by the neighbors in the quarter."[58]

Batma in the early 1980s (courtesy Rachid Batma).

In fact, Batma's narrative presents a defiant attitude towards authority. Once he has become aware of the inherent unfairness of those in power, including of course the figure of the father, his rebellion becomes more radical, his suffering more intense while adopting a determined position to revolt against the exploiters among whom he considers his father. This attitude in Batma's case is a trope in Moroccan narrative. The father figure has always occupied a central position in the North African and Moroccan novel. As Mohammed Zahiri explains, there is an obsession with the father figure in the novels of Moroccan writers. The father is not merely the unquestionable head of his household. He generally represents the oppression inherent in the dominant political, social and cultural order.[59]

This brings into mind, for example, Mohamed Choukri in his *For Bread Alone*[60] wherein the narrative is vehemently trying to uncover textual denial of colonial, familial and social regimes from the very beginning. Choukri's narrative perceives the unfair authority of his father since an early age and his threatening shadow will remain decisive in weaving the textual discourse of his work. Within the same vein, and in his *Hijra ilā ardi al-aḥlām* [Migration to the Land of Dreams],[61] Sellam Chahidi is faced with instability and disillusionment at all levels, especially at the emotional level. He undergoes shockingly traumatic individual experiences both at home and abroad. His emotional failure becomes evident from the beginning of his nomadic life, distinctively due to the imprint of his parents' instable matrimonial relationship: "I have always believed that marriage would be no more than what I had witnessed during my childhood between my father and mother; violence and irresponsibility."[62] It becomes important to note that in Chahidi's narrative there is a strong emphasis on the image of the father at the expense of a semi-conscious omission of the mother and a confiscation of the wife.[63] The mother figure is consequently obscured and minimized, if not eclipsed, in the first part of the autobiography. Her shadowy presence is substituted by that of the father on different occasions and the reader becomes aware of the author's denunciation of the symbols of repression through the rejection of the father's authority.

Tahar Ben Jelloun, one of the most renowned contemporary Moroccan writers, has dealt with the theme of fatherhood in its various incarnations in much of his work wherein the exploration of patriarchal structure is most explicit.[64] In *La Nuit sacreée*, Benjelloun offers a real negative image of the father. Against the course of events in the narrative, the dying father confesses that he has forced his seventh daughter Zohra to turn into Ahmed, the son he could not have. This symbolic raping of the daughter's identity in the narrative reveals a more complex father figure that is cruel, autocratic and rapacious.

In Batma's case, the significance of the father figure within the family structure and his role as the ordinary conveyer of traditional culture are apparent in the text; but at the surface of the textual layers, one senses an inestimably affective distance between the author and his father, revealed mainly through the uncertainties and latent manifestations of the text—a distance that further contributes to the sense of an overwhelming emotional alienation from home. Nevertheless, the mother, as a figure of memory, in Batma's text becomes the central reference in the process of remembering. She is often described in emotional ways as the home's main pillar and the center of attention of the neighborhood, either in the countryside or in the city. Her commitment to customs and tradition makes her indispensable for the development of the narrative, and for the communal sphere of where she raised her children. The presence of the mother in the text becomes essential in reviving the everyday life of the Moroccan family and in giving it some sort of continuity as well. What we discover with the author is a symbolic mother, representative of the traditional Moroccan woman who devotes her entire life to her home. The conjured memories of the mother in the text are closely related the authentic space of the Oulād Bouziri as a "lieu de mémoire" that embodies the lost past; the authentic and uncontaminated rituals, space, times, life that have altogether disappeared with the move of the family to experience modernity in the city life.

Batma's narrative moves on to talk about the artistic conflict that occurred in France between Seddiki, the manager of the theatrical troupe, and the actors. The disagreement started when the director himself made an interview with a French newspaper; the actors believed the article that came out to be a strong defamation against their dignity as the manager declared

Larbi Batma and Omar Sayed during their stay at Eden Hotel, Paris for a recording session of their famous song *Mahmūma* (ca. early 1980s) (courtesy Rachid Batma).

that the entertainers in his troupe were just miserable mice that would serve for the testing of his theatrical plays. During the presence of the troupe in France, the author evokes his initiated contact with Boudia, an Algerian theater manager and actor who belonged to the left-wing intelligentsia in Paris and who was assassinated by the Mossad for political reasons. Batma talks about his relationship with this emblematic figure and how the assassination shocked him in the process.

In the last part, the author-narrator charts the beginnings of his musical band and narrates the troubles and obstacles that came on the way when he, and other actors, decided to start a musical band. They were all encouraged when they released their first songs. Those who discovered their lyrics thought that the songs were different and discussed other topics than those musically established at that time, "the songs discussed the sufferings and daily concerns of the poor."

"There is no artistic creativity without sorrow,"[65] Larbi Batma would tell us in his autobiography; or as Edward Munch has put it, "Art grows from joy and sorrow; but mostly from sorrow. It grows from human lives."[66] Batma discovers the potentials of his voice in the ostensible emptiness of a small village called "Oulād Bouziri" one night when he was singing to "Chhiba," a girl who was living with his family. He confirms that she was the first one to notice his voice. Though commonly considered insane in the neighborhood, the girl was exited and amazed when she first heard him singing; and that whenever she sang, she would ask him to sing after him and repeat the chorus.

> That night while "Chhiba" was singing, I was rehearsing some lyrics of the same song. She noticed my voice; yes, my voice was first discovered by an insane girl, whenever she sings, I keep singing after her. She would often stop and listen to me. From time to time she would ask me to repeat the chorus.[67]

Batma's artistic memory has developed through the vivid and colorful rhythms of popular songs and through improvised spontaneous tunes. The radio that kept broadcasting songs on a regular basis at that time, as television was not yet available for poorer classes, recurs in the depth of this memory. Though the school did not allow learning any form of artistic expression at that time, Batma demonstrated strong keenness to music earlier in his age. As a child, he would go to the village huts and picked up cane from the stalk and made flutes. Also he had a clear fondness to singing whenever he heard a rhythm, be it even that coming from the sound of a train's wheels while traveling from his native village to the city.

Batma's Text "the Departure" can be read from various perspectives. The first one affiliates this novel to the literary, esthetic and artistic genre that accommodates the literary experience of the author whereby the writing "self" becomes absorbed within social, historical and cultural intricacies and complexities of a postcolony in disillusionment and of a nation in frustration. It can also be categorized within the confession literature or testimony literature genre, and as an autobiographical piece loaded with mystic and folkloric meanings. The autobiographical genre cannot by any means be the only critical and theoretical stance through which the novel could be viewed as there are still other symbolic junctures that crisscross the epistemological boundaries of the text and which are nonetheless considered unusual to the genealogical construction of the autobiographical writing in general and to the narrative writing in Morocco.

Larbi Batma's artistic career and literary experience belong to another genre other than literature, as he started as a theatrical actor and a vocalist of popular chants who wrote *Zajal*, informal Moroccan poetry writing. I believe that it is the first time a Moroccan artist engages in the ritual of writing a narrative oriented towards documenting and recording wherein writing becomes a pretext that provides a clear and authentic image about the writing self and about other people he got acquainted with in the course of his life, as well as about events he took part in, about practices he was involved in, experiences that he constructed and lived. Writing in this sense goes beyond critical theorizations to drift into a new literary horizon that parallels his text, or at least that surrounds it: popular chanting, folk music, theater and cinema, artistic life in general; besides, he provides a clear picture about social issues during various transitional stages, especially at the level of cultural reference in the early seventies and beyond. Hence Batma inaugurates what may be termed self-literature writing or individual mode of writing, which once was dominated by politicians and community ideology writers.

At the level of reception, Batma's text is not purely literary though it may be qualified as literary since it creates its own literariness that transcends typical stylistic narrative conventions and extricates itself from highly embellished language. It is a textual weaving of an individual drama of struggle, disillusionment, hope and despair that adopts impulsiveness and innateness as a guiding principle during the writing process. This spontaneous mode of being while writing is reasonably inescapable in the case of Batma as it finds its esthetic expression within the depth of this artist's experience. Such a vain and self-conscious experience reacts against the museumization of any forms of literary writing or literary genres and stands in opposition to any inflated and hyperbolic writing styles. His writing comes as it is, untainted, stripped off of rhetoric, and hence, coexists and engages in dialogic interaction with several languages and several linguistic registers. Perhaps what becomes easily grasped by readers is an ideal language of essence immersed in a Sufist discourse that goes beyond parodying or mimicry. It is and unmasked language that believes in truth and in human values. However, the use of unpremeditated, un-oratorical language does not preclude the amplification of questions about individual existence within a network of intersections where metaphysical and anthological anxieties and obsessions are embraced by an instinctive, pristine language with its conceivable structures and significations.

"The Departure" as a title is loaded with intense meanings that both are transparent and suggestive, and subject to various interpretations—namely affiliations of the text to the author, the author to the text—the relationship between the text and the reader—then the reader and the text from the perspective of all possible levels that engage a critical deconstruction without basically overlooking the horizon of expectations forged by the text with itself in the light of the negotiation of endless binaries that complicate the narrative and deepens it further. As "the Departure" invokes nomadism and travel, it also builds up an imaginative world of possible affiliations and textual connections to powerful psychological and anthological moments of anxiety, anguish, dislocation and threat. These offer a single reading of the text and the title, and a reading of the text as a whole entity disassociated from the title. Hence, the title and the text could bear various interpretations as signifiers in this particular narrative fail to homogenize interpretive taxonomies of reading.

> I see them now between my ribs.... I can see my early beginnings full of hopes, running across the hills of Oulād Bouziri, a child from the vast Chawiya plains, hanging around the 'Oum Rabiaa' river banks.... Rahal ben Larbi, my grandfather's name who adopted my mother [...] Rahal my father's name, Hadda my mother ... departure, borders, hardship ... names that denote violence, discomfort, volatility ... this is how my childhood was, departures from Casablanca to my countryside village.[68]

Then, what kind of departure does Batma's text invoke? Is it about the movement of the narrator, the character, the author from his native village to the city, and then to other locales inside and outside Morocco? Or is it a symbolic departure in the collective imagination that transcends the author's memory as an enigmatic individual within a complex society. I think that the symbolic dimension of the movement is horizontally constructed to bring together insinuations about the title. In fact, the physical and the symbolic coalesce, and as readers we cannot poetically grasp the interplay between representation and reality from within the textual poetics of the narrative unless we become aware of the intersections between the figurative and the material; and through the combination of the autobiographical discourse and other discursive representations about arts, existence, writing and imagination, love and death in the autobiographical circle of Batma's account.

These intersections as a whole overlap with the discourse of lamentation and grief reiterated in the narrative: grief on the journey from the village, mourning the loss of the grandfather, the father, then the mother, and even the dog named "Mssika." Mourning the loss of his best friend Boujmia occurs on various occasions as well. He writes:

> Boujamaa died and after his death, many wonderful things such as friendship vanished as well. Until now, I have not found a friend like Boujamaa.... God's mercy be upon him. I was younger than he was, but he believed in my ideas and my future ambitions.... The blow was sudden and harsh.[69]

The discourse about death in Batma's text and language, and also in the overall narrative structure is not isolated from the thematic concern about departure and separation. It indicates a narrative mode that goes beyond imaginary loss, defeat and submission to embrace a discourse on Metaphysics whereby the author is positioned between two worlds; one tangibly known and physically narrated, and a second one caught between desires, revelation and morality as clearly evidenced in various sections of his autobiographical account. Readers of Batma's text will immediately get aware of the author's unremitting battle with death; an inevitable end that is perceived in the narrative as constantly delayed and deferred through occasional reliefs and momentous comforts derived from the innocent and beautiful memories he narrates with utmost sincerity until we get to a very revealing statement wherein he declares that "a patient like me cannot express a wish for tomorrow ... because he knows he's convicted to death! ... Besides, someone with a disease like mine cannot know when the end would be, just waiting for death."[70]

This is unusual to Moroccan writing; it is probably the first time a Moroccan writer expresses intense images about a situation where death and life of the author come at odds in critical moments of revelation and confusion. Death and life in this narrative become invisible characters that have powerful presences and powerless abilities in translating reality in plain and blunt truths. It is through these clashing discourses of life and death that "The Departure" as a text can shake and even disturb reading practices that work against oblivion. It is, after all and regardless of the human condition and situation under which it is written, an account that stands as witness to the postcolonial Moroccan political and social conditions that Batma and his band (Nass el-Ghiwane) are part of. When readers start questioning this text in the light of narrative writing, they become aware of the strategies deployed by the author, though unconsciously, in blending both the autobiographical and the testimonial discourses. Suffice it to reconfigure the permeated meanings encompassing the author's name and his text, with the help of internal and external textual indicators, to discover this particular and exceptional mode of writing. As a postcolonial subject, Batma offers a life narrative that textures extraordinary opportunities of situations to narrate a legacy of social injustice and oppression, of violence and social sufferings.

Also, as a testimonial narrative, Batma's text moves across various spaces and within unlimited boundaries of memory to produce intimate attachments between characters who testify and those who bear witness to legacies of dispossession, sufferings, injustice and cultural disintegration in postcolonial Morocco.

The discourse of writing in Batma's case, based on the intrinsic connectedness of temporal and spatial relationships that texture the narrative, is loaded with intense and thickly condensed moments that produce drifts and shifts in the genealogical order of the account, especially when death as concern and obsession is evoked. In deep moments of meditation and confusion, the author states: "Now, I am trying to write down the days that have gone by and I am in a duel with death; but the only wish I have is that death disowns me for a while to inscribe those moments and memories and express my hopes."[71] These moments of despair, melancholic hope and desolation go also hand in hand with the discourse on arts throughout the whole narrative; a technique that informs Batma's book and which is concurrently meant to distort the conventionally and structurally hierarchical discrepancies between what is revealed, what is thought, what is remembered and what is witnessed as actually happening.

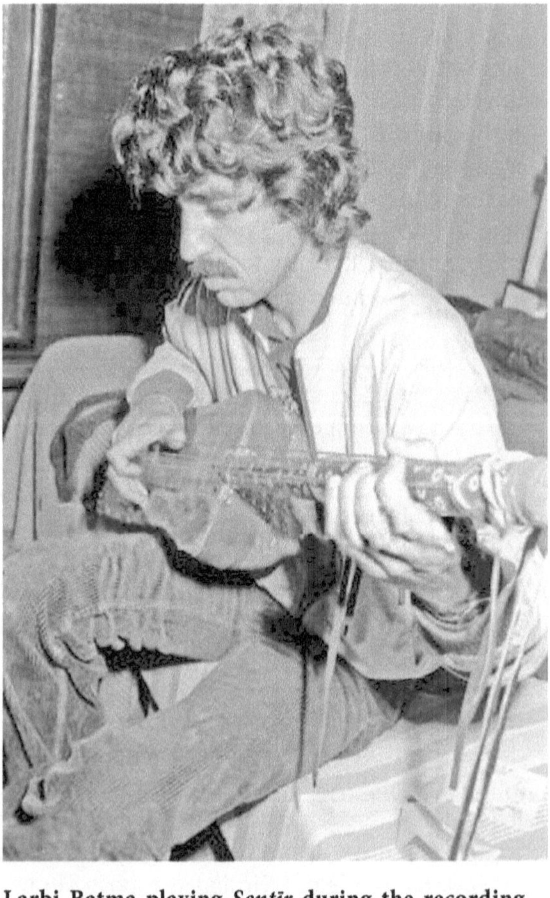

Larbi Batma playing *Sentīr* during the recording of *Mahmūma*, Eden Hotel, Paris (ca. early 1980s) (courtesy Rachid Batma).

These are central discourses in Batma's "the Departure" and nothing can match them in tone and emotional expression more than the discourse on love; the transcendent love of the father, the mother, the grandfather and brothers, and of the people who lived with the writer and whom he loved. He declares,

> Every Saturday, we would wait for my father to come back from the city. Whenever we heard the evening train's sound, my brothers and I, attended by my mother, God rest her soul in peace, stayed in front of the house covered by the breeze of a pitchy night while keeping our eyes on the hills that stand between the house and the train station. As soon as we get a glimpse of my father's silhouette, we all rush towards him cheered and followed by the sound of the barking dogs. We hug him and he hugs us, and at home we get candies, clothes and books.[72]

Batma is a multifarious and complex writer whose "the Departure" combines the authoritative presence of nature as perceived by the artist's emotions pulsing between the lines of the book so that the reader feels a reddening horizon, hotter earth, blossoming roses, and children's laughter; and between the qualitative presence of the human being as drawn by the writer's imagination through vivid characters from the unfathomable Morocco. Batma's characters live in the countryside or at best on the margins of the city, but still leading their own life that is so different and complex. His writing becomes typical as we move further into the hidden transcripts of his text. What we discover is his way of combining, in moments of bitterness and deep thought, both the child-like uncontaminated sensation of someone who comes into contact with the spell of nature and human emotions that encompass mystical revelation of undisclosed wounded souls, pains and sins.

Batma had stark aversion to talking about death. In his interviews after the publication of the book, he always insisted that *Al-raḥīl* was not about death as such. He probably was not afraid of dying as much as he felt too embarrassed to talk about it. In his text, life and death intersect in a single moment of confusion whereby death becomes an inevitable end, an inescapable fate, a collective human identity that charts the individual's borders and destiny and in the meantime triggers virtuosity, creativity and exception in life. This intricate and multi-layered elusive feeling about death that the artist perceives ambiguously is what makes the author see death as "a white cloud":

> *lmūt jāya ki sḥāba bayḍā*
> *tabqāw beslāma yā-hl al-ma'rūf*
>
> Death is looming around like a white cloud,
> Rest in peace grateful souls

Batma's text remains a narrative of grievance, moaning and complaint of a whole generation more than a mere autobiographical work. It is a historical document about various spaces wherein the national and the historical overlap to give complex insights about the post-colonial condition of Morocco. Although Nass el-Ghiwane prefer to attribute their musical performances and lyrical potentialities to the group as a whole, it is a well-known fact that Larbi Batma was the main song composer in the band, especially after the death of Ahgour Boujemaa. This is not meant to undermine the contributions of the other members but rather to highlight his vital role as the "hidden" poet of the group. His poetic voice is not accidental nor are his thematic preoccupations coincidental; they are a product of his deep entanglement in the social and historical reality of his country. As a child, he underwent various migrations and suffered from diverse hardships. This is not to be taken as merely a personal space whose construction goes back to colonial times, but rather as a collective space, whose significance derives its meanings from the concerns of a whole generation, the postcolonial—an historical era, the post-independence era, and a whole nation, the Other process of Morocco.

Batma's personal life was complex, as his autobiography attests. Its complexity is to a large extent an embodiment of the complexity of post-independence Morocco. His linguistic "I" in the narrative as a discursive representation is not to be taken as simply the real historical "I" who lived in a certain period of time, that is to say as an authentic "I," but rather as a political "I" through which the discourse of opposition got constituted into his popular poetry writing experience. Such a political "I" encompassing the disillusioned Moroccan after independence does not stand for simply the individual memory of Batma, but rather helps reconstruct the memory of independence as well.

Batma's individual "I" is not the artist's pure "I," an "I" that is governed by art for art's sake. It is rather the political artist's "I" that is structured by art for the sake of politics, not in the literal sense. Artistic creativity for Batma becomes a cultural space and an esthetic tool through which he critiques the existing social formation. This "I" is historical and real, but it is not to be taken as such. It is the starting point through which a perspective on history is open, whose specific location is the peripheral popular consciousness.

Those individual memories that echo Batma's historical reality are significant. They are not interesting as ends in themselves, that is, as authentic narratives about the past as it really was. They are important rather as means through which that past can be reconstructed, not the past of an individual, but the past of a whole society at a specific point in history. Hence, the individual becomes an icon about a whole community. Batma is not to be viewed as just a distinguished artist. He, in fact, embodies a political statement about the Moroccan nation after independence. Such a political statement is not a final truth in itself. It is rather one perspective, that is significantly enough to represent popular consciousness. Those individual memories played a vital role in the constitution of the voice of opposition within Batma's subjectivity, a socializing process that was doomed to reside in the periphery. Hence, the reconstruction of such memories is extremely interesting to account for the discursive surge of opposition within the Ghiwanian songs. What is at stake is not the reconstitution of their individuality, but rather the reconstitution of their historical significance as sites through which post-independence Morocco can be not only questioned, but also re- inscribed, rethought and redefined from the perspective of the peripheral position of popular consciousness.

Al-raḥīl also offers fragmented moments and glimpses from the encounter of Batma with French women he met during his stay in France in the early 1970s. This section in the book, though small as it appears, is a rich experience of a young Moroccan stranded between two cultures. His experience moves across episodic boundaries of alienation, while negotiating spaces for self-assertion, existential struggle, meaning and survival in Morocco and Paris. It stages the mobility of fantasy and desire, remaps the topography of the body and disturbs the paradigms of adventure. This episode gives clear indications about the protagonist's journey from economic hardship in Morocco of the 1970s, to a life of mobility from Morocco to France while traveling with Seddiki's theatrical troupe. When the troupe got into trouble with the manager due to the circumstances previously mentioned, and also because of cold weather and the scarcity of theatrical performances that the troupe was supposed to give for North African immigrants, performers started to quit gradually; some went back to Morocco, few others overstayed their legal sojourn for some time and then left.

Batma and Boujemaa spent over three months together in Paris, wandering and hanging around, leading a bohemian-like life before leaving back home. It is during this period that both of them came into immediate contact with France, as a foreign place. In this particular episode about a temporally instantaneous life abroad, Batma's autobiography offers an interpersonal account about a particular place and a particular time; a brief story dealing with spatial and temporal impacts on an individual's alienated and disintegrated self. This sub-narrative about his nomadic wanderings takes shape only through a fragmented account of the places he visited, the people he met in the *banlieues défavorisées* (disadvantaged suburbs), and the descriptions he offered about Paris and other locales. These locales are delineated by the author as hostile spaces of racial violence and epistemic hypocrisy with no promising possibilities for reconciliation. His struggle to straddle the two worlds of Self and Other is what guides the movement of this sub narrative in the autobiography. Batma's textual imbrications give problematic insights into the author's northward mobility, into experiencing new ways of seeing and being; and into processes of reacting against France's inscriptions of its Otherness. In the course of events, Batma meets queer and strange French girls that are reduced by the narrative into a set of repulsive, sexually perverted "objects" who would find delight in making love in toilets after stealing from stores with the narrator.[73] Evelyn and Cathy illuminate the sub narrative with interesting facts that harbor sexual enthrallment, adventure, unrestricted freedom, and queer encounters in colonial metropolis. Batma, on the other hand, harbors the typical oriental male fantasy about the west and in particular about an exotic otherness.

For the author, the French girls he managed to strike up a relationship with are most closely associated in his text with symbols of disloyalty, falseness and betrayal. For the French girls, Batma best epitomizes the oriental Other who would set them free from their psychological disorders and liberate their sexual troubles. What these cultural encounters between the author and the French girls indicate, since most of the time they lead nowhere, as they seem to turn out into stories with unsuccessful endings, is that there is a deep-seated malaise in the French society that hampers the integration of two distinct cultures. Integration seems to be impossible to be fulfilled because the idealized images about the West are proven to be illusive and in crisis. What the narrative brings to the surface, instead, is a pathologically disordered culture in need of recovery and salvation.[74] What brings these girls together with the narrator is bodily pleasure and bohemian adventurous escapes from the confines of society, and sexual promiscuity.

Underneath textual structures, there are hidden gaps in the narrative that refer to the author's unconscious concern with sex as a liberating force. This is of immediate relevance if, for example, we consider Tayeb Salih's masterpiece *Season of Migration to the North*. In Salih's work, the main character, Mustafa Sayed, tries to symbolically reverse the history of western colonialism by indulging in sexual adventures with British women. The sexual and textual encounters in Batma's case are interwoven with situations in which affiliation and filiation are utterly intertwined. For Batma, the motherland is a space of filiation and the migratory experience is an act of affiliation based on a conscious choice of self assertion, sexual adventure and novel artistic experiences. This process of becoming turns into a subject position in transition, occupying a third space whereby the filial sense of belonging and affiliating mode of becoming undergo moments of anxiety and tension throughout the episode set in France. Occupying this third space is empowering, as it helps develop a double consciousness that creates a distance from the hierarchical parameters between here and there, between now and then, and between the lost and the would-be recovered. The liminality of transition between here and there becomes even more complex in Batma's text, particularly because he celebrates a nomadic view of postcolonial identity, rejecting both filiative and affiliative processes of being and of becoming. As a nomadic subject, the author is fixed neither at home nor in the host country. He can neither totally occupy the center nor the cultural space of origins from which his journey started. Lack of "coherence and unity" in both locations, as Salah Moukhlis assumes, sets the author "on a perennial quest for a sense of stability that will never be achieved."[75] He is a marginalized outsider who is always on the move to create spaces where his identity can be reinvented and redefined. The cultural visibility of the author through his artistic potential, performing in the streets of Paris with a French girl and composing the lyrics of his songs to be played by Nass el-Ghiwane later, gains much power in the narrative and turns his marginality into a "signifying liminal space" of opposition and subversion where some sort of unconstrained freedom is achieved, dichotomies are deconstructed and hierarchies are subverted. The west in Batma's case is not solely a fascinating terrain where he can satisfy his sexual and social frustrations, but also a realm of poetic inspiration and artistic creativity. In a fragmented matter of fact, Batma remembers how he left the troupe and left back home. However, immediately we learn that he planned another trip to France to join his friends in the theatrical company who stayed for better life. His subsequent trip to Paris is thus represented as a way of expressing his refusal to comply with a reality of social and political stagnation in Morocco. Unlike Khatibi's autobiographical narrator in *La Memoire Tatouée* [tattooed memory] who initiates a northward journey to Paris in search for a more existentialist understanding of identity, Self and belonging, Batma's main objective in his journey is the quest for an artistic inspiration, for creative freedom and for personal adventure.

In this section, Batma is primarily concerned with the specificities of place and with how a subject in moments of transition is shaped both in and out of that place. The author is trying to bring forward the idea of the self-in-motion, or the troubled and unsettled self, and the whole cultural discourse about Otherness in the imperial center. His sub narrative draws on a literal and symbolic protagonist's journey, "shuttling between places, to dramatize the contradictory formations of the postcolonial subject between cultures,"[76] as Lisa Lowe puts it. Batma records his personal movements, his emotions, his individual and cultural backgrounds, and his struggle for hope and determination. There is an autobiographical desire in Batma's text, or an inherent impulse rooted in the quest for self and the desire to document a life beyond borders as well. It is an individual's journey in constant motion struggling to acquire agency and voice outside the confinements of the postcolony. Batma feels both dragged and pushed by the strangeness of the place. Although he feels some attraction to France, he cannot refute his grounding in homeland. In this sense, and from time to time, he engages in metaphorical returns to his ancestral home in an attempt to capture the voices, sensations, and memories of the past through the poems he used to write and the lyrics he composed during his "exilic" stay in Paris and Grenoble wherein he tried to recapture a sense of origins and roots through his affiliation to Moroccan,

Arab, Palestinian communities together with his friends Boujmeaa and Boudia, the Algerian pan-arab activist.

In reading between the lines through this section, one feels that there is a tension between the narrator's dreams and the real world of the colonial center to which he has been drawn. These strained moments become more disturbing when he discovers that Europe, as a luring space to the colonized, is an imagined reality, a constructed idea, a fantasized dream. While enduring an imposed experience of alienation and dislocation, the narrator becomes aware of the racial violence to which he was subjected; "*sale Arabe*" (dirty Arab) was an epithet that struck him during his stay, and which was strong enough in demythologizing the European dream of a postcolonial subject in search for expressive modes of creativity in the colonial center. Also significant in the author's space of literary nomadism is his refusal to yield physically and metaphorically to a western culture that has failed in many ways to recognize and accommodate cultural and geographical differences. This is best illustrated through his rejection and displacement of one of the most popular beliefs among Moroccans that the key to success becomes possible only through imperial metropolis where the promises of a better life are abundant away from home that, in turn, offers nothing except false hopes and empty promises. But when he becomes aware that it is in his homeland that regeneration and rebirth are supposed to be fulfilled, he dropped out the idea and simply decided to travel back to Morocco.

Unfolding Al-Alam (Pain) for Esthetic Narration: Autobiography of a Prophesied Death and a Narrative of Illness in Performance

Anyone who is familiar with and attracted to Batma's *Zajal* writings for Nass el-Ghiwane, as I was, and anyone who has always valued his poetry in particular for the breathtaking simplicity and splendor with which he could develop his impulse and effect in this subtle genre, cannot help reading Batma's autobiographical memoir with much admiration. Batma's autobiography is as effect-laden in writing as are his best poems for his musical band. It is in subject and tone indistinguishable from much of Batma's poems written with sincerity, acute details and dire metaphorical rendering.

In his *Al-raḥīl*, Batma takes a daring gaze back into his beginnings and traces his life backward while memorializing those disturbing moments in which he hardly escaped the unbearable grabs of the specter of poverty, social turmoil and political unrest. His narrative offers significant events that have shaped both his individual and collective life in postcolonial Morocco. He has managed to take his readers into a heart-rending journey about his life experiences since childhood until he was diagnosed with a fatal disease; a disease that was enabling enough in triggering his writing potential. Yet, of all the events narrated in the first part of his account, nothing would match his profound concern with death in the second part of his narrative.

In talking about death as concept and metaphor in American autobiographical writings, Thomas Couser has clearly stated that

> The expectation of death may impel the writer, as though the composition of an autobiography might help him to compose himself in the face of death[...]. More importantly, the form and content of the narratives are often significantly shaped by the writer's preoccupation with death, even though the event itself eludes direct treatment. Two problems overlap here in an interesting way. As a mortal, the writer may seek to come to terms with death. As an autobiographer, he may want to write a conclusion, which in its finality and significance, will somehow be equivalent to his own death.[77]

Such is the case with Batma's *Al-Alam* (*Pain*) wherein death becomes necessarily attainable as a conclusion. The second part of Batma's autobiography is a short narrative that came out with Toubkal Publishing in 1998 after the author's death. It is an excruciatingly painful memoir wherein sufferings string one narrative event to the next within a gloomy setting peopled by fading characters that seem to endure the specter of death on a daily basis. Batma's feelings on the subject of his own death are expressed plainly with no metaphorical twists or turns that would fail to reveal the more profound breakdowns of his condition. The structure of this narrative, which weaves temporal shifts while moving from one painful moment into another, focuses on events that highlight the pains of experiencing unstable and interrupted flow of emotions in waiting for an inescapable end. The main question that Batma's account attempts to raise is how the author/narrator in *Al-Alam* has managed to confront his own end with its real agonizing trappings, while his language remains defiant and very powerful all the way through.

Al-Alam compiles scenes from the hospital where the author was being treated, and it repeatedly deploys pieces from the narrator's instantaneous prayers and meditations in the form of poems to break from scenes taking place at the hospital and to shift into monologues that narrate melancholic situations and wistful sorrows. Batma has written about his own death, something unusual in autobiographical writing in general, and in Morocco in particular. According to Barrett John Mandel,

> It may be possible to write an autobiography without consciously dwelling on the subject of death, but it is surely not surprising that in fact most autobiographers are extremely aware that they are writing their own stories just somewhat sooner than someone's else writing it for them.[78]

If autobiography writers are interested in stories of life and about life as lived and experienced, and if they seem to be unable to reflect on the profound emotions which must inevitably suggest a brief discussion or even allude to the subject of their own departure from the world, Batma, on the contrary, has been very conscious of the last episodes of his existence and has written about the end of his own life. Batma's text, hence, creates an aggressive, if not vulgarized, rhetorical space where the narrator's body and mind, past and present, memory and oblivion collide together to turn into a battle zone upon which an endless war is fought against the multiple incarnations and permutations of the deadly disease.

Within the same vein, *Al-Alam* is entirely devoted to the author's psychological and ontological experiences as a dying patient in a hospital where he spent the last moments of his life. It also offers flashbacked episodes about his state of mind during his stay at home for short breaks while waiting to join the clinic for chemotherapeutics sessions. What is striking about this second part is its theatrical diction and structure—it is divided into scenes that blur temporal and spatial boundaries to produce a narrative loaded with strong emotional moments wherein the narrator/protagonist reveals heart-rending, tear-jerking events inside the hospital and at home in his apartment in *Rue Oran*, overlooking Gautier district in Casablanca.

Rue Oran, is a symbolic street where Batma and his friend Ahmed Snoussi, a humorist and satirical artist who was banned from Moroccan television for the ideological and political discourses his art delivers, share the same building. *Quartier Gautier*'s onomastic diversity and multiplicity of meanings it purport points to the intricately differentiated contours of colonialism, neo-colonialism and postcolonialism on a local scale; it is a neighborhood for the well-off and also for people from various strands, populated by Moroccan Jews, Spaniards, Italians and French. Gautier as a constructed space in a metropolitan contact zone of colonial memories and postcolonial stories allowed Batma to envision a world of contradictions on a daily basis and visualize the contrasts that have produced stiff spatial lines of isolation characteristic of colonial legacy. That's where he wrote most of his poems and theatrical shows in the early 1980s when he first settled there.

Al-Alam as a short but extremely emotive and upsetting narrative makes strenuous semantic efforts, through the choice of words and expressions that actually call for careful interpretation, to depict the narrator laboring dynamically and in an unrestricted linguistic style with his fatal disease. In reading *Al-Alam*, one is taken into the puzzling world of hospitals wherein the author is attempting vigorously to explore the defying moments of locating his traumatic experience as a dying patient in an expressive context. Some of his close friends, those who kept visiting him regularly said that he was writing the last chapter of his life and was so weak that he could not move his hand. Sometimes he would keep writing until the pen fell down. Abdel-Ilah Ajil, a friend and member of a theatrical troupe who directed one of the author's plays, tells us that Batma has an incontestable obsession with writing and states that most scenes of the TV serial that he wrote for Moroccan television, *Janb al-bir* (beside the well), under the direction of Farida Bourkia, were improvised and written at the time of screening. Bourkia, according to the same source, was flexible enough in giving Batma's improvisations an esthetic authority because she understood that he was a bundle of ideas that would at any moment twist the narrative of the serial into productive and powerful tales. Batma in his *Al-Alam* incarnates that obsession with his writing, struggling to capture details of his pain to give shape to moments that might otherwise look shapeless and incipient. In so doing, he seems to tell his readers that this is not a story of life and death, but an account of what it means to be alive; it is a way of being alive. Writing can resurrect and keep hope for and about life. Batma's narrative about a prophesied death turns into a descriptive terrain of last events and a consolatory force to the self, even if the descriptions remain temporary and confusing, and the consolations turn out to be transitory because of the inevitable tragic lot of death.

In *Al-Alam*, another journey about torment, physical helplessness and psychological torture sets up to build a narrative of events towards an unavoidable destiny. The text is limed in time but extends its textual fabric over pain and sufferings all the way through. It sums up the events of a journey into the world of a malignant disease and its treatment wherein recovery is almost impossible. It is a real gloomy moment of transition of a troubled memory wherein "a black curtain raises, on a black stage, lit with black lights, to give way to a black actor, wearing black, to enter."[79] One of the most important and obvious symbols that overwhelm this quote is the aura of darkness.

Darkness and light in literature typically represent and two conflicting forces that epitomize good and evil, knowledge and ignorance, love and hate or happiness and despair. Darkness can stand for a state of confusion, uncertainty, tragedy, alienation and depression. Certainly, in Batma's text, it stands for the combination of all these; though it becomes a powerful symbolic metaphor that lends itself to one single interpretation. It is the metaphorical and metaphysical embodiment of the shadows of death. This is a very revealing quote that adopts theatrical structure and sums up in meaningful terms Batma's state as noticed and perceived by the dying patient he was. It also highlights his Sisyphus struggle with cancer to invest what remains of time in order to create meanings for a certain life. Essential to *Al-Alam* is that it is fraught with tension, conflict, contradictions and desire in a troubled memory that refuses to surrender. These conflicting desires and contradictions remain deeply faithful to questions and quests that do not seal off Batma's memory, but involve it concurrently in a struggle with the world of hospitals, with what he calls the pliers of medicine.

Al-Alam starts with the narrator's intention to rewrite the other remaining part of a life awaiting documentation. The idea of engaging in writing came to him when he was alone home revisiting the first part of his autobiography and reflecting on its reception by the readers. Since everybody, as he believes, thought of the book as real confession about an individual's journey into death, Batma insists that the other chapter about his life should be taken as a journey into sufferings. These sufferings started when he first heard about his disease. The news came from a nurse he met when he first entered one of the city's hospitals for a quick surgery to take out a cyst from his neck. Though the surgery was successful, the biopsy tests proved otherwise. The nurse revealed the bad news over a phone call that lasted for few minutes. From this very moment, the narrative adopts incredibly gloomy descriptions of situations and events to come later; regular visits to hospitals and clinics inside and outside Casablanca would give the narrative a set of ambivalent feelings and emotional twists. The narrative captures one of those moments of absolute hopelessness when the narrator finds himself torn amid an endless chain of questions about his plight as a helpless patient. He is shown in a terrible moment of despair close to the beach writing few stanzas of a poem that he never finished, according to him. He tore the papers into small pieces, threw them into the air and headed towards the nearest bar. Immediately, the narrator's tormented mind takes the readers into the limitless and relentless space of the city to talk about his friends, some of whom he discovered by chance, and for the first time, as patients in hospitals being treated and fighting against the same disease, others who, in the course of events, had already passed away.

Batma tries to give shape to his experience during the whole time he spent at the hospital taking chemotherapeutic sessions by fashioning and refashioning himself through the retelling of a story that, in effect, is meant to re-create life and reproduce a new experience that writes the author's self into a new narrative about life. The narrator is aware that he is caught within the cleavages of impossibilities and hopelessness. So, the narration of his sufferings and pains since the very moment he was diagnosed with cancer is an instance of an individual who does not, and cannot, obscure the truth about his fate as a dying patient. His autobiographical account, namely the second part, *Al-Alam*, registers particular moments about orientations, (re)orientations and (dis)orientations towards life as experienced by a body in torture and torment. Still, that very body believes that he can write a narrative of his own even in moments of extreme anxiety and concern. For him, the task is worth undertaking since the experience is of vital importance to document but whose outcome remains undoubtedly uncertain and unknown.

The narrative sometimes moves into flashbacks to relate events about the author's moments caught within the plies of a rotten medical care while moving from hospital to another. *Al-Alam* is an intricate narrative that portrays the author's inner conflicts; the artist's state of mind battling against his Self, against his predicament as a Moroccan subject, and against a deadly disease. It is also an authentic story that documents the ordeals of Moroccan artists living on the margins of a society caught within the cleavages of poverty, destitution and exclusion.

Batma kept writing about his terrible moments in spontaneous and simple ways to uncover the ordeals of a desperate patient awaiting death. In this case, *Al-alm* is not about successful accomplishments or about triumph over hardship and misfortune; it is less about finding any ultimate meanings to life and to existence. Much more than this, it is an affirmation about the incompleteness of life with its unpredictable turns and shifts. Such unpredictable turns are worth narrating, according to Batma who also keeps struggling to narrate an un-narratable illness, albeit his illness is narrated from an artistic perspective where he easily catches moments that give him insights into the deadly disease, and which could by no means be narrated as such from someone with no artistic flair or powerful feelings.

Writing in Batma's case becomes a means to flee, perhaps to defeat, the tragic labyrinth of death. He knew how the game began and how it would end, and was quite sure that he would not get out of the maze safely. His narrative captures flashes of utmost hopelessness, loneliness and desolation about a tragic situation of suffering wherein the act of narration becomes an inducement for patience, oblivion, desires and hopes. It is also a vehement denunciation of Moroccan post-colonial condition noticeable enough in contradictions and ironies about values and mores that ridicule medical care and doctors whose hypocrisy and greed have altered the profession.

While writing, a hazy sound of a song by the Egyptian singer *Mohamed Abdelwahab* suddenly came from a neighboring house—*yāmsāfer li-wahdek* (lonely traveler). He knew that he was a traveler himself whose departure is naturally certain and whose return is definitely impossible. This inescapable ending develops all the way through the narrative and threads the text with sorrowful moments of mourning and melancholy. This is a "bare autobiography" with no frills and no alterations but with great

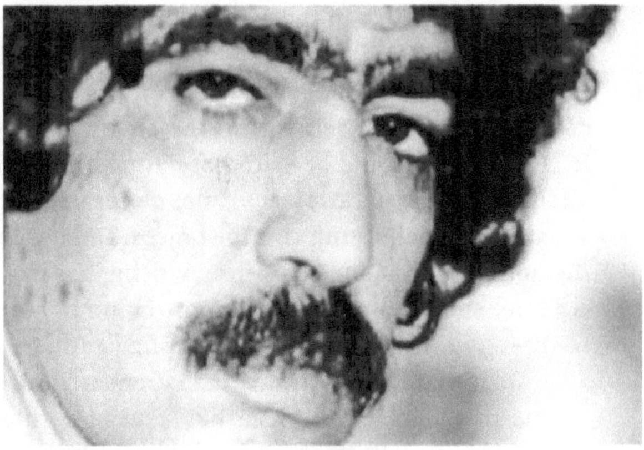

Larbi Batma in 1992 (courtesy Rachid Batma).

faithfulness to every single moment captured by the author. It is bestowed with spiritual liveliness and with quintessence purity and nobility that confront the disease with utmost audacity. Readers of Batma's *al-Alam* will discover not only a very sensitive author who documents his death with depth of thought and with a powerfully poignant language, but also a narrator who excels in narrating with minute details his bohemian life, alcohol, drug addiction, women, success and failure wherein fate overlaps with dreams on life and thoughts about death.

As echoed in his autobiography, writing for Batma is not an easy process to achieve but it is fraught with brutality and pain. Writing about human condition in his case needs strong will and authentic drive to talk about the dismays of a "malignant disease inside one's self," as Batma puts it. In his *al-Alam*, Batma does not experience a transient death but he undergoes atrocious moments in thinking of and writing about a death that takes time to disclose its revelation, to the extent that it turns to be a real companion in a journey where no return is granted. His mode of writing, thus, becomes an alleged reason to procrastinate the secrets and mysteries of death. Viewed from this perspective, the whole narrative offers powerful instants about a moment of vision wherein life and death converge together to produce a complex knot of uncertainties about the condition of an artist in agony. This also converges with powerful feelings about absences and presences, dreams and hopes, written with explicit language that plainly displays things as they are supposed to occur.

Also, one may venture to say that writing about Batma, the individualized (I) in the narrative, is writing for that very (I) as well. Batma writes for himself. He turns the writing endeavor into a means of liberation and a releasing force that both alleviates the tension of the disease and the infirmities of a tormented body, and loosens the horrendous obstacles of everyday life. Hence, writing also in the case of Batma literally turns into a means to deliverance, to salvation, and to redemption. From self-destruction, indulging in drugs and alcohol, the author moves, through a re-creation process, to the construction of the self within the circumspective inscriptions of memory. In this sense, it could be said that Batma, through the process of writing, has attempted to break away from the pattern so often assigned to people who are aware of their dying circumstances, and has in certain sense gone beyond the notion of existence. For him, writing has in fact become a source of self-comprehension, a means of appropriation of language and of re-routing and re-directing the violence of a looming death.

Most significantly, however, Batma's writing of *Al-raḥīl* has been a means of empowerment. From an earlier stage of his life, the narrator perceived the unimaginative power of words (when he first witnessed the killing scene of betrayal during the colonial era). His aim has undoubtedly been to cork, albeit for a short time, his fate. He has chosen to shake the power of words to change the course of his own fate and redirect it away from its doomed itinerary. It is the writing process that has enabled him to salvage from the emptiness and oblivion through the retrieval of fragments about his life and through the reminiscence process of memory. In writing his life story, Batma has recovered himself from oblivion and has created for himself a new space; the space of a challenging writer who is trying to forge an existence and an identity for himself and for his characters whose historical reality would have certainly gone unnoticed.

By the end of his *Al-Alam*, Batma reveals that he has completed the second part "in a relatively short time, seven days," a seven-day time span that probably would remind readers in the Arabo-Islamic world, in an inverted manner, of the myth about the creation of the universe. His seven days are nightmarish; thinking about suicide, scenes and events from the hospital about the patients' suffering conditions, endless questions about his ordeals. These were all part of expressively interwoven details caught by an artist's perceptive eyes. He states that what scares him most is the emptiness of the place, the silence of patients in the middle of the night. Every night he often thinks whether he would be able to live for the following morning; and in fact, as he kept hoping to wake alive, the disease kept consuming his body and soul while writing his autobiography of pain; while writing what I venture to call an upcoming after-life poem.

What is also particular about *Al-Alam* is that it is a narrative that is caught up in mournings and dwells much on loss and forfeiture. The idea of loss in this thrilling narrative involves the narrator in a mediating state of mind that is too much concerned about an inevitable ending. This is an anticipatory loss that is reiterated on various occasions, if not in the whole narrative. The loss of the mother in the course of events, the loss of some friends, Driss, Abdelkader Massa and many patients sharing the same room with him, and who started "to fall down like autumn leaves,"[80] are all instances through which the narrator tries to come to terms with his predicament, and through which he mourns his once-healthy self as well: his long and curly hair that starts to fall, his unrecognizable posture, his skeleton-like body, etc. In doing so, Batma tries to compensate for the loss through writing. As readers, we soon become aware that if the narrator involves himself in narrating loss, he would never end up; he instead struggles to delay events where loss is eminent to complete his work. In other words, nothing is striking in this narrative more than an atmosphere of death that takes over the esthetics of the narrative. This certainly accounts for blanks and voids in his memory that impacts on the structure of his work.

In fact, the structure of his autobiography disturbs and unsettles the chronological fabric of events through the retrieval of incidents from a flashbacked memory either in the first part or in the second part of his autobiography. In terms of form, one would notice how Batma uses an indirect mode of narration coupled with monologues (in the form of prayers) and dialogs. The author also uses *Zajal*, theatrical style, filmic situations inherent in movie making, and scenic montage style that are altogether features of the narrative mode construction in novel writing. These features indicate the extent to which Batma's work is clearly influenced by drama and movie making where he has been involved actively during his artistic career.

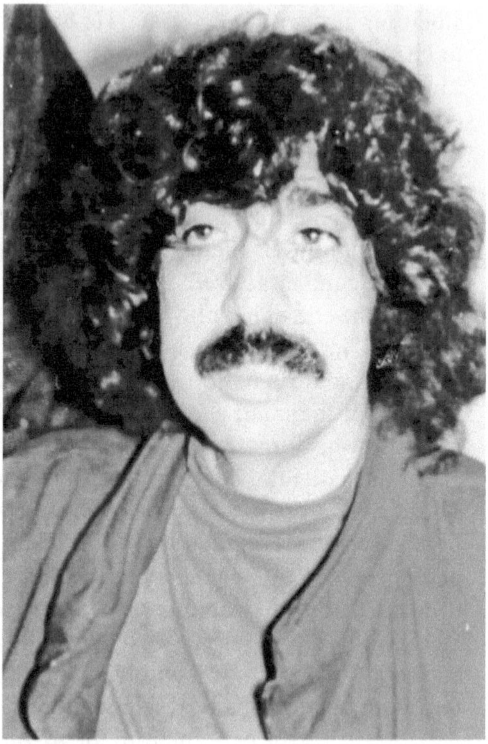

Larbi Batma after the publication of *Al-raḥīl* (1995) (courtesy Rachid Batma).

Batma has been frank in revealing his mistakes, his weaknesses and fears. The language he uses is clear and simple, and fluctuates between elevated classical Arabic and authentic Moroccan vernacular. His writing style tends to be more reportable and direct in its structure because the author is involved in writing a true and honest story about life.

◆◆ III ◆◆

Euphonious Voice(s) from the Margin

Nass el-Ghiwane and the Making of Alternative Popular Music

Popular music that embraces the traditional—and which is typically characterized by the synthesis of entertainment values and the artistic manifestation of the life of people—is a powerful medium of expression with wide appeal, through which individual and community affiliations and shared histories and cultures are performed, contextualized and problematized. It is not only a cultural phenomenon that needs to be taken for granted but it is also a complex process of symbolic meanings that involve the manipulation and reinvention of the constellation of values and standards that contribute to the making and to the framing of individual and collective imagination of a given country.

In his editorial note to Andy Bennett's *Cultures of Popular Music*, Stuart Allan states that "popular music" is one of those phrases that purport meanings that are both accurate and indescribable at the same time. People are aware of what they mean when they say it, yet rarely do they find themselves in complete agreement about a clear-cut definition of the term. "Popular" and "music" both revel meanings that "carry the burden of a troubled history," each of them having been made the subject of intense cultural conflict over time, space and place.[1] However, there is no doubt that popular music has turned into one of the most outstanding leisure resources in late modern society. The rhythms of the popular permeate people's lives in various ways and have become an omnipresent aspect of their day-to-day experiences and existence. In every country people gather in venues for special occasions to listen and dance to their favorite music. As Andy Bennett contends, "the summer months bring festivals where music consumption is mixed with relaxation and socializing as people forge new friendships and associations based around common tastes in music, fashion and lifestyle."[2]

Equally significant about popular music is the way in which it operates at a collective level in forging communal consciousness and in pervading identity construction. In his introductory note to *Klām al-Ghīwan* (Al-Ghiwane's lyrics), Hassan Nejmi states that when the Greek artist Mikis Theodorakis started documenting his artistic and musical biography, he found out that the documentation was nothing more than fragments about his own life experience. Every song he wrote, every tune he composed and every work of art he completed were just broken moments of his human experience. His musical style was permanently inspired by the slithering flashes of collective and personal experiences he went through, as stated in his *Chemins de l'Archange* [the Archangel Paths] wherein he declares that "the very moment he started writing, he discovered that he was as if he were in the process of rewriting the history of Greece with all its thrills, surpises and ordeals."[3] This is exactly how the experience of Nass el-Ghiwane is.

Writing about the artistic experience of Nass el-Ghiwane is in fact reflecting on and setting about a critical moment in Moroccan history, as the members of the group who came up from the depths of despair of the 1970s-Morocco and ignited popular zeal and collective spirit of Moroccans were in essence starting a novel expressive trend of a social, cultural, artistic

Nass el-Ghiwane: Beginnings in 1970 (courtesy Rachid Batma and Omar Sayed).

movement and transformation in the country. Nas el-Ghiwane's musical style has largely contributed in the regeneration of Moroccan music. The group, as an important cultural spirit and not simply as a phenomenon, has set up a horizon of expectations wherein several esthetic movements of cultural expression blossomed and which, in turn, became an important medium that allowed the masses to be heard through the revitalization of poetic, lyrical and musical folk heritage, and also through the rejuvenation of belongings and roots in a context that has witnessed transitional changes in terms of artistic vision, esthetics and practices. Although the features that conditioned the emergence of Nass el-Ghiwane might seem unpretentious and taken for granted at first glance, the choice made by the founding members of the group and the itineraries that led to the rise of the band itself are at the heart of the transformations that affected the cultural landscape of the nation. It is undeniable that the destiny of young boys from Ḥay Moḥammādi neighborhood already manifested itself when four of these had already shown substantial and exceptional maturity whereby the diverse multi-cultural and artistic geographies from the precincts of deep Morocco overlap to become mutually intertwined. Beyond these geographical manifestations of the band's members who came from different origins and various parts of the country, Nass el-Ghiwane's experience was an expressive discourse about the cultural and discursive practices in the 1970s-Morocco, as this historical juncture witnessed the birth of artistic parody and satire through stand-up shows; it also witnessed a rebirth and revival of theatrical, filmic, poetic, critical and narrative discourses. These were all feeding up protest movements, and social and cultural expression with all their predicaments, constraints, violence, and counter-violence.

Hassan Nejmi who has been pursuing research on Moroccan popular music and other Moroccan popular issues states that Tahar Benjelloun, the Moroccan francophone writer, has once declared that Nass el-Ghiwane musical repertoire has been faithful to the roots and to the collective imagination of Moroccans. Benjelloun has described the members of the group as troubadour poets who have excelled in the promotion of local rhythms and in the making of festive performances through a revival of poetic archives of ancestors. Edmond Amran Al-Maleh, the Moroccan novelist and prose writer, has also stated that listening to Nass el-Ghiwane's music is throwing one's self physically and spiritually into rhythmic states that carry both body and soul through eternal and sturdy lyrics that are evocative of violent and soft insurgency at the same time; through texts that are instantaneously nostalgic and life celebrating. Moulim Laroussi has also gone further in describing Nass el-Ghiwane as artists who do not speak the language of reason, but the bodily one.[4]

In fact, the emphasis on the body in performances and artistic practices is not a new undertaking in cultural and performance studies. The physical presence of performers acting live performances for audiences is one of the most fundamental prerequisites of any onstage event. The performer's body, in this instance, becomes a source of signification and multiple implications. The role of the body onstage offers various expressive possibilities that communicate visual ephemerality; a short-lived experience and an all-encompassing transitory moment of representation. The language of the body in the Ghiwani case, as Moulim Laroussi has put it, does not emanate exclusively from the fact that the members of the band themselves started their artistic career as theatrical actors with Tayeb Saddiki, but essentially from the mystical and Sufist dimensions the Ghiwani musical expression embodies and enhances in performances through a distinctive and wide-ranging Moroccan poetic style that is musically established in its identity and foundations. Hence, in the Ghiwani jargon, the body becomes a palimpsest where past experiences would be completely erased, and where new mystic ones could be inscribed. The possessed body has to yield itself to a state of fulfilled trance. As Farid Al-Zahi has accurately confirmed,

> It is obvious that the mysterious, vague and ambiguous image of the "possessed" evokes, above all, the exposure of the mind to madness, of language to body, and of exoteric knowledge to the esoteric. The "possessed," whether in the folk conception or in the "scholarly" sufi conception, is a suggestive character whose surface may vary from its depths, therefore it is necessary to deal with it-to discover its "truth"-in terms of the conformity between lack of conformity; between form and meaning, between the signifier and the signified, between the truth and figurative expression.[5]

In one of their famous songs, *Al-hāl* (Transe), Nass el-Ghiwane's poem includes a sentence that reads as follows "Al-hāl ya-hl Al-hāl, li mafih hal yadbel," and which could literally be paraphrased as "calling for the possessed, bodies with no trance would be dying." The death here is symptomatic in the meaning it purports for a dying rose. Nass el-Ghiwane as already possessed performers onstage enunciate a collective call that invites possessed bodies to engage in a ritual of trance; it is an invitation that comes abruptly without knowing its origins. The utterance which the "possessed" enunciates is a subjective sentence that assumes … a response tantamount to a terrifying question: the question of all questions … [wherein] The "possessed" is a being absent from its self and beyond all responsibility."[6]

In here, the main and foremost importance of Nass el-Ghiwane in the Moroccan cultural landscape lies in the member's poetic expressive potential to stir trance-like states, in their musical making and arrangement that enhances an aura of spirituality, and in their performative enactments on stage that pushes possessed bodies further and further into an infinite transformation where words are transmuted into movements and where the body is transfigured into verbal proclamations. There is no doubt that Nass el-Ghiwane continues to take over Moroccan popular music in Morocco. Beyond the esthetic implications of their music and the poetic incarnations of their songs, the band's music has largely dominated the political and social conscience of Moroccans for over decades now. Hitting super stardom in Morocco during the 1970s and the 1980s is not incidental; this musical group has composed and sung indefatigably while drawing from folksongs, religious and oral poetry from *Malḥūn* using an old diction blended with traditional melodies and rhythms that are in turn drawn from the diverse cultural musical repertoires of the country such as Gnāwa music, Amazīgh music, Ḥassāni (Sahara) music, Ḥmādsha and 'Aisāwa styles. By forefronting national genres, rhythms and instruments, Nass el-Ghiwane performed the unity of the nation and initiated a counter discourse against the State's epistemic violence. The band's musical repertoire recoups and inscribes moments of social and cultural trajectory that recognize the neglected history of the ordinary people. The foregrounding of the body in Nass el-Ghiwane's performances turns also into an artistic expression that is deemed capable of transgressing the boundaries of established discourses on the aesthetics of bodily representations to become a site of disruption, dismantle and interruption. These disruptions and interruptions are enhanced through musical effect and paraphernalia where body and soul, physical presence of the performers and emotional detonations are mutually brought together. Music of Nass el-Ghiwane amplifies how the body's inscriptions and meanings are disclosed, while expressive moments of trance revelations, vibrations and embodiments enfold in.

In listening to Nass el-Ghiwane's music, one can just wonder at the intricate discourses the songs reveal. The critiquing of the failure of promises about Moroccan modernity is at the heart of these discourses. Of paramount signification, Nass el-Ghiwane performed against the background of political disorder, social inequity and intense oppression. The band's songs speak directly to people in a language that is meant to be blunt and plain in exposing the nation's predicaments enclosed within the bounds of paranoia and violence. In fact, since independence large proportions of Moroccan society (the urban proletariat and the peasantry) have remained voiceless. Their culture became undermined by the class aspirations of a nationalist, bureaucratic bourgeoisie. This cultural cooptation replicated, in the Ghiwani spirit, the process of an internal colonization initiated by the ruling class. It was in response to a vast inhospitable surroundings that a generation of young Moroccan artists began to think about the production of a new art and its theorization which refuse the subjugated status of a perpetually peripheral culture.

The artistic rise to fame of the Moroccan popular band "Nass el-Ghiwane"[7] in the beginning of the seventies and during the last decades of the twentieth century meant a real musical revolution and an authentic social

Nass el-Ghiwane's initial lineup in 1970. Top: Omar Sayed, center: Mahmoud Essaadi, right: Larbi Batma, left: Abdelaziz Tahiri, front: Boujmia (courtesy Rachid Batma and Omar Sayed).

and cultural phenomenon in Morocco and in the neighboring Arab countries. The vicissitudes of the lives of the band's members, albeit tragic at times, have contributed to further shape the legendary spirit of the group's originality as one of the most important musical genres in twentieth-century Morocco. This band and many others following its lead unsettled the artistic and thematic concerns of Moroccan popular music and became an icon of the new Moroccan culture after independence. It quickly achieved national and pan-Maghrebi fame remaining popular inside the country and among Maghrebi communities of immigrants worldwide. This reputation and influence of Nass el-Ghiwane as a popular group is not fortuitous. It stems from the fact that it has furnished ample terrains for the emergence of an alternative music in the 1970s made up of diverse genres that lie on the margins of mainstream culture. Also, their popularity is due to the use of deeply-rooted traditional musical genres and instruments from a variety of regional Moroccan traditions and made them the basis of their musical repertoire. Besides, their popularity lies not only in the use of extensive research in cultural heritage and local rhythms and tunes, but basically in their use of lyrics loaded with social and political contents which looked at the tense socio-political conditions and at the curtailment of public liberties in the 1970s and 1980s with subversive criticism. For Carolyn Landau, "Nass el-Ghiwane is considered by many Moroccans to have been the first Moroccan to exemplify or signify a national identity that embodied the multifarious cultural and musical nature of Morocco."[8] Their music as an iconic signifier for the multiplicity underlying the construction of cultural identity incorporates various musical instruments, dialectical metaphors and dialogical references from cultural memory that were novel to Moroccans' artistic taste when the band first appeared. Authenticity is also a concept that has always been associated with Nass el-Ghiwane's musical appeal. As Simon Frith assumes, "good" popular music is authentic—not to people's socially decontextualized sensibilities, but to "a person, an idea, a feeling, a shared experience, a *Zeitgeist*." Bad music, according to Frith, "is unauthentic—it expresses nothing." In common with the critique made of popular music as a whole, "bad" popular music is taken to be standardized, its creativity and distinctiveness quashed by the music industry. The final dismissal is that it is 'commercial.'[9] In Nass el-Ghiwane's case, it is important to stress the authentic poetic value of the songs they compose, as they embody not only a distinct and impressive popular music genre, but a pattern for both the very concept of "authentic" popular music, which stems directly from a long Moroccan poetic tradition, and the basis for a narrative of Moroccan popular music as a cultural system.

In order to understand how Nass el-Ghiwane first came into existence, it is of immediate importance to go back to the sixties and the seventies of the twentieth century and situate this artistic experience within its socio-cultural contexts both globally and locally. In Europe and in the United States of America, the sixties of the 20th century witnessed the rise of a rebellious generation that was dissatisfied with the outcomes of industrial and capitalist societies. The post-war generation felt that its hopes started to be frustrated as its ambitions began to fade away because industrial and technological progress was achieved at the expense of humanity.[10] Within this complex historical moment which witnessed the formal end of colonialism in its military aspect, the rise of the liberationist thinking movement around the world, and the emergence of political, social and economic crisis, evolved a powerful sentiment among western societies that science and technology brought nothing but destruction and disasters. Such a discredited view of modernity is what is eventually reflected in philosophical and intellectual theories purporting alienation, estrangement, objectification and individualism. This condition would give rise to philosophical movements like existentialism and irrationalism, as we all know.[11]

Nass el-Ghiwane, as an artistic revelation, had clearly and undoubtedly been bound up with the global movement of youth culture that emerged in the 1960s in the United States and Britain, and which by the 1970s had witnessed a zealous expansion throughout the world. The youth movement, clearly visible in and incarnated by musical bands such as the Rolling Stones and the Beatles, was deeply rooted in political struggles such as the American civil rights movement and the movement against the American involvement in the Vietnam War. This was more evident a youth culture wherein people's appearance and choice of music could convey in clearer terms all sorts of political and social meanings. The songs that were produced at the time in the west were an important aspect of this movement and were characterized by powerful poetic discourse about social disapproval, political protest and individual disenchantment. The 1960s also witnessed an eccentric mode of expression visible enough through rock music and other musical styles that broke through to mainstream popularity and developed counter-cultural discourses against authority and hierarchy.

It should be noted that the 1960s were both a period of global great political and social disturbances and a realm for new counter cultural lifestyle visible enough in popular music. The pop star's lifestyle was imitated and perpetuated by many youths, and aspects of that lifestyle did indeed become assimilated into the cultural values of society. This assimilation is readily apparent in the growing acceptance of countercultural style and fashion into the mainstream, including longer hair on men and women, large-bottom trousers, or long-colored shirts. Dress, as marker of identity, became significant in the perpetuating of difference through a different lifestyle from the ordinarily adopted.

Also, during the 1960s such music worked as an inspiration for the

Hippies who incarnated new liberal ideologies while leading a bohemian life-style that symbolized peace, love and freedom. Journeys to the East or Orient in Edward Said's model of analysis were seen as redemptive for the western's spiritual loss. North Africa, among other Oriental geographies, was a common destination to the Hippies who saw in these alienated settings sanctuary sites of freedom away from the authoritarian codes that regulated individual relations in the metropolitan centers. Euro-American Hippies alienated by their own culture have long been drawn to Morocco and have seen in it a haven providing self-fulfillment, individual prospects and bodily pleasures.

These youth movements, either through music or through Hippie life-style, largely influenced rebellious identities around the world that aspired to denounce corrupt authority and colonial legacy. The postcolony also witnessed the circulation of such cultural practices, though invariably in different configurations. Music was a core component of the movement. In an interview with Elias Muhanna, Omar Sayed one of the founding leaders of Nass el-Ghiwane confirms that in the Sixties,

> the world was changing so quickly; we were not impervious to what was happening in Europe and America. On the contrary, we were very much influenced by it [...] the hippie revolution arrived in Morocco by way of Casablanca. We were listening to Western music, the Beatles, Jimi, and the Stones.[12]

The most notable influence of the Western musical culture, and by implication the hippie culture, was their circulating culture of male fashion. Their relatively long hair, when they burst into the scene in 1964, was a shocking fashion statement, one that was quickly adopted by other rock bands of the time, and by the 1970's, long hair became standard fashion for men. It was a culture in circulation that was adopted by Nass el-Ghiwane in its esthetic dimension, and not as a literal political orientation. This does away with the allegations that the hippie mode was behind the rise of the Ghiwani revolution since the former is known for "its deteriorating taste and its excitement of inner fantasies and tendency towards a loud and noisy tone."[13] Although there is some resemblance between the western bands, Beatles-Rolling Stones, and Nass el-Ghiwane in terms of hairstyle and outfit, each music band responded to their immediate social, historical and cultural contexts. While the Beatles came as a reaction against the post-war spirit of the western individual crisis, Nass el-Ghiwane emerged in a postcolonial Moroccan condition, where frustration, defeat, social desolation, and political anguish were dominant, not only due to the tragic downfall of pan–Arabism movement, but, and this is more important, to the interrupted narrative of independence as well. The esthetic impact of the hippie lifestyle on Nass el-Ghiwane is undeniable. Yet, this global flow at the time was not behind the rise of Nass el-Ghiwane's experience, as some might claim. This experience was rather an outcome of the local culture, which was determined by historical and cultural circumstances and which was also affected to a certain degree by the common historical legacy shared within the Arab world.

As far as pan-Arabism is concerned, the Israeli victory over the Arabs in 1967 constituted an extremely shocking experience of defeat, which was not just a military act, but also a cultural and a civilizational one:

> At the National level, this period was that of defeat and shock par excellence. The defeat of 1967 crushed minds and emotions in one of the most disastrous setbacks the Arabs have ever known in their modern history; a defeat that had gloomy consequences at the national level, which was closely linked to international variables.[14]

Morocco, as an Arabo-Islamic country, experienced the 1967 defeat with deep frustration. This historical moment of defeat to pan-Arabism had a powerfully pernicious influence, not just over political leaders, but also over people as Muslims and Arabs. This historical situation was translated in the popular memory through Nass el-Ghiwane as well. As for Morocco, the post-independence era was characterized by disillusionment, anxiety and traumatized expectations, which generated intense social and political conflicts. After 1956, the country was vulnerable to intense social turmoil and continuous social upheavals because of the frustrations of independence whereby those who resisted the French colonizer were neither rewarded nor even recognized, while those who cooperated with colonial authorities ascended to both political and economic power. This situation was at the genesis of Nass el-Ghiwane's emergence as a popular music band. Indeed, The Ghiwani group and fans, finding their historical legacy in Moroccan resistance movement, continued the nationalist fight through art. They shared almost the same ambitions of the political process defended by such leftist activists like Mehdi Ben Barka and Omar Ben Jelloun, and all those who were assassinated, detained or exiled.

Nass el-Ghiwane's sudden occurrence was, consequently, involved and entangled within a global context, where the hippie culture as a fascinating fashion was adopted for esthetic expression. The impact of Jamaican reggae music symbolized by such renowned artists as Bob Marley and the Wailers was clearly noticeable. In fact, Nass el-Ghiwane's rejection of the corruption that they believed to inflict the regime was echoed in reggae music of the Wailers. Both groups sang out against corrupt institutions, social injustice and rotten political systems. Both groups, albeit in various ways and through the powerful use of metaphorical language, engulfed their critique of social and political condition within mystical spirituality that stimulates trance. Such moments of trance at least in Ghiwani music need to be understood not as mere spiritual exorcism of possessed bodies and minds, but as rebellious acts that targeted to give voice to the hopes of Moroccans who were dissatisfied with social inequities and oppression.

Yet, what really constituted the origins of Nass el-Ghiwane's experience as a major force in Moroccan popular music was the cultural dynamic of the local, which was characterized by defeat, disillusionment, frustration, anxiety and injustice. Nass el-Ghiwane also existed in very challenging conditions of sporadic censorship and political repression in the country. Due to these circumstances, this highly appreciated musical group became one of the major voices of resistance and opposition in post-independence Morocco. Such a voice was not just an outcome of a reaction against the social system, but an inner dynamic that evolved within the Ghiwanis' individual memories of colonial and postcolonial moments. These memories are not to be taken for granted as individual stories. They are rather political statements about how the voice of opposition got constituted as a major preoccupation in Nass el-Ghiwane's lyrics and melodies. Nass el-Ghiwane had been a revolutionary drive in Moroccan society not simply because their artistic repertoire articulated issues pertaining to social and political divisiveness in the country; but because they occurred during an era when traditional Moroccan music was not fully recognized artistically speaking. The "high" and canonized culture of music of the time found its artistic roots either in the long-held tradition of *al-andalusi* (Andalusian music) or in the art music of the *Mashriq* (Eastern/Oriental) Arab world.

In Morocco, as is the case in the other countries of the Maghreb, Andalusian music is also understood as one aspect of a broader Andalusian culture that traveled to North Africa from cities in al-Andalus after the Christian reconquest, especially after the fall of Moorish enclaves such as Cordoba (1236), Valencia (1238), Seville (1248), Granada (1492), and the expulsions of "Moriscos" (Muslim and Jewish converts) from 1492 to 1611. This kind of music in Morocco is called "al-mūsīqa al-andalūsiya" (Andalusian music) whereas others call it "al-āla al-maghribiya" (Moroccan instrumental music) or simply "al-āla" (instrumental music). "In modern Morocco, the cities of Tangier, Tetouan, Chefchaoun, Fez, Rabat, and Oujda are considered to have the strongest Andalusian heritage. These cities are also the home of the majority of musical ensembles that specialize in the performance of Andalusian musics."[15] According to Jonnathan Shannon, the construction of an Andalusian identity through music began with the efforts of French and Spanish colonial authorities: directors of conservatories, scholars, and festival organizers to document Morocco's musical heritage during the French Protectorate over Morocco. Shannon argues that

> the reasons for creating such an identity are complex. Some scholars suggest that the focus on the medieval (i.e., Andalusian) aspects of the music was meant to deny the contributions of Moroccan Arabs to the repertoire in the intervening centuries. Perhaps it

> was an Orientalist-tinged nostalgia for the golden age of al-Andalus, a trend echoed in many modernist works in Spain in the first third of the twentieth century (as in the works of Federico Garcia Lorca and Manuel de Falla). And perhaps it was just another example of the well-documented French colonial strategy of divide and rule that was aided and abetted by scholars from historians to ethnologists.[16]

According to the same sources, the rise of a decidedly Moroccan Andalusian musical tradition in the period of independence coincides with the historical construction of "Andalusian" as an ethnicity in the modern Moroccan nation-state, along the lines of how "Berber" (now Amazīgh) identities have been constructed to fit into larger national narratives. Yet, what is also evident is that this musical patrimony that characterizes the Moroccan musical landscape turned into a canonized genre that is viewed as "higher" musical culture of educated urban elites.[17]

With reference to "high" culture, it is important to invoke that before the rise of Cultural Studies as a new critical and cultural academic discipline that seeks to explore issues of representation of marginalized cultural identities, culture was viewed as a tradition based on hierarchical economy whereby texts were classified on the basis of their esthetic attributes. This view was led by critics such as F.R. Leavis, who in turn drew on the Arnoldian perspective.[18] Its main assumption was to fix culture as a set of canonical texts whose positions within literary and cultural tradition are decided by the power of literary and cultural institutions. F.R. Leavis had an inclination towards setting up the canon—a nation's privileged treasury—to be consumed by all social classes as a "high" cultural tradition that has to circulate in schools and universities. Such a circulation of the canon underlies the repression and subordination of the popular. The esthetics of the popular as advocated by this interpretation becomes relegated to a second-hand position where literary production and artistic imagination about and by the popular are viewed with a sense of ordinariness and inferiority, and hence the maintenance of hierarchy as a political economy.

The Leavisite's perspective involves a particular reading of history and interpretation of society. History in this sense is based on the economy of hierarchy and hence society is to be led by the cultural elite whose position of academic education and sophisticated literacy guarantees their right to leadership. The core, indeed the main limitation, of such a reading is that it views and structures history from above. Cultural studies perspective on culture, on the other hand, which finds its shifting legacy in Raymond Williams' view of culture as "ordinary," subversive as it is of the logics of canonical culture characterizing the Leavisite's position, undoes and disturbs such binary opposition of essentialist and flattening distinction between high and low culture. By so doing, it democratizes the concept of culture, a perspective that goes beyond the idea of demeaning anything dealing with or coming from of the masses.

Williams assumes that current usage of 'culture' falls within three "active categories," or into some combination of these. Culture is "a general process of intellectual, spiritual, and esthetic development"; it is also "a particular way of life, whether of a people, period, or a group"; and "the works and practices of intellectual and especially artistic activity."[19] These definitions, particularly the second and the third focus on popular culture and de-associate culture from its elitist configurations. Raymond Williams' interpretation of culture reads history from below and hence deconstructs the essentialist position of the canon-based attitude that privileges certain texts on the basis of their esthetic formal properties that account for their literariness.

Now coming back to the years following the independence of Morocco from 1960s to early1970s, just a few years before the emergence of Nass el-Ghiwane phenomenon, the cultural enterprise in Morocco incorporated musical styles in hierarchical classifications. Andalusian music with its connections to the glorious moments of Moorish presence in Islamic Spain was considered "high" while Moroccan popular music was viewed as "low." Traditional regional styles of music continued to be an essential part of the cultural fabric of everyday life but, on the media, at festivals, and in performances on stage, these genres were considered part of the national folklore. This categorization de-contextualized and de-historicized Moroccan musical genres that were meditative of the daily life and culture of the majority of Moroccans. During this period, three basic orientations characterized the esthetics of musical expression in Morocco.

The first eminent orientation was clearly visible through a musical stream that refashioned its musical taste through the *Mashriq* (oriental/Eastern) esthetics, namely Egyptian music and tunes. The majority of Moroccans at that time found their artistic delight in listening to prominent Egyptian singers such as Um-Kaltoum, Abdelhalim Hafid, Farid al-atrash.... These and many others impacted heavily on musical creativity and on the esthetic sensibilities of musicians and listeners as well. They inspired Moroccan artists and artistic expressions in various ways, but basically through the adoption of horizontal classical Arabic poetry and through a persistent exploration of the standard classical themes such as *wasf* (description of nature and beauty), *ghazal* (love), *madih* (eulogy) ... etc. Artists of the time were careful enough in coupling the cultural specificity of Morocco with the oriental archetype of inspiration. Ahmed al-Bidaoui remains an important epitome of this trend. This period was seen by many Moroccan critics as being dominated by mediocrity in artistic production as artists were mere imitators of Oriental experiences and did not fully investigate the extensive cultural and artistic heritage of the country.

The second orientation drew its musical repertoire from the popular through the exploration and blending of local musical rhythms from various parts of the country. It targeted the creation of a new idiosyncratic musical style that considers Moroccan cultural diversity. Artists such as bouchaib al-Bidaoui and Houssine Slaoui were influential enough in creating a new musical esthetics whereby new lyrical topics about Moroccan life issues were explored in a simple colloquial language through the use of popular musical instruments and through humor or social satire as basic expressive means. Within the same vein, another genre characterized Moroccan music and was a source of inspiration to the founding artists of this orientation. The Moroccan *cha'abi* (referring to the popular), also called *Al-'ayṭa*, was famous in Moroccan urban and rural sites. This style is often attributed in the country to female professional entertainers or *Shikats* (pejorative and defaming connotation). These and their musical style often appeared in festive occasions such as wedding celebrations, baptism ceremonies or in festivals around the country. During this period, *Al-'ayṭa* repertoire expanded and new lyrical subjects were explored thanks to Bouchaib al-Bidaoui who adopted this genre and its rhythmic patterns and coupled them with other traditional styles.

The third orientation, however, tried to position its artistic concerns in music amid the two previous ones. This was best exemplified by Mohamed Fouiteh, Maati ben Kacem, Brahim al-Alami who were the first to set the foundations of what would later be classified as the new modern Moroccan music.... These artists adopted an in-between space in the use of an Arabic language that lyrically fluctuates between *dārija* (the colloquial) and *Foṣḥa* (the classical) with variations in thematic innovation while maintaining a forceful but rational appropriation of popular rhythms and tunes. Yet, although these new streams attempted to create new styles of music in a quest for the fostering of a discourse on music identity that targeted the Moroccanization of musical enterprise, the period witnessed a widespread of Oriental music (*al ughniya al-sharqia*) and remained artistically prevailing among Moroccans, namely through its thematic concerns that celebrated excess of passion and overflow of feelings which did not represent the people's daily anxieties and trepidations.

As Nass el-Ghiwane's inspirational style is informed by *Al-'ayṭa* music, it is important to reflect on this traditional genre. *Al-'ayṭa,* or sung poetry from the rural parts of Morocco which literally means a cry or a call, is believed to be the quintessential expression of the identity of the country. Many scholars have gone further in the analysis of *Al-'ayṭa* poetry and agree that the texts of this deeply rooted genre use poetic vernacular capable of stirring powerful emotions through metaphorical imageries and through the evocative rhetorics of symbolism that appeals to the senses.[20] This genre has always been associated with women performers, often referred to as *Shikhāt*, or dancing women. The *Shikhāt* are Moroccan professional entertainers;

female singers and dancers whose performances are musically complemented by a troupe of male instrumentalists for mixed audiences, and whose artistic and bodily spectacles "articulate some of the more powerful metaphors of Moroccan identity."[21] Traditionally connected with the Moroccan countryside, the *Shikhāt*, according to Alessandra Ciucci, "are considered the entertainers of choice at life-cycle celebrations and at private gatherings for the disadvantaged as well as for the most privileged."[22] Though they represent models of the transgressive female dancers in Moroccan society, with unlimited freedom that violates the borders of social restraint,[23] their dancing and singing performances are central to official and non-official festive celebrations like festivals, marriage ceremonies and birth and circumcision parties.

Academic scholars and researchers on Moroccan traditional forms of entertainment have assumed that the traditional practices in the performance of *Al-'ayṭa* in Moroccan amusement poetics and esthetics reveal the process of cultural transformation that occurred following the encounter of both Arab and Amzigh cultures. The effects and influence of this acculturation process in Morocco's historical, cultural and esthetic experience resulted in a dialogical interaction of expressive forms of entertainment and produced dynamic texts of vernacular poetry that became rich material for artistic expression.[24] In his *Ghinā' Al-'ayṭa: Al-Shi'r Al-Shafawī wa al-Mūsīka al-Taqlīdiya fi al-Maghrib* [Singing Al-'ayṭa: Oral Poetry and Traditional Music in Morocco], Hassan Nejmi has studied the historical, cultural and political implications behind the rise *Al-'ayṭa*, and offered an extensive reading of this musical genre as a complex form of poetic and esthetic expression in Moroccan traditional music. He assumes that nineteenth century was an important juncture in the development and promotion of *Al-'ayṭa*; it was ultimately a century of *Al-'ayṭa*. This musical genre flourished with the arrival and reign of Sultan Sidi Hassan, known as Moulay Al-Hassan (1873–1894). Sultan Sidi Hassan largely contributed in opening new political, social and literary horizons for the country in spite of foreign threats from imperial powers. In this period, forms of entertainment, esthetic, lyrical and musical expressions, particularly *Al-'ayṭa*, witnessed considerable prosperity and were encouraged nationwide.[25]

The spatial configurations of *Al-'ayṭa* as a musical genre are basically the invention, if not the off-spring, of the Moroccan society, and *Al-'ayṭa* celebrations are group festivities and gatherings wherein individual delight and enjoyment is fused with the group's and gives everyone the possibility of momentary escapes from the monotonous irregularities of the mundane life. Such is the case with Nass el-Ghiwane's music whereby the symbolic performances of the band's members take on a collective ritual that yields itself to rhythms and tunes which put people together regardless of their age, ethnicity, class or gender. The incorporation of *Al-'ayṭa* in Nass el-Ghiwane's musical repertoire has been done selectively and with great artistic care. Yet, what is basically evident in their music is that it offers powerful metaphors that embody rural parlance through the choice of meaningful imageries that are meant to yearn for, experience and voice the countryside. Also, the integration of traditional music in Nass el-Ghiwane's songs needs also to be ultimately understood within the ideas set forth by leftist Moroccan intellectuals of the early 1960s and late 1970s who demonstrated vehement anti-colonial positions that were geared towards the retrieval and rediscovery of Moroccan traditional culture which the narrative of independence had constantly overlooked. Abdellatif Laâbi comments on these ideas;

> We know that cultural imperialism expresses itself as the colonizer's attempt to graft imported elements of the colonizing culture onto the colonized, elements that are alien to the latter's mental habits and psychism. This violent grafting aims to provoke a chasm between the individuality of the colonized and all that may link them to their own culture, their own memory.... In order to oppose dispossession, the colonized should follow a double course. On the one hand, they try to question the Western culture that schooling ingrained in them. On the other hand, they initiate a movement of rediscovery of their own culture. The cultural patrimony of the colonized is investigated and rehabilitated. In this energy of rediscovery, it is brandished under the eyes of the oppressor as an object of pride.[26]

In addition to the three basic orientations that characterized the esthetics of musical expression in post-independence Morocco, it is within this historical and cultural context, captured in Abdellatif Laabi's words, that the essential need for authentic Moroccan music based on Moroccan musical and cultural heritage emerged. This need was basically triggered by an infallible desire to produce an artistic discourse capable of embodying, stirring and transmitting the hopes and despairs of the people. It was also motivated by strong ambitions to create artistic mediums genuine enough to build on the deeply-seated expressive melodies and rhythms in Moroccan musical memory while taking extensive advantage of the existing repertoire of world music. The Moroccan postcolonial musical condition is best exemplified by a member of Nass el-Ghiwane Omar Sayed in Ahmed El Maanouni's documentary film *Al-hāl* (*Trance*):

> People who were born in 1946, or '45, or '47 or even '48, the youth of that generation, the forties and fifties if you will, were all fond of oriental arts, that is to say oriental tunes and melodies: Mohammed Abdel Wahhab, Farid al-Atrache, Asmahan, Fairuz, Leila Mourad, Abdelhalim Hafed, Umm-Kalthum.... Fond of it to a point you can't even imagine. And I myself was among these people, to the extent that I went to Casablanca's radio to sing oriental melodies. Who saved me from this- in fact I wouldn't call it a disaster, but it would have been a great error had I not stopped- it was Boujemaa may he rest in peace. [...] He told me: 'You are a Moroccan, you must look for some of your own Moroccan stuff, in which you'll find yourself, and sing your own popular art first, before you go looking for art and tunes from other countries.[27]

It is clear that the rise of Nass el-Ghiwane was conditioned by such context that manifested both the need for authentic musical culture that would challenge the prevailing musical orientation of Moroccan popular music, and a real artistic determination to go beyond the dominating styles of music that failed to establish a voice for/of the popular. This artistic divorce and sudden break with the predecessors' artistic practices in Moroccan popular music would later be felt through the on-stage performance esthetics when the group first played for audiences. Nass el-Ghiwane appeared as a small but unified group that enhanced the aura of communal harmony characteristic of Moroccan traditional music performers such the Amazīgh *Rwaiss* in southern Morocco, *Gnāwa, aḥwāsh* dancing ... etc. Their dressing, their long undone hair, their posture as they stood during their performances rhetorically declared the birth of a new genre that broke with the already existing professional performers of popular music. Within few years, the band has managed to set a new artistic movement that soon stirred a revolutionary style in Moroccan music through the revival of musical styles (*Malḥūn, Al-'ayṭa, Sufist poetry*), and through the use of folk instruments such *Hajhūj* or *Sentīr, Bendīr, ta'rija, Ṭbilāt* and *Ṭbel* which were not considered by the predecessors in their musical repertoire. They also adopted the colloquial Moroccan *Dārija* instead of classical Arabic as a reliable means for the transmission of their messages to the layman. Other artists and musicians emerged from the margins throughout the country and followed the lead of Nass el-Ghiwane. Lamshāhab, Izanzāren and Jīl Jilāla adopted the Ghiwani style and addressed thorny social issues that inflicted Moroccan society.

There is an interesting idea that lurks behind Batma's writings and Nass el-Ghiwane's songs in general. Though the band's poems and lyrics, entranced depressed and sad hearts through poems that ripple with andulations from innate melodies and rhythms which emanate from the bottom of the country, Moroccan audiences still insist on reading the songs of the band, particularly Batma's poems, through the dense and tense socio-political condition of the 1970s and 1980s. The lamentation over lost youth and frustrated ambitions in the postcolony conditioned the Ghiwani repertoire which professes in its overall ideological inclination the ability of the individual to change the order of things and make one's own destiny.

For example, the song titled *Māhamūni Ghīr ar-Jāl ila Dā'ū* [I am only concerned about men if they are lost] was read as a subversive political statement and a dissident critique of the repressive attitude of the regime towards its leftist opponents who advocated public liberties. Batma stated in his autobiography that he had composed the first stanzas of this poem at the back seat of a car in France when he was with his friend Boujemaa. During his stay in Paris, Batma was dating a Bohemian French girl; but soon their relationship came to an end after she had let him down. The message the song pretended to transmit, according to Batma in his autobiographical account, bore the revered and ever-lasting truth that friendship was much more important than a short-lived passion.[28] The textual meaning of the song was displaced from the framed context of the lyrics and mapped onto the larger political situation of the country in the 1970s. The Ghiwani fans reinvented the song and projected new meanings to denounce social injustice and political repression.

Hence, the Ghiwani art, as envisaged by the band, was not indeed for the sake of art as esthetics, but for art as politics and at the service of political situation in the country.[29] Though not overtly stated when the members of the band talk about their artistic experience as they often try to undermine the political and ideological connotations associated with Nass el-Ghiwane's songs, Batma is clear about it in his *Al-raḥīl* when he states that "my songs instructed an entire generation that was sleeping in a pool of brackish waters under the waves of repressive politics. When they heard my songs they revolted against those waves and abandoned the brackish pool."[30]

Within the same vein, it is interesting to point out that postcolonial artistic movements in Morocco have been viewed as driving forces and genuine catalyzers in the struggle against all forms of domination through the "promotion of narratives that reinvent the nation's symbols and images and redistributes them to the community which in turn appropriates those symbols as integrated part of its identity."[31] As is the case with Nass el-Ghiwane's song *Māhamūni Ghīr ar-Jāl ila Dā'ū*, and many others such as *Jammāl* (camel rider), *Bṭāna* (sheep's hide), Said Graiouid argues, while referring to another musical repertoire, that a post-colonial example of this "push-and-pull" relation between texts and the community's interpretation can be clearly detected in the case of a popular song which appeared in the 1950s, *Shibāni* (old gray-haired man), by a Moroccan female artist, Hajja al-Hamdaouia. While the song in its syntactic structure was mostly about enticement imageries and erotic metaphors, the Moroccan audience reinvented the piece and twisted its meanings to read as an ironic symbol that parodies the new Sultan the French protectorate enthroned after they had exiled the legitimate one. Hence, this "common popular love ballad became a text of resistance nationalist militants used to rally the people for the struggle for independence."[32]

As Hassan Bahraoui has also argued—and as was the case with The Beatles in England, who relied mostly on the writings of both Paul McCartney and John Lenon—Boujmea, Batma and Tahiri

> were composing songs, most of which were derived from folkloric sources of cultural memory. They twisted the lyrics to acquire contentious meanings.... Politics in this case should be understood in its intrinsic state wherein the borrowed poems are loaded with significant meanings initially suggestive of everyday hardships. In most cases, these

artists worked on the transfer of meanings from old texts that they have mobilized for contemporary issues, an act that is carefully carried out with consensus and harmony.[33]

This act of transfer blurs the boundaries between past and present, traditional and modern, history and memory, esthetics and politics. Hence, the meanings associated with Nass el-Ghiwane's songs are open to various interpretations; yet, there is almost a widespread belief among Moroccan fans that Nass el-Ghiwane's writings have a strong inclination to delve into political issues. The members of the band have adopted a stance in which the message as a mirror to political reality, rather than the sheer entertainment value of their music, is the central concern. Their poems and music recount extremely intricate and powerful narratives that uncompromisingly denounce the injustices of history, society and politics in the country. Although many of these artists come from different social, ethnic, linguistic, and cultural backgrounds of the country, they are ultimately unified and quite explicitly engaged in countering the official mechanisms of exclusion, repression, and control over power.

As far the beginnings of the band are concerned, the whole story goes back to a June afternoon in 1971, when a group of five young boys from the

Nass el-Ghiwane after the departure of Mahmoud Essaadi (ca. early 1970s). From right to left: Omar Sayed, Abdelaziz Tahiri, Boujmia, Larbi Batma, Allal Yaala (courtesy Rachid Batma and Omar Sayed).

Casablanca working-class neighborhood enthralled the *Theater National Mohamed V* audience in Rabat which refused to listen to the Moroccan national orchestra then programmed with varieties from Oriental music repertoire. The group debuted with songs such as *Qiṭati Ṣaghīra* (my cute Kitten), *Ṣiniya* (tea tray) along with others like *Bani Insān* (people of humanity) and *Allah yā-Mūlāna* (God the protector). These and many others to come led the band to fame. They soon changed the Moroccan musical landscape of the country and left unimaginable imprints in the Moroccans' collective imagination. *Qiṭaṭi Ṣaghīra* [my Cute Kitten] for example, with its simple musical and lyrical sentences, was meant to announce a sudden break with the musical practices that were strange to Moroccan music of the time.

qiṭaṭi ṣaghīra
wa-smūhā namīra
la'būha yū-sali
wa heya li ka-ẓili
tūẓhirū al-mahāra
kay taṣīda fāra[34]

My kitten is cute
Her name is Namira
Playing with her is such a delight
She follows me like my shadow
She shows her skills to hunt a mouse

The simplicity of the theme and the way in which it was sung were in fact revolutionary for Moroccan music. My "kitten" is a spontaneous artistic melody that announced the beginning of the liberation of Moroccans from the profiling and uninformed taste and musical esthetic imposed by the colonizer or by the Moroccan ruling bourgeois class after independence. Such authentic meanings would also be visible in other songs that formed an avant-garde breakthrough. The set unsettled the prevailing musical experiences and disturbed the Moroccan artistic and musical landscape that was drawn stationary by the existing artists of the time. In addition to songs that are loaded with religious signifiers and meanings like *Allah yā-Mūlāna* which praises the Prophet, Nass el-Ghiwane have equally drawn the Moroccans' attention to celebrate and think of the tray (*Ṣiniya*) as an invaluable motif of love and family unity.

Ṣiniya's cultural and social implication in Morocco goes beyond the fact that it is a mere kitchen utensil used to serve food or drinks. When a family gathers around a tray on which tea is served, they perform an ethical and a very sacred social ritual in the Moroccan culture. It symbolizes unity, hospitality, generosity, and company. But also, during the "years of lead" which witnessed arrests, torture and imprisonments, the song was widely interpreted beyond the communal ritual and daily life practice that the tray symbolizes. There are images and stylistic signifiers in the poem that allude to untouched tea glasses, empty ones left aside as a social commentary on how the "beloved ones" went missing the chance to share the ritual due to their sudden and unexpected absences.

This famous song, despite the rich and dense political implications it might trigger, has a significant story behind. As Batma tells us in his autobiography, the first verses of the poem were hummed by a beggar, Ba-Sellam, who was touring Ḥay Moḥammādi bare-footed, singing and asking people for charity.[35] Batma who was home when he immediately heard the man passing by and rehearsing the first strophes came outside and invited the beggar in for tea. The beggar soon became a close friend to the family, drinking and smoking with the father, sometimes with the young Batma, whenever the occasion arises. For Omar Sayed, Ba-Sellam (meaning *father* Sellam) used to tramp the whole neighborhoods of Casablanca and his presence was almost neglected as nobody ever cared about what he was saying. This man and many more like him were often taken for granted as beggars and rarely did people feel concerned about what they were talking about. Ba-Sellam used to croon wonderful verses from Moroccan traditional poetry and no one ever paid attention to what he was saying except Batma who had an exceptional aristic flair and vision.[36]

The founding members of the band were all from the same neighborhood, though originally from different parts of Morocco. They all grew and lived in Ḥay Moḥammādi, referred to as *Carriére Centrale* (Central Slums) by the French colonial authority. When France gained control over Morocco, French authorities furnished strategic cities with new urban architecture and established what they called "la ville nouvelle" with broad avenues, modern buildings, hospitals, schools, and military barracks. The French protectorate system in Morocco aimed at conserving the Moroccan cultural uniqueness while containing it within a European urban style. Such urban design placed European administrative quarters outside traditional Moroccan medinas and enhanced the viewing of difference. In 1950s Casablanca, and during the last decades of colonial rule, the French encouraged low costing houses in the outskirts of the modern *ville nouvelle* to meet the urgent demand of workforce for industrial centers. Ḥay Moḥammādi became a working-class district for people who joined the industrial zone of the city. Even after Independence, Morocco continued the French's urban policy as the government encouraged suburban housing for the rapidly growing flows of immigrants from the countryside into the cities. The spatial organization of the city in postcolonial Morocco perpetuated and maintained the French divisive policies of urbanization. The ruling class reproduced and perpetuated colonial attitudes and politics of division that forcefully enhanced social disparities. During an interview with Hind Semlali and Mathias Chaillot for "Made in Casablanca" online magazine, Omar Sayed states that

> Our generation and that of our parents have closely witnessed both the pre and the post independence experiences in Morocco. Our parents fought for the return of the exiled king Mohammed V, but they all felt that they were abandoned as they soon found themselves put separately in a marginalized neighborhood, Ḥay Moḥammādi. Soon, the feeling of being left over developed within this bidonville dwellers. For us, as children, the revolt had to be built there because of this marginalization. But it was not a political revolt; it was an artistic and musical rebellion, an accumulation of feelings and emotional states. After 40 years, I have now become aware of the weight of our songs, our lyrics; everything was much more mature than our age. We only were 16 or 18 years old, we sang what we felt, we were not aware of the difficulties, of the engagement, of the heaviness of our words. And yet, it was the first group in Morocco to denounce corruption.[37]

It is often claimed that neighborhoods inhabited by working-class masses usually give the first sparks for each uprising against authority, oppression and manipulation. Because Ḥay Moḥammādi was one of these neighborhoods, peopled with dense working population, it is obvious that it often turned into a stronghold of resistance against colonialism; besides being a fertile space for the formation of political parties and trade unions that sometimes led revolutions. This is what inherently resonates with the Ghiwanian

Nass el-Ghiwane (ca. early 1970s) after Tahiri's Departure. From right to left: Larbi Batma, Abderrahman Paco, Allal Yaala, Boujmia, Omar Sayed (courtesy Rachid Batma and Omar Sayed).

song. Ḥay Moḥammādi was representative of post-independence Morocco in terms of struggle over power. Resistance fighters soon became marginalized and calls for change escalated the pace of arbitrary arrests and physical torture. Hope for better life in the postcolony turned into illusive dreams, which gave rise to social discomfort and political conflicts, and produced tremendous feelings of anxiety, disintegrated ambitions, misery and rebellion.

Ḥay Moḥammādi as a working class neighborhood accommodated poorer immigrant populations from rural Morocco who fled their tribes to the city in quest for better life opportunities. Yet what they found was extreme poverty that challenged their existence as human beings. They experienced all forms of oppression, suffering and neglect; sometimes pasturing the piles of rubbish in quest for sustenance and provision. Immigrants came from various parts of the country, which meant a conglomeration of ethnic and cultural backgrounds forcing their existence together. Amazīgh from the Souss or Atlas areas, Sahraouis, Riffians, and Arabs were all part of a communal mosaic that shared poverty, sufferings, despair and unfulfilled hopes; but above all they shared their own culture, rhythms and artistic practices as well. As Omar Sayed contends,

> You have to understand the history of the neighborhood. It was a large industrial area; many people came from various parts of the country to find work, including my parents, who emigrated here. It was a real *melting pot*, everyone knew each other, and on Sundays, when they were off work, people came out and played music, each with the culture of their region; there was Gnāwa music, music from Souss, everything was mixed. Of course, as children, we were imbued by those rhythms.[38]

The members of Nass el-Ghiwane were all from various cultural, ethnic and linguistic backgrounds but had a common passion for art; Larbi Batma from *Chawiya*, Boujemaa Ahagour from *Tata* in the Sahara desert, Allal Yâlla from *hūwāra*, Omar Sayed with *Amazīgh* Background from *Ait Baha*, around Souss region, Abderrahman Kirouche (alias Paco) from a *Gnāwa* family in *Essaouira*. These discrepancies in roots and disparate geographies somewhat helped Nass el-Ghiwane to foster a new song wherein sounds and rhythms from different parts of Morocco are interweaved through artistic pluralism to produce versatile texts and rich popular esthetics drawn from cultural memory.

The members of Nass el-Ghiwane frequently emphasize the importance of Ḥay Moḥammādi to their work and highlight the influence of the quarter's main entertainment venue on Sunday afternoons through the popular spectacles of *Al-ḥalqa* that exposed these young future artists to a diversity of music and collective dances and to choreographic figures and chants developed during many centuries of artistic practice in the villages and bearing a spontaneous oral character of popular creativity. They were also inspired by a wide variety of musical traditions, including *Al-'ayṭa*, *Gnāwa*, *aḥwāsh*, *mizāne hūwāra, aḥaydūs, al-ḥawzī*, etc. The ethnic diversity of this music coming from Arab, Amazīgh and African traditions reflected the ethnic composition of Ḥay Moḥammādi visible enough in the identities of the five members of Nass el-Ghiwane. These incidental contexts, culturally loaded as they are, were significant attributes that would impact on the rhythmic textures and tunes of their music all along their artistic career. The members of the group invested their efforts in Moroccan oral folk tradition in an attempt to renew the links with roots and memory as sites of authenticity and legitimacy. Their musical repertoire also benefited a lot from the images and metaphors inherent in the everyday language extracted from the reality of the masses.

They also emphasize the importance of their mothers in fostering their artistic talent earlier in their childhood. Batma's mother, Lalla Hadda, and Boujmea's, Lalla Khdija, were all sources of inspiration and musical flair. These were Bedouin mothers who came from the countryside and were all fascinated by Moroccan popular music. They were illiterate, but they were sources of wisdom, kindness and compassion, and their everyday language was often encrusted with proverbs and sayings. The mothers in Nass el-Ghiwane's case were the first school; the founding pillars on which the Ghiwani movement would soon become widespread. Needless to mention that a couple of songs were first sung by these mothers in ceremonial activities or in family gatherings, and were later adapted and reworked by the sons. The members of the Nass el-Ghiwane are intimately connected with the figure of the mother in a symbolic relationship that transcends the mere family lineage. It embodies an esthetic that reformulates all that is associated with urban and refined life. The existence of such figures in the artistic imagination of the group's founding members, Batma and Boujemaa for example, transforms their poetry texts into a multisensory experience which complies with specific notions about performing the countryside as an imagined and constructed idea in the Ghiwani trajectories. The mobilization of expressive culture as a powerful vector in the Ghiwani song, initiated by the mother figure, is an important dimension that is meant to experience the countryside and, at the same time, to celebrate rurality as an essential component of Moroccans' cultural identity.

The members of Nass el-Ghiwane group represent the post-independence generation that had its own ambitions, dreams and constraints as well. They grew in a popular district and the only sources of entertainment they had were few youth houses (*Dār al-shabāb*), initiated by civic associations, and *Essa'da* movie theater. These worked to develop the musical and theatrical abilities of young people in the neighborhood and would turn into potential outlets for all artists in the neighborhood and would shape the artistic flair of many; including Nass el-Ghiwane themselves who in their earlier beginnings were trained in amateur theatrical troupes affiliated to youth houses and watched movies or spectacles played in *Essa'da* Cinema. Three young actors as future founders of the group (Batma, Ahagour, Sayed) moved from an amateur troupe in Ḥay Moḥammādi to the theatrical company of Tayeb Saddiki, Manager of the *Théâter Municipal de Casablanca* during the 1960s and one of the major figures in the development of "new Moroccan theater."

Saddiki was already touring the country with his *Maṣraḥ Ennās* troupe (theater of the people) made basically of artists from Ḥay Moḥammādi. The two founding members of Nass el-Ghiwane, Batma and Ahagour became close colleagues of Omar Sayed, a childhood friend of Ahagour's. They appeared in several professional theatrical productions for Saddiki and reached the peak of their theatrical success with their performances in Saddiki's play *Al-Ḥarrāz*. In 1969, Batma and Ahagour toured France with *Maṣrah Ennās* theatrical troupe and were already thinking about the idea of starting a music group to sing the lyrics they had composed during their theatrical career inside or outside Morocco. After an unsuccessful experience in Paris as both artists were unable to make a living, they came back to Morocco. Shortly after their return, Saddiki asked them to perform their songs in the *Café Théâter* he had opened at the back of the *Municipal Theater of Casablanca* edifice. "Māhamūni," "Yā Banī Insān," "Ṣiniya" were all sung to audiences before the beginning of each theatrical performance. These songs and many others, if not most of the band's repertoire encompasses symbolic and socially engaged and sometimes militant messages containing social criticism directed at Morocco's ruling class. They express a great deal of social engagement with Morocco's socio-political and economic situation. In his *Al-raḥīl*, Batma states that these songs "contain the suffering and everyday concerns of the poor man. We have discovered something that may be called "the song of the people."[39]

Taieb Saddiki (1939–2016), who founded Maṣrah Ennās in 1968, where Larbi Batma, Boujmai and Omar Sayed first appeared as theatrical performers (courtesy Omar Sayed).

Hassan Bahraoui, a Moroccan scholar and researcher who has talked extensively about Nass el-Ghiwane, states that

> With Nass el-Ghiwane, the Maroccan layman would spring up for the first time, with his hardships, as a thematic concern in a music that aspired for artistic expression, with no lucrative intentions; a music that targeted pure expression without crudeness in order to celebrate collective values against narcissistic drives and stardom motives.[40]

Later when given the opportunity to record their song "Ṣiniya" ("tea tray") at the National Radio and Television studios, Ahagour invited Allal Yâlla to join for the recording. Allal was a multi-instrument artist who had already set up a music school in the quarter, a shabby garage that he turned into a small school with few students learning to play the lute. He did not officially join the troupe until Mahmoud Essaadi left. After the Television recording of "Ṣiniya," directed by Hassan Bourjila at the time, the members believed that it would never be broadcast, but to their surprise, and within few days, the song became popular in the streets of Casablanca. The Moroccan TV station asked for a rebroadcast, something which never happened as the founding members were busy creating the group. It is during this particular time that other members were asked to join and Saddiki offered to produce a concert. Omar Sayed, Abdelaziz Tahiri and Mahmoud Essaadi consecutively joined the band and appeared at the early concerts in Casablanca, not as Nass el-Ghiwane but as *Al-derwish al Jadid* (The New Dervish). The influence of the band's radio broadcasts on audiences became apparent, and the two first performances given respectively at the "Nautilus Club" in Casablanca and at the Cinema al-Malaki in *Derb Sūltān*, a highly populated quarter, stirred huge crowds of spectators who discovered a new alternative style of music that defied the existing one at that time. The band's first concert at Vox Cinema was eventually a turning point for the group as they had to perform alongside stars of the so called *al-Ūghniya al-'Aṣriya* (modern music). According to Larbi Batma,

> That show was different from the ones performed before. It was a challenge between our new style and the "modern" one that was dominating at that time. It was the victory.... The public refused to listen to those who went before us.... At the announcement of our entrance, applauses and ululations burst forth in the hall.[41]

Nass el-Ghiwane's early performances in the 1970s received particular attention in the press and strong promising responses from the public. Abdelaziz Tahiri and Mahmoud Essaadi, and due to their artistic disagreements with the other members or probably because of discomfort about the critical and provocative nature of the group's lyrical topics, left the band. Shortly, the two were replaced by both Abderrahman Kirouche (Paco), who was already performing with the recently formed Jīl Jilāla, and Allal Yâlla. The legacy which is still remembered nowadays as the "old" or original Nass el-Ghiwane started. In October 1974, however, the group witnessed a tragic moment with the death of Boujama' Ahagour, the main founder of the band. His death remains up to now mysterious to Moroccan fans. Later, the band composed and sang a poem that marks disbelief towards his death, a strong metaphorical and symbolic allusion to a deceitful and treacherous act best symbolized by the snake in the lyrics. It is entitled "Annadi ana" (I am calling), and starts this way,

khayī māt al-bāraḥ
ol-yūm jāt khbārū
khayī māt maḍyūm
nāssi ahlū ow-karū
lā, lā khayī māzalt m'āya
walā anā mṣadaq māzalt ḥdāya
gūlt al-khayī ḍrab al-ḥaya
gūlt al-khayī rāṣ al-ḥaya.[42]

My brother passed away yesterday
The news just arrived today
My brother died of agony
Leaving behind his family and places
O brother, you're not at all with me
Or is it just me who can no more trust the loss
I said to my brother hit the snake
I said to my brother, the snake's head.

Ahagour's presence with the band was certainly very short, almost three years and a half, but it has set out the artistic and musical path to be tracked by the other members for years to come. Very particular about Ahagour was his everlasting smile, and above all his tenacious obsession with *Zajal* writing drawn from old folksongs, and from Sufist religious brotherhoods and *Malḥūn* versed poetry. He was also obsessed with traditional Moroccan melodies and rhythms informed by an eclectic synthesis of style from diverse regional and cultural ethnic Moroccan troupes. He sang for hope, peace, victory and failure, beauty, love, the land, and the country. His songs will be a constant reminder of authenticity and an immortal link to Moroccan roots.

Since the Sufist tradition overwhelms most of Nass el-Ghiwane's poetic diction, melodies and performances, it is of immediate relevance to talk about Sufism in Morocco to highlight its connection with the Ghiwani spirit. Sufism is a broad spiritual tradition that began crisscrossing the Muslim context in the early 9th century and continued to permeate much of Islamic religious traditions. Sufists and their followers claim mystical and close communion with the divine through various ways. They have traditionally organized themselves as *tariqas*. Every Sufi way points to a Muslim historical founder, a master who is believed to have attained a unique level of intimacy with the divine, beyond that which can be attained through ordinary devotions,

Nass el-Ghiwane during a concert in the 1980s. From left to right: Allal Yaala, Larbi Batma, Omar Sayed, Abderrahman Paco (courtesy Rachid Batma and Omar Sayed).

demonstrated his spiritual status via lifestyle, special signs or wisdom, and gathered followers.

Sufi orders share broadly similar practices centered on collective sessions about chanting and venerating God's names and divine attributes. This ritual that enhances the veneration of and meditation about the name of God is meant to call forth his blessings as well. The repetitive chanting and the rhythmic melodies, conveyed through the use of simple musical instruments in the gatherings, create an ecstatic trance that is described as moment of a spiritual experience or gift enabled by the divine in favor of his lovers. Many Sufi traditions use percussions, wind or stringed instruments to accompany their chanting, but this is frowned upon by the more austere orders who regard the use of music as Islamically illicit or at least potentially arousing to spiritually doubtful passions, as Jonathan Berkey claims.[43] In Morocco Sufism is often associated with burial sites of sanctified and divine masters who came to be known as marabouts from the Arabic word *mūrābit*. That word literally means "the one who takes camp," or "the one who is garrisoned." This appears to be in reference to Muslim missionaries who settled in and Islamized the harder-to-reach rural areas during the Muslim conquest of North Africa.[44]

As Jane E. Goodman argues, marabouts are members of patrilineal descent groups that claim genealogical ties to the prophet Mohammed. In Morocco, while all members of such descent groups are referred to as marabouts, only a few individuals became the legendary saints, called *Aṣāliḥīn* or *al-awliya,'* around whom a mythology has developed and at whose tombs veneration occurs on various occasions. A simple marabout may turn into a saint through his divine ability to emit and glow with *baraka*, which Geertz has defined as "personal presence, force of character, moral vividness."[45] Baraka in the case of maraboutism is associated by wonder-working: causing springs to appear on rocky grounds or curing illness and reversing misfortuness. Jane Goodman also states that

> marabouts also accessed and administered the sacred, serving as village shayhks, delivering Friday sermons, overseeing holy days, teaching the Qur'an, undoing "evil" magic, and managing activities at their ancestor's shrine. Studies of maraboutic groups have emphasized the ways in which they exercised their (supposedly) closer ties to the divine to play key roles in local political economies.[46]

Nass el-Ghiwane has found its way through these various marabout incarnations and other traditional practices of music-induced possession wherein mysticism becomes endowed with revolting poetic diction. They have managed to revive cultural memory where there is an increase of more popular forms of ecstatic trance, and have forced their inspirational moments through the workings of *Hadra* and *hāl* (trance) associated with mystic divinity and maraboutic practices. This kind of trance in the Ghiwanian tradition is secularized and desecrated outside the maraboutic spaces or *Zawiya(s)* (a retreat for religious brotherhood)[47] and taken onto the stage to be performed in eventful performances that are endowed with metaphoric combinations and associations which embrace social and political concerns about the country.

In his foreword to "Omar Sayed Raconte Nass e-Ghiwane" (Omar Sayed narrates Nass el-Ghiwane), Martin Scorsese states that Nass el-Ghiwane

> went back to their roots, to Berber rhythms, Melhoun sung poetry, Gnāwa dances. I think one of the band members described Nass el-Ghiwane's extended compositions and improvisations as their own version of soul music. I was fascinated to see that they used mostly traditional instruments—the *Bendīr*, the derbouka, the *da'dū,'* the guembri, and, most intriguing of all, a fretless banjo employed as a variation on a western lute.[48]

In fact, Nass el-Ghiwane's music has challenged the parameters of Moroccan popular music in terms of musical arrangement, thematic concerns and song forms. The band plays and associates instruments from various folk traditions that had rarely been used together. The two primary melodic instruments they use are the Gnāwa *Guembra* or *Sentīr* and the *snitra* (a fretless six-string adaptation of the American banjo that has been reworked by Allal Yaala to give identifiably Moroccan solos). The percussion instruments they use are the *tam-tam* (pair of pottery kettle drums—used basically by the 'Aisāwa religious order); the *Da'dū'*, also called the *Harrāz* (large single-headed cylindrical drum used by multiple drum ensembles, such as the *Huwāriyāt*, the *Haddāwa* and *Ḥmādsha* religious orders); the *Bendīr* (round frame drum with a gut snare strung across the inside of the skin head—used by a number of traditional genres); and the *ta'rija* (small-sized vase-shaped drum used by numerous traditional genres such as *Shikhāt* (women dancers) and *A'bidāt arma*.

The improvisation of Sufist soul music in the case of Nass el-Ghiwane is not fortuitous. It is deeply rooted in the various melodic and rhythmic styles that the country has been exposed to years back into time. Morocco as a site of complex history that crisscrosses the boundaries of nationality and extends beyond mere geographical locations is a network of traveling cultures that played a central role in the shaping of the Moroccan esthetics as a multicultural terrain. According to Clifford Geertz, Morocco's position as a borderland open to influences from multiple sources, has fostered both cosmopolitan openness and parochial defensiveness. Talking about Moroccan culture is also invoking Morocco's interconnections to such elusive and difficult to encapsulate "mega-entities" as the Mediterranean, the Middle East, Africa, Arabs, France and Islam.[49] This assertion also invokes Arjun Appadurai's assertive remark that all local cultures exist within webs of cross-societal bonds.[50] The "flows" between cultures that Appadurai invokes have largely impacted upon musical culture in Morocco, and Nass el-Ghiwane's music cannot acquire sufficient meanings without such ground. The profound influence of sub-saharian rhythms and tunes on Moroccan music in general and on Nass el-Ghiwane in particular cannot pass unnoticed.

When looking at how Nass el-Ghiwane's song is constructed, one would certainly notice various overlapping constituents that build on together in intricate ways to give an overall musical effect. In terms of rhythmic constructions, Nass el-Ghiwane adopts quick but simple rhythms that reverberate with acoustic harmony empowered by the traditional instruments deployed. These instruments chosen by the group in their beginnings were thought to be unfamiliar and were deserted, as they did not seem to be in compliance with modern esthetic tastes. These, however, were, and are still, carefully manipulated by the group in cautious ways to yield agitating "internal metaphors" and rhythms which arouse an emotional experience that immediately lead to a state of complete mental absorption, an unconscious, cataleptic and hypnotic condition that takes body and soul into trancing moments of utmost immersion. This state of heightened emotionality which evokes ecstasy and enchantment is underlined by Jonathan H. Shannon in an insightful article talking about performance in the Arab world. Jonathan refers to this internal sensation as *ṭarab*, translated as enchantment and which refers to "a type of aesthetic bliss or rapture with respect to an art object,"[51] or with respect also to a style of music and musical performance in which such emotional states are evoked and aroused in performers and audiences. For him, reactions following a musical performance can be considered as building up

> a metonymic or part-whole relationship between the listeners and the overall performance: the shouts and gestures that occur within the context of a performance may come to stand for the performance itself. In a similar manner, a given performance may come to stand for an entire genre and indeed, for "heritage" and "cultural authenticity" as a whole. It is this music-culture synecdoche that allows a given performer or performance to insinuate him- or herself, or itself, into the social consciousness as an element-cherished by some, vilified by others-of the culture of a community, city, or even nation.[52]

The expressive power of the deeply moving emotional state and absorptive function of the Ghiwani rhythms which lead to a state of trance are further intensified by the collective mode of performance of the group's members wherein voices lap over the sounds in meaningful ways to create imbricated sequences of powerful moments where body and soul transgress the boundaries of time and space and become possessed by the spell of music. As Hanoun Mbarek has accurately pointed out,

> Since singing is initially viewed to be a phonic and auditive rhythm, and since this rhythm can never be detached from the rhythmic beats of the body, Nasss el-Ghiwane have played a significant role in redefining the dynamics the the body so that the rhythmic component gets empowered. So, their music opened spaces to dancing; the dancing state that follows ascetic chanting of Sufists and dervishes. Performance with Nass el-Ghiwane becomes a moment of liberation, not only for the band, but also for the audience, a moment of deliverance that detaches the body from its consistencies, a moment of dancing, vociferation, denunciation, and creativity.[53]

As far as the texts are concerned, Nass el-Ghiwane use the everyday language that crisscrosses the limitless precincts of time and space and brings old diction to serve current issues about Moroccan society. In fact, what is interesting about Nass el-Ghiwane's text is that it has redefined the status of the Moroccan vernacular and has reinvented its aesthetic purposes. With Nass el-Ghiwane, the Moroccan *Dārija* has acquired its artistic and rhetorical value through embroidered expressions that generate ornate images and embellished details through a systemic adoption and adaptation of an old style that characterizes oral tradition and popular culture in Morocco. The language used by the group is known as being dense and impenetrable, though well acquainted and thoroughly conversant. It is loaded with meanings that embody human values and complex concerns that sing for love and anger, anxiety and serenity, violence and peace. Popular sayings and wisdom of the ancestors are at the heart of the Ghiwani diction. Language in the Ghiwani tradition transcends the secular and the profane while pushing the listeners, in moments of contemplation and meditation, further and further to embrace the mystic and the sacred in their connotative dimensions. As Hannoun Mbarek has clearly put it, "Nass el-Ghiwane are constructors of language. The language they use is constructed, threaded, figuratively and polysemously built. It makes us think of possible ruptures with Arabic."[54] Nass el-Ghiwane, he adds, have chosen to seek refuge in *Dārija* as haven of creativity wherein words and expressions are intertwined with powerful images and metaphors to create internal and external harmonies that keep questioning the instabilities in souls. Hannoun also argues that

> We feel that we are taken into a mystical space through the use of the sacred language, the language of troubadours; a language that enthralls and impresses, and breathtakes both bodies and souls. It is the language of the unusual … it is loaded with connotations that are not immediately perceived … connotations that are replenished when reread or viewed from other epistemic angles … these possible implications drive us into other possible worlds.[55]

Such implications of possible worlds are quite eminent when one attempts to reflect about the experience of Nass el-Ghiwane in another language, rather than Arabic. Writing in a foreign language, especially in English, about the artistic experience of the Moroccan folk band Nass el-Ghiwane is not as easy as it might sound. The challenge comes full circle when one thinks through the poetic imageries and esthetic configurations of the bands' poems. Hence, documenting Nass el-Ghiwane's experience is also looking closely at the band's lyrics that are originally written and sung in Moroccan vernacular (*Dārija*). This is ultimately a very demanding task, an unmanageable one, when one considers the almost untranslatability into English of their poems that are deeply immersed in Moroccan popular culture. The connotations and moods that can easily be revealed by *Dārija* are almost impossible to capture in English. Besides, the act of translation in this case becomes real transformation, deformation and displacement of the meanings that the Ghiwanian poems purport to convey.

The complexity of Nass el-Ghiwane's lyrics and music stems from the fact that they use an authentic subtle lexis dipped in mystical opaqueness suffused with meanings from folk culture that cannot be fleshed out if not associated with their historical, regional and cultural contexts. Hence, perhaps one of the main compelling questions readers might ask while going through this book is why does this research endeavor take the trouble to investigate the experience and musical repertoire of Nass el-Ghiwane instead of looking at issues other than folk music? The answer to this valid question can be responsively articulated through a reversal display of the interrogative mode: Why not explore the experience of this artistic Moroccan band as a Moroccan who has experienced and lived an immediate experience with the band's context and conditions that made it rise and flourish.

Nass el-Ghiwane's musical repertoire is informed by clear musical strategies that enhance Moroccan culture and tradition. Through a deliberate and conscious choice of performing a coherent style of Moroccan music, albeit blending various traditional musics and poetry from old repertoires, the band remains singular in enunciating a coherent identity and in celebrating locality. The arrangement of older popular/traditional Moroccan rhythms from various parts of the country, while manipulating poetic images and metaphors to suit current social and political issues in their performances, Nass el-Ghiwane create a unique discourse about national unity and identity distinctiveness.

Identity in the Ghiwani discourse is articulated not only through the incorporation of rhythmic instruments that are deeply rooted in Moroccan musical landscape, but also through the redefinition and reinvention of old poetic orality that characterized traditional music. In Morocco, the improvisation of lyrical poems has been a long tradition sustained and perpetuated by the peasantry mode of rural Morocco. For example, there is an improvised poetry that is sung in rhythmic lyrics by harvesters during summers, and also by shepherds portraying idyllically the pastoral life. Harvesters and shepherd are by nature illiterate Bedouins from rural parts of the country but who are poets as well. The sound of sickles striking repeatedly against wheat and barley during harvesting times can often be accompanied by songs that are usually improvised to celebrate the countrified mode of life. These songs, though improvised most of the times, are suffused with religious and mystic chants that ask for God's mercy, or help and forgiveness. Batma has stated on various occasions that his poems come from the depths of his soul ready to be written and sung. He often insisted that Ghiwani poems are always ready-made inspirational voices that are inherently contrapuntal and readily tuned inside the Ghiwani poet. What these inspirational moments need is only an artistic valving and creative pumping when an overflowing void manifests itself inside; "you just cannot get it filled up if there is no emptiness within; these are inexplicable spiritual and musical pleasures,"[56] as he once put it. Batma is undoubtedly referring to the circumspective forces that ignite the creative potential in the poet as a peasant wherein improvisation and verbal artistry become instrumental in producing meanings. This oral genre appropriated by Nass el-Ghiwane can be clearly felt in one of their songs titled *al-Ḥaṣāda* (Harvesters) whose origins are credited to Batma's mother who improvised the song.

Nass el-Ghiwane's poems and songs emit dense rhythms and melodies from the precincts of deep Morocco. Such density is awe-inspiring and mystically trancing in a way that turns their poems into expressive rhythms about human condition in a postcolonial locale of shattered dreams and delayed expectations. The band first emerged in a time of intense political, cultural, musical and intellectual ferment to reproduce the integration of identity within spatial boundaries that have been dismantled by the colonial presence and by the conflicts over power in post-colonial Morocco. The band's artistic and musical experience has reinitiated identity cohesion and spatial assimilation through the use of authentic rhythms, simple linguistic mediums and through original folk instruments. In other words, it has instigated a post-colonial emergent self with a new identity predicated on the rediscovery and on the revalorization of identity's own cultural heritage. Hence, Nass el-Ghiwane's instrumental artistic choice to go back into folk memory and reinvestigate it is in itself a genuine investment in the collective linguistic heritage of Moroccans visible enough in the oral tradition and in the use of an everyday language that builds into images and metaphors about the little ironies of life. The band has also invested its efforts in rearticulating popular rhythms, melodies and tunes that are deeply rooted within Moroccan culture and memory.

The distinctiveness of the "Ghiwanian" artistic experience in Morocco and in the Arab world is mainly due to the thematic and rhythmic concerns raised in the band's lyrics, melodies and rhythms. Nass el-Ghiwane's songs are replete with religious signifiers from Sufi brotherhoods' musical, ceremonial and artistic traditions. The rhythmic melodies of *al-Ḥamdūshi*, *al-'Aisāwi*, and *al-Ḥaḍārī* overwhelm Ghiwanian lyrical structure. These have always had more powerful effects on Nass el-Ghiwane's musical Practice. Mahmoud Guettat states that "The development of these brotherhoods didn't only have consequences on the political and social life of the population. It contributed as well to the safeguard, even the enrichment of the musical patrimony."[57] Also, *Tagnāwit* (Gnāwa identity), or Gnāwan-ness in Deborah Kapchan's words, and its African roots is clearly visible and of vital importance in Nass el-Ghiwane's musical and artistic repertoire. Indeed, the band has always made a conscious effort, through research in Gnāwa's artistic practices and musical manifestations, to incorporate in their own music Gnāwa esthetic styles and components such as instruments, melodies, and rhythms.

The Gnāwa are a population of Morocco. They are dark-complexioned people historically known as ex-slaves whose musical rituals celebrate significant mystic figures and involve trance and possession by various divine spirits. David Goodman notes that Gnāwa musicians have created, despite this fact is not historically proven, an imagined ancestral linkage to Sidi Bilal al-Habashi[58] whose divine blessings bestow the Gnāwa's experience with a special mystical and spiritual dimension. Their possession ceremonies, often referred to as *Derdba* or *Līlla*, enhance a Sufi-like organizational practice, though they do not claim to be affiliated to a Sufi order as such.

While indications about the ancestral and topographical origins of the Gnāwa are still missing to scholars worldwide, it is clear that their roots of sub-Saharan origins are undeniable. Some scholars such as Deborah Kapchan,

A troupe of Moroccan Gnāwa troubadours with percussive instruments: *Qrāqab* (castanets) and *Ṭbal* (drum).

Viviana Paques and David Goodman have suggested that Gnāwa presence in Morocco is related to a history of the trans-Saharan slave trade. Kapchan, based on Paques' assumption in her *les Esclaves de Dieu*, asserts that the Gnāwa are ritual musicians who were brought to Morocco mostly as slaves in the 15th and 16th centuries from the Songhay region of West Africa and who hold mastery over spirits to cure possessed bodies through a rhythmic music that induces trance.[59] Goodman has also noted that performance lyrics during the ritual ceremonies indicate received references of the Moroccan conquest of the Songhai Empire in 1591 and the northward movement of people that resulted basically in hiring black slaves for the military and the constitution of the *'Abīd* (slave) Army. Ziad Bentahar contends that there are indications of a sub-Saharan legacy in Morocco prior to 1591. As early as 1185, for instance, the Almohad sultan Ya'qub al-Mansour ordered a south-facing city gate named Bab Agenaw to be built in the city of Marrakech. The similarity of "Agnāw" to "Gnāwa" and the probable connection to 'Ghana' suggest that the term was used in connection with sub-Saharan Africa and its populations in Morocco well before the conquest of the Songhai Empire.[60] For him, there is no doubt that the origins of the Gnāwa are connected to sub-Saharan Africa and this fact is predominantly eminent in Gnāwa ceremonial activities. In the *Līlla Gnawiya* (Gnāwa night), the lyrics used very often refer to the Sudan and to the venerated saints and people of sub-Saharan origins, particularly *Bambara*. Moreover, many terms originating from sub-Saharan African languages are found in Gnāwa chants. The word *Gembri*, for instance, probably comes from *Gambare*, the Soninke word for lute.

Yet, what is worth noticing is that Gnāwa are generally viewed as authentic musicians. Their music is characterized by a distinctive identity visible through the use of beats, lyrics and instruments. In the 1960s, their music has become increasingly popular with the Moroccan public and international audiences as it has been incorporated by many music bands ever since. The visibility of such music in various Moroccan musical genres endows Moroccan musical identity with an undeniable African cultural identity.

Nass el-Ghiwane's experience has benefited a lot from this African musical identity as well. They familiarized the audiences with the beats and sounds of Gnāwa through their adaptation and incorporation of Gnāwa musical instruments, rhythms and melodies. Also, the presence of Abderrahman Paco, a *M'alem Gnāwi* (Gnāwa master) as a bass player within the band adds an interesting dimension to the affiliation of the band to African Gnāwa cultural heritage. In his autobiography, Larbi Batma invokes how the band first thought of incorporating Gnāwa rhythms through the use of an authentic Moroccan acoustic instrument to complement their songs. While they had a variety of purely Moroccan percussive instruments to choose from, they had some difficulty finding stringed instruments that were authentically Moroccan. So they decided to use the Gnāwa *Sentīr*. He states that "Boujemaa and Tahiri went to Marrakech and met with a Gnāwa *M'alem* named Baqbo. They bought a *Sentīr* from him, an instrument that was at that time common and known only among the Gnāwa brotherhood."[61] As said earlier, after the departure of Moulay Abdelaziz Tahiri, Paco joined the group. Larbi Batma has reported that

> after listening to his playing, we decided to include him in the band and to give an artistic twist to his instrument and to his playing because he only played in the Gnāwa manner and we were in need of a *Sentīr* player who would play in a completely different way that fits the Ghiwanian fashion. This is how we took a different start.[62]

Besides being a real authentic Gnāwa master and a charismatic figure in the band, Abderrahman Paco was also a song composer, especially after the death of Boujemaa Ahagour. In fact, two dominant trends in song composition identify Nass el-Ghiwane's music and both are motivated by a strong revival of popular poetry, popular proverbs and popular diction rhythmically dipped in melodies that revisit Moroccan cultural and musical patrimony. The first trend is best exemplified by Larbi Bama who constructs his poetic images using a deeply-seated rural *Dārija*. The second one with its mystical dimension in a Gnāwa fashion is epitomized by Paco. The dominant musical inspirations of the group are the musical traditions of the *Tariqa* (religious orders) represented by the *Gnāwa*, *'Aisāwa* and *Ḥmādsha*, orders. According to Abdelhai Sadiq, the songs that incarnate the spirit of these orders are transmitted through the scenic presence and vocal input of the members and their instruments.[63] Nass el-Ghiwane were thus influential in adopting the Gnāwa background in Moroccan music. They have largely contributed in shaping Moroccan musical landscape and gave their music a sub-Saharan dimension that would be adopted by many other bands to come. They have also largely contributed in displacing and in combining Moroccan musical genres traditionally associated with various social and cultural groups in Morocco. As Fuson declares,

> Melodies from the urban elite traditions of Melhoun and al-Andalus were displaced from their traditional ensembles and performed to the accompaniment of the Gnāwa *Sentīr*, the *Ṭbilāt* of the *'Aisāwa*, and the *Bendīr* of the common folk. Similarly, Nass el-Ghiwane displaced melodies from the Gnāwa and *'Aisāwa* by singing them in a unison group style more characteristic of the Arab-Andalusian style. Lyrics from old and stately poetic styles were displaced in time and verse from their original contexts and heard in songs alongside everyday Moroccan street Arabic.[64]

In rhythmic melodies that reiterates the ceremonial activities of Gnāwa fashion, Nass el-Ghiwane retrieves moments of cruel tyranny and slavery through a song entitled *al-ṣaḍma* (the shock), as if history were meant to repeat itself, and as if sufferings enacted by oppressive individuals were unavoidable blows to live with. Shock from injustice and its painful ramifications is the overall feeling that grows through the recurring melancholic tunes of the song.

hmūmk f-ḥyātk ṣadmātk
o-f'āyel khūtk hadmātk
mṣāybk o-ḥwālk nadmātk
shūf kif mwāj a-danyā khadmātk
o-ma danyā ilā smiyā
tghāṭī bihā 'lā ojūh ẓalmātk.
t'āmiti o-takhfiti waṣṭ a-ẓlām
bqiti jothā f al-khlā marmiyā
ḍayā'ti mn ḥyātk 'wām
tahti bin nnas 'awām
yazīk mn al-klām al-khāwi![65]

Worries in life have shocked you
the deeds of fellows brought your collapse
Your misfortunes and feats are a pang of guilt
Look how the wavy life tricked you
The world is but a nominal cover
on the faces of your intimidators.
Thoughtlessness to retreat amid darkness
You've become a corpse dumped in wilderness

Years of your life went astray
Wandering around among the others
Break that shallow talk!

This Gnāwa tone, carefully reworked by Nass el-Ghiwane and which reinstates the feeling of oppression and helplessness of an unfair life, neither mourns nor surrenders to the despotic condition. It is, however, laden with signs of spectacular powerful tales of resistance against alienation, dispossession and dislocation lived and experienced within the postcolonial order. Through this song, we can feel a strong selective outlining of the various forms of social domination combined and harmonized with aspects of resistance; an outstanding musical manifestation of dual relationships that are recurrent in Nass el-Ghiwane's thematic concerns. The complexities of these relationships are both mystified and expanded by a lyrical discourse of protest in Nass el-Ghiwane's musical repertoire.

Moroccan Gnāwa musician playing his *Sentīr*. The caption reads "Scenes and Types—Black musician."

In fact, Nass el-Ghiwane as a musical "phenomenon" is an extremely interesting artistic and cultural experience where another version of Moroccan history is inscribed, recorded and saved; a version of history initiated from below, that is to say, from the perspective of popular collective consciousness. Reducing it to mere esthetic monumental experience is simplistic and reductive since it excludes the political implications and the cultural affiliations overlapping with artistic breadth. It is more than being just a medium for musical entertainment. It is rather a cultural space where history, politics, society and nation are brought into an intricate set of complex connections, contrasts and contradictions. The political implications of the Ghiwanian experience, not in the literal sense of course, goes beyond simple estheticization to emerge as an oppositional driving force that articulates the discourse of protest as an irrefutable trait of the Ghiwanian song.

Discourse is a very problematic term. It is one of the least settled categories of linguistic, philosophical and sociological debates of the last fifty years. It has often been defined as text from within the perspective of modern linguistics, which evolved as a reaction against De-Sausure's assumption that the sentence is the ultimate unit of language. The Foucauldian view of discourse in its essence enhances the idea that

> social institutions produce specific ways or modes of talking about certain areas of social life, which are related to the place and nature of that institution. That is, in relation to certain areas of social that are of particular significance to a social institution, it will produce a set of statements about that area that will define, describe, delimit and circumscribe what is possible and impossible to say with respect to it, and how it is to be talked about.[66]

This statement underlies that discourse is closely linked to the power of social and cultural institutions where the "content," "function", and "social significance" are what matter most. Going beyond the "form" and "materiality" of language, the Foucauldian perspective refers to discourse as a mode of talking that finds it expression in text, but underlies the perpetual presence of the social institution, according to its place and nature, as a powerful denominator of surveillance and control that governs avowed and disavowed statements and shapes up truth within power relations networks. The truth is not transparent. It is rather a site of struggle that is shaped up by the functional role of social institutions.

Protest as discourse in Nass el-Ghiwane's experience means a "mode of talking" about the complex social reality of post-independence Morocco that allowed for the rise of artistic forms of expression from the periphery. The Peripheral site as a social space of artistic and cultural expression is entangled within complex dynamics that constitute the voice of protest as a discursive practice, characteristic of Nass el-Ghiwane's songs. Targeting the discourse of opposition and protest is not an end in itself. It is rather a means through which postcolonial Morocco can be revisited and reconstituted through the Ghiwanian music as a discursive practice that rethinks Moroccan history from below.

During the 1960s of the last century, Morocco was entangled in a political and social context marked by conflict and repression, popular discontent and unrest that culminated in subsequent political arrests and a sequestration of the rudimentary liberties of the citizens. The cultural situation of this historical period was also of vital consideration as it also motivated and fueled up the outbreak of mass uprisings. The existence of several factors constituted a fertile ground for the growth of protest, popular anger and resentment. On the one hand, there was a postcolonial awareness that started to build up owing to the outstanding role played by intellectuals, teachers and students in framing the masses and their contribution to the dynamics of the struggle in Moroccan society. On the other hand, several accrued adverse circumstances have made education tragic, particularly with respect to indicators of poor academic achievements, high illiteracy rates and expulsion from educational institutions. This situation was also at the heart of intensified popular anger and mass demonstrations and led to uprisings wherein citizens expressed their discontent and their rejection of the political system. The state intervention was brutal in crushing out these forms of popular protest. The overall cultural, political and social situation in the country led to a movement of protest in High Schools and at the universities by the students who expressed widespread frustration against the political policies of the country. These students were enticed by leftist ideologies and engaged in a series of strikes and mass events. The 1965 uprising was one of the most noticeable movements as stated earlier. This protest against the political system

> became a characteristic subject of the growing countercultural, alternative musical mode led by *Nass el-Ghiwane* and later *Jīl Jilāla* and *Lamshāhab*. The new Moroccan "pop music" attracted a large group of fans, especially among the young.... Nass el-Ghiwane emerged at a time when King Hassan II survived two coups d'état, and the political challenges of different groups were animated by different motives. Despite explicit censorship exerted over artists and politicians in this period, these groups were able to perform publicly and even at times at national celebrations and through TV and Radio because of a milder official policy.[67]

It is worth noticing that protest in Nass el-Ghiwane's work is a predominant structural issue. It is so because aspects such as opposition, rebellion and resistance characterize the rise of this unique experience whose work cannot be adequately appreciated if it is not problematized and historicized in terms of the individual members' personal memories; their experience cannot be appropriately understood if it is not contextualized within the narrative of post-independence Morocco with its achievement and failure, ambition and frustration, avowals and denials.

Opposition and protest as discursive practices in Nass el-Ghiwane's songs is a prominent feature that takes various configurations along history. All such configurations, entangled in historical and cultural events and processes lead to the construction of the notion of Moroccanness from a different perspective. It is not the official narrative of Moroccanness, but rather a popular one wherein the center is reshaped from the position of the periphery. One of the major aspects of opposition within the Ghiwanian experience is the articulation of poverty as a postcolonial reality that cropped up as an outcome of a political process which interrupted the legacy of resistance movement. The lyrics of a song entitled *as-sāyel* (the inquirer) investigates the issue of poverty inflicted on a postcolony of disdain and repressed dreams.

al-faqr nakba l-ṣḥābū
mayḥla dimā mrār
qūmān fnāt gālt annār
qūm ḍaḥā b-shbābū
o-mazāl al-faqr qahār
hūmā qallā o-ḥnā ktḥār
hūmā li-jābū sbābū
amā 'amlt lakhyar
[....] *anā ḍayf allāh ghithūni*
[....] *lā mḥāba wa-lā maḥbūb*
[....] *al-ḥāq gafa marhūb*[68]

Poverty is calamitous to the poor
It can never be sweet, it's sour forever,
People died; voiced out fire
They sacrificed their youth
And still poverty is a scrunching burden.
They are a minority and we are the majority
They brought its causes;
is there any safety?
I am the God's guest, do save me
Heartiness has vanished, no more beloved ones
Rights have been threatened

In rhythmic musical beats iconic of multiple Moroccan musical identities that incorporate diverse musical references, the song alludes through powerful imageries to the sufferings of Moroccans living at the margins of society where poverty remains a real predicament. Concern about poverty keeps interrogating other issues in the song such as resistance to the colonizer. People who resisted colonial encroachment to free the country sacrificed their lives, their youth in order to set up a stronger nation where such disastrous inflictions as poverty could have been the exception and not the rule. Post-independence condition is constructed in the song as being crushed down by paucity despite the legacy of resistance movement that targeted not simply the end of military occupation, but also building a new Morocco where self-esteem and social justice were meant to be enjoyed.

Poverty and beggary are calamitous; they are the outcomes of the complex historical and political processes of postcolonial Morocco where the minority, namely the feudal ruling bourgeoie class who cooperated with colonial authorities, had immediate access to political power after the colonizers' departure. The majority, despite its glorious history of resistance against colonial authority, was doomed to endure poverty and destitution. So, poverty is not a natural lot in Nass el-Ghiwane's undertaking; it is rather a political upshot whose moral and ethical responsibility is anticipated by the feudal bourgeoisie that sustained the same power relationships that characterized the colonizer's attitude towards the native before independence.

In a Sufist and mystical twist, the song calls for divine care and protection. The guest of God longs for a spiritual shelter against depravation, a religious duty invoked by the song as a retreat from poverty. This spiritual invitation is not simply a mere religious emotion nor is it a forceful state to defend the right for a descent life, but it is also a clear indication about a crumbling political system and its fatal failure to deal with issues disturbing the postcolony.

This song also records a historical moment wherein tenderness and sympathy, warmth and solidarity have vanished. The communal life that Moroccans used to experience has totally crumbled down. The individualist spirit has radically superseded the traditional mode of being. "lā mḥāba wa-lā maḥbūb" (Heartiness has vanished, no more beloved ones) is a cultural statement that cannot be understood properly if its derivative meanings are not explained within the cultural context in which it is used. "Maḥbūb" here has much to tell about the structure of the family, a structure whose common core is the filiative associations that bound up family connections. This filiative order in the song is unsettled, if not broken and taken over by individualistic and opportunist culture which is mainly founded on personal desires and self-gratifying egos.

Post-independence Morocco and its people were frustrated and disillusioned by the narrative of independence, and were attracted and moved by such Ghiwanian texts: texts about corruption, injustice, moral decadence and rotten politics. They were the first Moroccan music band to articulate overtly the voice of the people, their worries and sufferings, even in the most forbidden issues that very often led the band to problems with the authorities. They were the voice of the oppressed lower classes and were prohibited for some time to put their records for sale and to play on venues for the vital energy of rebellion they displayed to their public. Through this song and many others, they exposed the decadence and the corruption of the postcolonial regime and its bureaucratic leaders characterized by repressive politics and individual opportunism. They express a great deal of social engagement with Morocco's socio-political and economic situation though the members themselves often argued that their movement was apolitical. Omar Sayed for example reflects on the meanings of a famous verse in one of their songs. The stanza uttered in the beginning of the song states that we "are leading a life of a fly in the sheep's hide" *(a'ychīn a'īcht dabāna f-l-bṭāna)*:

> Many people tried to find a political agenda to that song, but they were totally missing the point, which is unfortunate because we were in all honesty trying to say something much more important. They thought we were saying that the flea was sick of living in the sheep's hide [...] we were trying to say that this hide that the flea is living in was once a sheep. The hide remains but the living thing is one ... we were living within the remains of something that no longer exists....[69]

Btāna in Moroccan vernacular (*Dārija*) stands for a rotten and smelly sheep's skin. The lyrics of the song move on for an openly declared denunciation of injustice that is eminent in the progressive moral and political engagement of the band: *āchmen farq bīn a-nta, o-nta, o-nta, wā-na* (what is the difference between you, you, you and me?). No matter how the metaphorical meanings of the verse are understood by Moroccans, and although Omar gives a deflected version of the stanza to minimize the subversive nature of the band's movement in the Seventies, Nass el-Ghiwane's message remains politically oriented and gives insights into the socio-political condition of the country. As might be the case, Nass el-Ghiwane's movement was not an open movement of protest as many saw it. In the case of all the paranoia and fear of the 1970s and 1980s, it is inevitable that the political agenda would clearly be attached to al-Ghiwane's songs though the members had never the intention of writing political songs. They all grew up in the streets of Casablanca and their songs represented states of vagabondage, misery, anguish and frustration as Omar himself confirms:

> We were street kids from the poorest part of Casablanca, and we sang from that perspective ... take the songs *Fīne Ghādī biya Khūyā* [where are you taking me, brother?], or *al-Mādī fāt* [the Past has gone]. These were songs about uncertainty, and anxiety we felt in that moment, because everything around us was changing so rapidly. The world of our parents was slipping away and we were heading to ... who knows where?[70]

The discourse on authenticity as expressed in Omar's terms asserts claims to heritage and pristine life decidedly prevalent in the Ghiwanian repertoire and spirit. The esthetics of authenticity in Nass el-Ghiwane's songs is a double age process that reconfigures political and social discourses to be impervious assertions on authenticity and heritage as ways out to the Moroccan post-colonial condition and predicament. It is true that Nass el-Ghiwane's songs try to transmit people's grievances and sufferings through artistic and musical practices; still, their lyrics remain potential sites about social struggle and political upheavals. Their music continued to be a site of protest where struggles for and against corruption, humiliation and contempt were implicitly displayed but easily felt. Their movement remains at the genesis of the social, political, cultural and economic injustices that have weighed down the post-colonial Moroccan society.

The post-colonial experience in Morocco, as is the case in other post-colonies, was traumatic and the political transition to the modern nation state was broken and was characterized by cynicism and unfulfilled expectations as the ruling bourgeois class sought to re-build an authority that perpetuated the same hegemonic practices of the colonizer, while citizens sought to decolonize the post-independent nation and re-construct a nation about being and belonging. In fact, in looking closely at the experience of Nass el-Ghiwane, one will soon find out that this experience is a foundational juncture in contemporary Moroccan history of arts and music. These young artists inspired in Morocco of the 1970s a sense of community and managed to express a new cultural and artistic turn that was indicative of a new transition in Moroccan society.

In their immersion within traditional Moroccan artistic forms, Nass el-Ghiwane strategically drew on *Malḥūn* traditional poetry and its renowned poets who appeared in the precolonial era and who are (were) believed to represent indigenous wisdom, humble life style, and above all a nobler spirituality than ordinary people. The genre of *Malḥūn* for Moroccans also reflects an authentically pristine national folk canon that is still kept as an invaluable cultural memory to be saved. In the case of Nass el-Ghiwane, *Malḥūn* background in melodies and lyrics was mainly deployed to answer questions of identity in post-colonial Moroccan society. The band mobilized cultural heritage as a decolonization process with a probing attempt to provide a sense of authenticity, allegiance to roots and celebration of un-spoilt past in order to revive popular awareness and cultural nationalism.

The Nass el-Ghiwane movement has drawn on spiritual and mythic cultural and musical repertoires to construct an authentic Moroccan culture through the adoption of *Malḥūn* oral tradition. This renewed interest in *Malḥūn* poetry by the band, selective as it was, was meant to restore a Moroccan identity against the invasion of other musical styles associated either with French colonial authority or with the *Mashriq* musical and artistic culture. The selective use of the *Malḥūn* repertoire in the Ghiwanian style appears in several songs. *Ḥan wa-shfaq* (Take Pity and Care) by Sidi Qaddur al-'Alamī (1742–1850), for example, is an extraordinary text that was reworked by the band with the objective of renewing the *Malḥūn* cultural legacy and with the objective of giving a new artistic twist to traditional poetry. The song opens as follows:

rfaq yā malkī b-'abdak
wa-a'ṭaf yā ṣābgh l-niyām
yā badr anbā man l-ghtām
yahdīk allah lā t'addab qalbī qāṣīt mā kfā
nta l-mawṣūf bil-mḥāsan
wana al-malsū' bl-oghrām

o-a'yit ankādd la-sqām
a-mā bardt man jmār f-qalbī muḥāl tanṭfā
nbāt nsāhar l-liyālī
o-dumū'ī ḥāyfa sjām
nabkī o-nūḥ f-l-rsām
'ala maḥbūb khāṭrī man jār 'liyya o-lā 'fā
imta yā mālkī nshāhad
kadak yaḍwī 'la l-rsām
mā bīn mḥāfil al-riyām
o-nqūl brīt man 'lālī w-nsīt mḥāyan l-jfā[71]

Be kind, my possessor, I am your servant
Have some care for your colorful eyes
O moon of the news that brightens in the darkness
God guide you, don't torture my heart, I've had enough
You're alluring in charms;
And I'm hooked in passion
I am tired battling against the stages of illness
No ember in my heart cooled off
I spend sleepless nights,
my tears flowing endlessly
I cry and moan in the darkness
for my beloved who shows harshness and no mercy
When, my possessor, shall I see
your posture shining on the traces
Among the hordes of gazelles
and I can say: I was healed of my illnesses, and forgot any coldness

It is clear that the whole poem revolves around the presence of a woman. Her metaphorical presence is used interchangeably with the memory of the beloved. This classical image in Arabic poetry is also viewed as a metaphor for the homeland, beautiful and distinguished among its neighbors. On one level, this is a love song, but when one considers the performance context of 1970s concerts and mass media recordings that are played to this day, the song takes on public meanings as well. In addition to the interwoven textual threads of a love story, this poetry becomes a call to oneself and others to have compassion and return to the community and to shared ideals. Reference through precolonial reality visible enough in *Malḥūn* poetry is a call in Nass el-Ghiwane's undertaking to go back to roots through authentic esthetics as a way of constructing Moroccan cultural identity.

As mentioned before, Nass el-Ghiwane started as theatrical performers. Their first theatrical contact with *Malḥūn* was eminent in a famous play titled *Al-Ḥarrāz* (the guardian) written by Abdeslam Chraibi and directed by Tayeb Saddiki for his theatrical company. Performers in the play, including the founding members of Nass el-Ghiwane and other artistic bands to appear later such as Jīl Jilāla, sing selections from *Malḥūn* poems such as *Ghita*, *Faṭma*, *Malika*, *Al-Ḥarrāz*, *Allah ya mūlāna* (God Our Lord) and *Dif Allah*

(God's Guest). Besides its *Malḥūn*-based poetry, *Al-Ḥarrāz* builds its theme on a love story whereby the lover tries various ways out to gain the beloved *Aiwisha* held against her will by the Gardian.

The most popular band in Morocco that followed the lead of Nass el-Ghiwane and which made extensive use of *Malḥūn* in its musical repertoire is Jīl Jilāla. This band is mostly famous for involving a female artist (Sakina Safadi) in its earlier stages of self-definition. Formed in both Marrakech and Casablanca in 1972, Jīl Jilāla grew out of a theatrical troupe that invested much of its theatrical writings on Sufist and *Malḥūn* poetries. The band's early repertoire drew heavily on Sufi imageries and diction and produced theatrical performances that acquainted audiences with traditional and popular styles of theater esthetics.[72] The members of the band named themselves Jīl Jilāla (generation of Jilala) in homage to a Muslim brotherhood called Jilala whose founder, Moulay Abdelkader Jilali, known for his opposition to oppression and injustice came from Baghdad and settled in Meknes.

During the 1970s, Jīl Jilāla and Nass el-Ghiwane were the two most popular and leading musical groups in Morocco that established a mainstream trend in popular music. Both groups spoke of social injustice, human values and political issues, albeit they presented different orientations in terms of texts, tastes and esthetic styles: Nass el-Ghiwane, as provocateurs of Moroccan music, were highly estimated for their rebellious diction that addressed the working-class rebels; Jīl Jilāla, on the other hand, presented and represented a more tamed stylish class orientation which was distinct in outfit and lyrical discourses. Despite the competitive, sometimes conflicting orientations of the two bands, some members of theses groups have witnessed shifts and drifts while playing with one side and then migrating to the other. This phenomenon was in the earlier stages of the makeup of both bands when the members were still in the process of defining their musical career and style. Two musicians have played with Nass el-Ghiwane and with Jīl Jilāla—Abderrahman Paco and Moulay Abdelaziz Tahiri. Tahiri, who played with Nass el-Ghiwane at their first concert, became a member of Jīl Jilāla in 1976. He played a pivotal role in moving the band in a new direction away from performing songs of social protest and commentary and built a repertoire based upon modernized *Malḥūn*, a genre of sung poetry that had fallen into neglect in Morocco.[73] Jīl Jilāla released two anthologies of *Malḥūn* songs—*Sham'a* ("Candle") and *Lūtfiya*—that were enthusiastically received by the public in the 1970s and 1980s. These albums introduced a new generation of music listeners to *Malḥūn*, many of whom assumed that Jīl Jilāla had created a novel musical style.[74] The *Malḥūn* poetry has also inspired Nass el-Ghiwane to foster a language medium that could reach audiences and link Moroccans across boundaries of region and ethnicity. Their songs reflect a process of selection and signification from various *Malḥūn* poems and other popular genres through specific linguistic choices that appeal to audiences socially and individually.

The Moroccan vernacular, given its fluidity and expressiveness, is a deliberate linguistic choice adopted by the band in its movement. In his book on Nass el-Ghiwane, Ḥannun Mbarek explains how the band's lexicon has managed to mobilize an arsenal of Moroccan vernacular idioms, proverbs and folk expressions to elevate Moroccans' opinions of their spoken language. He states that through Nass el-Ghiwane, Moroccans became open to the truth of the messages underpinning their lyrics, and "that our colloquial Arabic has its words and its images that are able to produce and construct beauty, while esthetically seizing what we did not believe it could seize."[75] He portrays Nass el-Ghiwane as reviving Moroccan *Dārija*, the language of the earth, of the ancestors, of the home and of the neighborhoods that developed here and there without official permission, elevating it, and returning it to its enlightened potential, even to a sacred and mystical degree.[76]

For Ḥanoun, the Ghiwanian tradition is a cultural revolution of popular awareness whereby the songs use standard images and metaphors to voice out unofficial views, anxieties, both personal and collective, whose genesis stems from the trodden-upon, from the subalterned population. The Nass el-Ghiwane songs mix up regional varieties of language and Culture. They drew on the global context of protest music in the late sixties and created a distinctive style that combined colloquial Moroccan poetry with musical elements and melodies from various mystic and Sufist brotherhoods. The use made of popular spiritual antecedents, visible enough in these religious brotherhoods, was reiterated in a 1980s article in the journal *Lamalif*. The written piece by Mohamed Jibril discussed *Al-hāl*, a feature-length film documenting the group Nass Al-Ghiwaine. Jibril states that

> Nass el-Ghiwanese familiarisent avec les habitants et les chansons et contes du 'cru' qu'ils se remémorent, nous indiquent les matériaux de base qui sont, ensuite, retravailés par eux. [Nass el-Ghiwane acquaint themselves with the inhabitants and the songs and stories of the "raw," recalling for themselves and indicating to us the foundational materials that are, finally, reworked by them].[77]

This "raw" folk style through its popular linguistic medium activated popular awareness and tastes as it created new musical turn that deviated from the typical Arabic music prevalent in the 1960s and 1970s-Morocco wherein musical production relied on oriental esthetics, as mentioned earlier. Probably, one of the most influential historical figures in Nass el-Ghiwane's poetry that used Moroccan vernacular is the sixteenth century mystic poet *Sidi Abderrahman al-Majdub*,[78] the wandering poet who was taken as an indigenous cultural model, along with his numerous other aspects of Sufi and native culture, and became one of the greatest inspirations for the band and the other bands that followed in their practice of adapting folk traditions to contemporary music. Through their contact with the oral poetry of this figure, Nass el-Ghiwane articulated discourses of protest and disillusionment and developed a cultural movement that foregrounded the voice of the lower classes while aspiring for freedom of expression, social justice and political revolution in the postcolonial world.

In fact, Nass el-Ghiwane can be viewed as symbolic embodiment of the vernacular poetry of the wandering poets. These troubadour-like figures, called *al-Majdoub* in Arabic or *amdyaz* in Tamazīght language, are famous for their wandering errands from village to village and for their nomadic lifestyle, singing songs that explore life issues and tribulations. They are viewed as living encyclopedias of popular wisdom all over the country. Like their ancestors, Nass el-Ghiwane are also involved in a dialogic un-interruption that resonates through Moroccan history, creating narratives that transcend boundaries of time and space. Their songs evoke issues of a remote past in a manner that breathes new life into ancient texts or provides historical grounding for current issues. Thus, the wisdom of the sixteenth-century Moroccan poet Sidi Abderrahman al-Majdoub is echoed in the poetry of Nass el-Ghiwane; an inter-textual significance that reflects the uninterrupted narrative of people's histories struggling for equality, social justice and human dignity.

Nass el-Ghiwane drew eclectically from Moroccan folk and Sufi heritage. Their music has a rich repertoire that includes laudatory songs inspired from various Sufi tariqas in Morocco. In fact, the Ghiwanian movement has instilled Sufi songs with social and political meanings that evoke the social injustice of despot regimes. The case of *allh yallāh mūlāna* creates an in-between space where the sacred and the secular are intersected to give a clear narrative of post-independence Morocco plagued with social disorders, cynicism and repression.

lāh –allāh, yallāh mūlāna
sīdi yā mūlāna, shūf mn ḥāl-anās
a'm lafssād ya la'bād, nāss khūtna faḍḥūna
bl-jmār al-wagād
wast ṣḍūrna washmūna[79]

O God, the great, our guider
O God our guider, your pity on people
Dissipation is widespread, our people have failed us
With hot cinder, they tattooed our chests

In Nass el-Ghiwane's musical repertoire, Sufi popular music exists in a cultural space between the sacred and the secular. It is a forceful space of interaction where the sacred is secularized and the secular is sacred. The interplay between Nass el-Ghiwane's popular music and the religious music sung at Sufi ceremonies is cautiously mobilized and negotiated in the band's lyrics and melodies. The messages that the songs purport to convey are often engulfed within a religious discourse of devotion, servitude and piety wherein the secular overruns the sacred and twists the meanings that negotiate musical boundaries. The following song gives clear indication:

sūbḥān allāh ṣayfnā wallā shatwā
o-rja' fṣal ar-bi' f-al boldān khrīf
o-mḍāt iyāmna srqatnā sahwā
o-tkhalṭāt ladyān shella līk nṣīf
[...] o-lḥākm tayṣūl tayqbāṭ a-rashwa
o-shāhd taydir f-sh-hada taḥrīf
fham al-ma'na o-'īq o-stāfd o-rwā
hadā ser al-klām ma rāmū taṣḥīf
yekfāk d-lbkā yā 'ayni, yekfāk ham d-alḥāl
a-ẓarf ghshamnī o-laḥni mābqa li amāl
lilāh yā li tas-alni lā tāleb al-mūḥāl
qaṣtī wāḍḥa f-jbinī mabqāt raghba talhīni
'al-lafrāq 'awāl.[80]

Glory to God alone, our summer has become winter
While spring in the country has turned into autumn
The days have gone by and we have been off track
The tyrannized judge is bribed
The witness distorts testimonies to speak truth
Understand the meanings, alertness is a must
This is the secret of words that can't be altered
Tired of tears, and of this situation
Rejected and hopeless
For those who need to know me
Do not ask for the impossible
My story can be read on my forehead
Neither desire nor envy allures me
Separation is my destiny.

In literature, seasons often provide a point of reference or emotional allusions in quest for individuation and self-determination. Engagement with yearly-based seasonality in this song alludes to an unsuitable four-season template wherein seasonal time provides a complex ground of an embodied temporal disjuncture. The four-season paradigm here does not inform a logical progression of nature, and does not refer to temporal movement and development; merely, the four seasons are unclearly defined and the metaphorical interplay of the images they purport is meant to enhance the Moroccan postcolonial condition. Seasons are used by the poet as a metaphorical device to mourn the socio-political situation of the country. They are deployed in this poem to catalyze the transformation of awareness towards contemporary social consciousness. In fact, as seasons denote a significant role in organizing the logics of time, and the sense of the development of the year through various phases of survival, in this poem they are meant to stand for a deflective chaotic system and for an unpredictable future of a society loaded down by social turmoil. This is evident in relationships between seasons that are recast in jumbled meanings whereby summer has turned into winter and spring into autumn.

The Sufi submersion in Nass el-Ghiwane's songs is often meant to serve as an introduction to thorny issues that kept gnawing the post-independent Moroccan society as is the case with *Samta* (the belt). *The Belt* articulates the disruptive circumstances of a socio-political system that gave rise to the phenomenon of clandestine immigration.

yā wālfi, rzaq shi f-shi o-dāym allāh
fetḥā f-galbi b-dekkā ṣ'ība
olla neḥki 'lā ḥbābī, ḥālī yā megwāh
khdāt-hūm al-ghūrba f- ṣenāra o-sbība
ṣār labḥar jebāna o-lḥūt jāh 'shāh
shāt b'īd o-lbūghaz rah fin rah
wa-fayn ghādī?
a-dra' 'yā o-lamwāj glība
al-markab yaghrāq o-lmūt qrība
wāsh shahdū ḥbābi bellāh?
māna waḥdāni, māna berānī
anā mūwāṭin, o-ṣamtā 'liyā
al-jenwī māḍi yajrāḥ yedāya
al-'imarāt 'aliyā, o-lakwākh mardumīn
lamsābeḥ dāfqā, o-fdaden maḥrūqīn
arḍī 'atyā, o-knūzha maftūḥīn
shamsī ḍawyā, labyūt maghmūqīn
bḥūri 'āmra, o-ḥnā jī'ānīn
denyā ghādiya yā-hli bḥāl al-maskīn[81]

O my beloved! Some live on others, God is eternal
A wound in my heart, left by a hard blow
Or, do I have to tell about my beloved ones ...
Taken by estrangement in a fishing rod
The sea has become a graveyard
And fish enjoys the meals
The shoreline is far and the Strait is just there ... over there
Where are you going ?
Arms are tired ... and the waves are rough
The boat is sinking and death is closer,
did they say their prayers before, for God's sake?
I am not lonely.... I am not a stranger
I am a citizen and the belt flogs me ...
the knife is sharp ... it has bled my hands
The buildings are high, the caves are collapsing
Abundant swimming pools but the fields are burned
My land is fertile, its treasures open
My sun is shining, houses are gloomy
My seas are rich, But we are starving
Life will fade away, like the poor's.

The belt as signifier in the poem herein has a powerful political implication and vital oppressive connotation. It is the belt of the police, security representatives of the state, and which stands as a repressive and disciplining tool. So, the belt becomes a political statement about the oppressive political system that followed independence. This system, where state institutions are violating people's rights instead of protecting them, sustaining poverty instead of fighting it, reinforcing social injustice rather than fortifying a state of law and rights, is held responsible for the clandestine immigration issue. This is the main problem that the song dramatizes in poetic imageries that cannot by any mean offer ample understanding when translated into English. The main implication of the song is that it vehemently attempts to question the validity, authenticity and efficiency of Moroccan official ideology of nation building and national belonging.

This song reveals the obstacles, and above all the predicaments, faced by those who illegally emigrate across the slender stretch of water between Morocco and Spain. The hundreds who attempt the dangerous crossing every year are known in Moroccan vernacular as the *harraga*, which means "the burners." The song takes as its subject matter the intriguing issue of Moroccans who embark on tiny boats to literally "burn" the bridges of their lives, their identity papers, in order to illegally creep into the neighboring western countries across the Straits of Gibraltar. The poem tells the story of Moroccans who feel useless in the mother country and who have, concurrently, turned into stateless objects as they, by the force of the circumstances, very often choose to die untimely deaths in the rough waters between two continents. It is about a fatal crossing, not by clandestine emigrants but rather by people who feel, in general, to be leading a clandestine life within the country. The poem highlights the fact that those who leave the country behind do so because they are hurt by a sharp knife that literally stands for uncomfortable reality since these "burners" are experiencing marginality, poverty, illiteracy, and despair in a country that offers nothing more than dejection, false hopes and vanished dreams. Taking a tiny boat for an unpredictable crossing, according to the song, is definitely a means through which the burners aspire to emerge from the clandestine state they are leading within the country in order to get recognized and self-assert their identity as human beings beyond borders.

Hence, this exceptional poem in Nass el-Ghiwane's repertoire records a failing experience of clandestine immigration; a tragic experience that does not only raise human sympathy, but also turns into a boiling question about the legitimacy of the postcolonial nationhood. The song gives a thrilling description about undertaking risky journeys into the unknown wherein shocking feelings refuse to stand still within the images conveyed in the poem about clandestine immigrants who in turn, driven by the circumspective forces of abject poverty and unbearable life condition within the postcolony, have become easy prey for sharks across the straits of Gibraltar. Such condition is highly pictured through a set of contrasts that give the postcolony a net of contradictions and ambivalences (My land is fertile, its treasures are open / My sun is shining, houses are gloomy / My seas are rich, but we are starving). The victims of illegal immigration are referred to by the poet as the "beloved ones," and the sea is compared to a graveyard. Immediately, one would conceive of the sea as a space for life and revival that turns into a political discourse wherein the official narrative of post-independence totally crumbles down. It collapses as the neo-colonial order has failed to abide by its promises for the independent nation. The Ghiwani poet wonders where those clandestine immigrants are heading. Their money is taken by the traffickers whose boat and paddles fail to face the stormy waves of the sea; their tragic end is closer and their chances of being saved are slim. The Ghiwani poet also wonders why these citizens of the new nation have accepted to lose their life that way; he pays testimony to such a tragedy, and constructs himself as a witness, a true and a honest one, as if he were in the court to effect justice. He assumes that it is his moral and political responsibility to keep a popular record of not just a tragic human experience, but also of a translational political act, which does not only defy geographical boundaries but defines the economic and historical relationship between the south and the north of the Mediterranean: The same relationship of power and mechanisms of hegemony that have defined colonial legacy in the country are taking a different configuration and a new historical significance. The ex-colonizer is yet in a position of power; his economic prosperity is tempting for the poor ex-colonized.

There is also an interesting thematic concern raised in this poem. The message is constructed through the montage of a series of scenes about a fatal voyage across the stormy waters between North Africa and Europe. These scenes are meant to be structurally fragmented in the ways the country's condition are. The irony is that the ultimate end of these fragmented identities taking daring journeys, and which on the other hand are not reclaimed once found dead in the shores, are to vanish into the unknown forever. It is through death that the whole effect of the poem becomes felt and perceived as we look closely at how it is esthetically built on metaphorical images and contrasts. These clandestine immigrants are trying to get recognized through embarking on fatal crossings and it is through the concept of death that the poem's scenes get reconstructed to reinstate a human dimension that would otherwise pass unnoticed if clandestine immigration were to be read from the official perspective of the country's narrative.

On the other hand, the boat, which is depicted as dipping into the rough waters of the Mediterranean, certainly illegal but a serious situation to be considered, is symbolically significant. It could be interpreted as an immediate result about a whole nation sinking since those Moroccan citizens have decided to leave a country that still needs them, however poor and oppressed they seem to be. The poem tries to delve into the inner side of the immigrant who undergoes a dual struggle as he/she does not feel lonely as long as it is a collective experience of adventure to security and better life condition. But still, he/she feels as he/she were a stranger, a foreigner, denied full citizenship as a Moroccan. Although they view themselves as citizens, they are not fully considered as such by the nation. The belt of oppression can still inflect its clatches on them; consequently living under perpetual threat. These citizens are pictured as being fully aware of their position as victims of a political system that is founded on oppression, condemnation and denial.

Throughout the poem, and as stated before, one can notice the workings of paradoxes and contrasts as a strategy deployed to lay down the overall poetic effects and meanings. The belt becomes critical of a binary opposition set up between the rich and the poor that characterize the country's social structure. The rich are defined as powerful (high buildings), and in full rest (swimming pools); this is while the poor are defined as weak (collapsing caves), in full desperate need (burned fields)."My land," Morocco, is fertile, but its open treasures are for the rich, who are paradoxically referred to as savage animals to stress their moral decadence. The sea, the Moroccan one, is very rich, but for the rich; this is while the poor have to meet their starvation. The fertility of the land and the richness of the sea are spaces of hegemony, but such power cannot be totally hegemonic. It is rather productive of resistance. Clandestine immigration, regardless of whether legal or illegal, though it entails escapism and defeat, is transformed by Nass el-Ghiwane into a voice of resistance. The Ghiwani poet negotiates a third position wherein he stands against both the oppressor and the escapist. Subsequently, and what is essentially to be stated is that Nass el-Ghiwane, through popular song, constituted a unique voice of opposition against the postcolonial condition in Morocco. Through opposition as a discourse, they construct a different narrative of Moroccanness that undoes the official one from the perspective of popular consciousness. Their discursive opposition finds its historical legacy in the national resistance movement and provides a rich musical archive that seems important enough to rethink Moroccan identity after independence.

Against the course of poetic orientation, an interrogative mode flares up in the clandestine narrative: "Has he accepted that?" is a question of protest against such non-dignified death. Although the Ghiwani poet in this particular piece sympathizes and identifies with the clandestine immigrant as a human case of tragedy, and as an instance to criticize political oppression in the postcolony, he does not categorically side with such an escapist act and non-dignified end. The Ghiwani poet, hence, does not celebrate leaving and departure, but rather calls for resistance and for opposition. This is not at all a situation that needs escaping, but rather a situation to face and challenge, as formulated by the poem.

Within the same vein, it is important to state that Nass el-Ghiwane's poems are suffused with lots of interrogative statements that dwell within the lyrical structures of the poem. Evocative as they are, many songs include an interrogative mode that keeps asking legitimate questions wherein the unrelentless search for definite answers becomes illusionary and futile. For the Ghiwani poet, it seems almost an unavoidable necessity to reiterate interrogations about the complexity of the condition. These appear as a set of open-ended questions that nurture the paradigmatic structures of the lyrics and enhance the overall effect of the poem. In discussing the issue of interrogative modes in poetic diction, Daniel Feldman confirms that,

> When one asks a question, whether in social speech or in poetic language, the question is meant not to celebrate ignorance but to struggle against it. Questions are not about the enigma of not knowing, but about exploring how we can know more. They serve not to venerate the mysterious transcendence of what we do not know but to expand the bounds of what we do.[82]

In Nass el-Ghiwane's poetic repertoire, as example, the following interrogations have appeared in various poems: *wach hna houma hna*? (Are we those we are?), *a'lach ana dhiya l-samt*? (Why am I victim of silence?); *fine li jam'o a'lik hal a-niya*? (Where are those who gathered around you?), *fin ghadi biya khouya*? (Where are you taking me brother?), *chkoune igoul walfi ana ikhoune* (Who would ever think the beloved ones would betray?) *chkoune f danya 'ala al-hak idafe'* (Who would defend the rights in the world?), *mal kassi hzine mabin al-kissane*? (Why is my glass saddened among others), *imta tbane salama*? (When shall peace show up?), *īmtā ibān ḍawnā kandīl madawi alā kol mkāne?* (When shall our lamp lighten the places?) … etc.

If we, as fans and audiences, attempt to loosen meanings from the intricate lines of the poems where these queries among many more appear, we certainly get overwhelmed with powerful and revealing images about uncertainty, reluctancy, doubt, unpredictability, ambivalence which inform the postcolonial imperative in Morocco. If we are allowed to get into the minds of the members of the group, we can probably get this answer to the Ghiwani's rhetorical interrogations: "we are singing for and amid our uncertainty." Also, if we consider Nass el-Ghiwane to be the quintessential popular voice for the voiceless during a specific historical juncture in Morocco known as the "years of lead," the interrogative tone that impels itself in poems mirrors an inquisitive logic that variously partakes in knowledge about the postcolonial condition characterized by disappointment, deception, repressed experiences, unfulfilled promises and frustrated dreams.

The melody of interrogation in Nass el-Ghiwane's poems opens an unpredicted horizon of expectations with possible meanings that audiences need to decipher. It calls for an implicit dialogic response which immediately engages the poet and the implied reader/listener into a conscious meditation of the constraining grid of social and political conditions of the country that spawn a round of circumstantial inquiries wherein questions produce more intricate questions, and wherein uncertainty leads to yet more uncertainty. Being the quintessential voice of the people, the rhetorical questions raised in the Ghiwani musical repertoire are asked for effect as persuasive devices to put emphasis on situations with almost any expected answers. These self-evident rhetorical queries reflect the uncertainties of the postcolonial subjects torn between the desire to understanding and the absence of clear responses to the hopes that left people within deep torment with no promising relief.

Nass el Ghiwane, the lineup in 2014 (courtesy Rachid Batma and Omar Sayed).

The lineup of the group, ca. 2014, after the death of both Larbi Batma and Abderrahman Paco, and departure of Allal. From left to right: Rachid Batma, Chifa, Omar Sayed, Hamid Batma (courtesy Rachid Batma and Omar Sayed).

Stories from the Margin: Nass el-Ghiwane Narrate History and Memory through Individual Representations of the Past

The members of Nass el-Ghiwane musical group, as stated earlier, came from various regions and embody the cultural diversity of the country. The rich cultural background of each member would later give the group both a homogenous musical distinctiveness and substantial heterogeneity in the formal construction of melodies and rhythms. Some members of the group were born in Ḥay Moḥammādi from migrant parents who first came from the rural parts of Morocco to Casablanca for better life opportunities; others came with their parents to settle in the city for the same purpose. Though their life stories are more or less different and their cultural backgrounds are diverse they share the same concerns, predicaments, dreams and aspirations as schoolboys, then as school dropouts and later as young theater performers and musicians. Their little stories articulate experiences, recount events and offer explanations and opinions; they are stimulating and worth recovering, documenting and reflecting on because they certainly add an interesting discussion as to how individual experiences shape historical, cultural and musical collective imagination in Morocco.

This section attempts to unearth the early beginnings of each member of the group and track their physical routes across various spaces inside and outside the city. It is concerned with few aspects of the members' life stories as told and narrated by themselves or testified by their friends during various media programs devoted to the beginnings of the group. My intention is dictated by a strong will to reconstruct these stories and document the individual experiences of the members of the group for readers worldwide. Their little narratives and enticing life experiences, ordeals, contributions and achievements offer suitable terrains to engage with the complexities of the postcolony, and raise fascinating questions about issues pertaining to nation, culture, history and music. These life experiences also offer interesting research venues on complex discourses about the postcolonial subject, as well as a rich heterogeneous background to theorize the Moroccan colonial, national, historical and cultural experiences beyond the mechanisms of hegemonic discourses dictated by postcolonial authority.

Nass el-Ghiwane's life stories are nearly and to some extent the same because they are set against the background of very confusing and ambiguous social, cultural and historical experiences. They are representations of a society whose collective memory is fractured by generational, societal and political divides. They are lived and experienced within a very complex background that has been characterized by various disconnections initiated by the colonial experience and perpetuated by the neocolonial mindset. When looking closely at these individual life stories while trying to reconstruct the textual fabric that brings them together, one might come to conclusion that they are all about the quest for self-discovery amid a disintegrated social class and uncompromising families in a seemingly brutal and indifferent country while quietly but clearly telling stories of the Moroccan nation. These life stories reflect personal experiences that also incorporate an assembled past which is constitutive of the construction of collective identity, and hence of nation building. The allegory between individual and national identity elevates their life stories from a typical narrative of anguish and torment into a thoughtful analysis of the formation of the postcolonial subject and agency.

What is interesting as well is the way the life stories of Nass el-Ghiwane's members speak of and to their context especially the background of an overdetermined situation to battle for national independence and cultural autonomy in the context of colonial encroachment and its discursive outcomes.

These stories tell much about poverty, physical abuse and educational neglect in a postcolonial setting. Their narratives of sufferings are told against the backdrop of their experience of the community inside the shantytowns where they grew up in Casablanca and elsewhere in Morocco. They emphasize the fact that these self-made individuals, with an early flair of artistic orientation, took their fate into their own hands when, out of extreme anxiety, they ran away from schools and led a shanty life to repossess power and agency. The memories they offer abound with ideas that tell much about transitional moments in Moroccan colonial and postcolonial histories and reflect on various issues that have plagued the postcolony in general—rotten educational system, neglect and hardship, aborted dreams, empty experiences of exclusion, individual and collective disruptions.

Also, when we look closely at the members' life stories, we find out that they explore representations of the past that operate as junctures between history and memory; they narrate and streamline the contradictions and conflicts that have afflicted Moroccan society during and after the colonial experience. Nass el-Ghiwane's narratives, which chart individual itineraries in the postcolony, are also impregnated with uncertainties that are symptomatic of colonial legacy. These uncertainties are clearly apparent not only within a colonial discourse of unbalanced power relations, but also and to a great extent within the postcolonial order which has reinforced, promoted and perpetuated the colonizing practices that have aborted desires and individual aspirations.

Omar Sayed, Ahagour Boujmea, Allal Yaala, Abderrahman Paco, and Larbi Batma whose life story has been dealt with extensively in this study, offer interesting personal and socio-cultural life stories that are worth retrieving in this book. The endeavor here is to pave the way to the setting for historiographical writing about these individuals' experiences that need to be read as sites of representation which offer the possibility of retrieving the postcolonial subject's overshadowed histories and stories. The experience of individual experiences in Nass el-Ghiwane's case challenges the ambiguous renditions of the past as envisaged by conventional historiographical writings and disturbs official history. These fragmented narratives offer ample possibilities to peel back the layers of the "epistemic violence" of postcolonial historiography, and counteract the intricacies of the "sanctioned ignorance" that has marked out the neo-colonial interpretations as well. They also emphasize the need for a serious academic undertaking to unearth the heterogeneity and complexity of the history of Moroccans. These subalterned voices in historiographical undertaking are important discursive modalities of representation where intertwined associations between history and power relations could be rethought and redefined. The experience of Nass el-Ghiwane has hardly found its ways into historiographical accounts, and the life stories of the members of the group have also been less tracked in academic undertakings.

Omar Sayed

nbāt nsāhar l-liyālī
o-dumū'ī ḥāyfa sjām
nabkī o-nūḥ f-l-rsām
'ala maḥbūb khāṭrī man jār 'liyya o-lā 'fā
imta yā mālkī nshāhad
kadak yaḍwī 'la l-rsām
mā bīn mḥāfil al-riyām
o-nqūl brīt man 'lālī w-nsīt mḥāyan l-jfā[83]

I spend sleepless nights,
my tears flowing endlessly
I cry and moan in the darkness
for my beloved who shows harshness and no mercy
When, my possessor, shall I see
your posture shining on the traces
Among the hordes of gazelles
and I can say: I was healed of my illnesses, and forgot any coldness

Omar Sayed, the manager of Nass el-Ghiwane musical group since 1970, was born around 1940 in Derb Moulay Cherif, Ḥay Moḥammādi, from a mother of Arab descent and a father with Amazīgh backgrounds. Omar's father, Si Abdellah Sayed, endured both the specter of poverty and the atrocities of the French authorities, as he was involved in the resistance movement against the colonizer. In 1954, just a couple of years before the formal independence of the country, the French authorities accused him of shipping weapons and ammunition to resistance fighters. He soon had to endure an exilic experience as he was deported to his native village, *Takerdoust*, in the outskirts of *Ait Bāhā* in Southern Morocco, leaving his family behind. By that time, Omar had already been living in a nearby shanty neighborhood with a relative from

Omar Sayed, the group's veteran (ca. 2011) (courtesy Omar Sayed).

his stepmother's side to whom he was given as an adoptee since she was barren. In his earlier years, Omar was torn between the two spaces of the city; between the family's home where his mother used to live before she joined the father in the village, and the would-be family with whom he stayed, going to school and doing menial jobs to survive.

Omar led a nomadic life of physical displacement and emotional instability earlier in his life. The feeling that grew within him as he started to become aware of his nomadism was that of disappointment and deprivation. He felt to be an orphan dropped out by a father who betrayed his emotional and filiative connections. Omar immediately found in Derb Moulay Cherif neighborhood and friends an alternative space to the parents' affection and to the warmth of the family life. His earlier years at school were characterized by disturbance, violence, tumultuous behaviors and disorder, which made his integration at school almost impossible. He still remembers how he once failed to do his homework, so the teacher fixed a slate over his back wherein was inscribed, "this is a donkey." The teacher took him to the other classrooms of the school and asked mockingly "who is this?" The pupils would yell in loud voices "this is a donkey."[84] This left a traumatic scar inside Omar who started to develop a feeling of frustration, fear and a psychological blockage. In 1958, he had to sit for his primary school certificate. The written exam was successful, but he failed to pass the oral one. Omar tells us that while he was leaving to school for the exam, he met a group of boys who were getting ready for a football match. As they needed someone to complete the team, Omar offered to play. He forgot about the test and, consequently, was sent away. He soon discovered the Americans' *Zabbāla* (garbage heap) somewhere in Ḥay Moḥammādi. This garbage heap was associated with American army landings in Casablanca sometime in the 1940s during the military Operation Torch led by George S. Patton. What attracted Omar, besides the food leftovers and desert that he discovered for the first time, were the illustrated comic books thrown in the heap. Omar found delight in collecting *Kiwi*, *Zembla*, *Akim*, *Blek le Roc* and many more. As he states, "I started to look at these books and enjoyed the stories. It is through these comics that I got acquainted with narrative techniques, plot, characters, acting and scenario writing."[85] These comics would also fuel up Omar's imagination with stories he used to write to his friends through letters he sent from his native village during summer school holidays.

In 1960, Omar Sayed was admitted in *Ibn al-Owam* agricultural school and lived in the boarding house. He loved the Chemistry class taught by a French teacher called *Monsieur Herbovoit* and excelled in the subject. The outfit of Monsieur Herbovoit influenced him a lot; and as Omar himself declares, "He used to wear long throusers and sandals, something unusual at that time; and these are what I am still wearing today."[86] Yet, as he was a cinema fan, he often skipped classes and went to watch movies at *Essada* Movie Theater whenever he saved money from the blankets he used to steal from the boarding house. When he got discovered, the administration sent him away. That's how his school life came to an end, and that's how his regular trips to the village became possible to visit his mother.

Unlike his relationship with the father, Omar was strongly attached to his mother, Lalla Daouia. As she was from Arab origins living in an Amazīgh environment, the mother according to Omar was also leading a distressed and grief-stricken life in the village.[87] What would often catch Omar's attention as a child whenever he joined his mother during school holidays was her loneliness and her long, continuous droning singing sounds that bore nostalgic tunes while doing the housework. Omar was very much afflicted and affected by her tunes which he discovered earlier as a schoolboy. These tunes and camouflaged mourning-like hums, as Hassan Habibi states "would later be reworked and readapted to suit the Ghiwani melodies. They have become an integral part and a metrical component of Nass el-Ghiwane's chants."[88]

Omar did humble and tedious jobs to survive and help the family. He worked as a porter at the harbor, as temporary employee in a factory, then as an apprentice for a butcher. In Ahmed Maanouni's *Al-hāl*, Omar states that he had to endure the filthiness of the place where he used to clean the stomachs and intestines of the slaughtered animals at the butcher's. This affected his eyes and had to live with short-sightedness ever after.[89] Omar Sayed considers Ḥay Moḥammādi as neighborhood to be his real school where he learnt so much. The theatrical performances of *Al-ḥalqa* in the neighborhood and movies at *Essaada* were an outlet of entertainment for Omar and his friends; he states that in those days "we were in front of real artists who narrated stories using powerful Moroccan *Dārija* full of meaningful images and metaphors; each circle had its own specificities, its mode of narration and its audiences as well."[90]

In fact, *Al-ḥalqa* was a rich inspirational venue that would later bring Omar's fascination with theater. He and his friend Boujemia soon started their *Rowād al-khashaba* (stage goers) theatrical troupe. On various occasions, Omar has declared that *ṭbal* (drum) was the means through which he came to strike an ever-lasting friendship with Boujemia. Boujemia, who lived four blocks away from Omar's home, was already known in the neighborhood for his artistic orientations; an intellectual man who had his own, but limited, friends whom he shared intellectual affinities with. To win his friendship, Omar once made a drum and went closer to Boujemia's home and started playing. The rhythmic sound of the drum heard outside soon aroused the curiosity of Boujemia who suddenly appeared from the window of his room, and then down to the street. The two became acquainted with each other and started an artistic journey together. This artistic journey with its beginnings in the neighborhood's Youth Houses, and around a barber's shop owned by an artist named Hassan, where the two would later meet Batma who had already been a closer friend to Hassan, would start an ever-lasting friendship between these three young men and would culminate in a new experience with Tayeb Saddiki's theatrical troupe in the second decade of the 1960s. Seddiki's theater was very fundamental to their artistic experience. It reworked and brushed up their sensitivity and ignited their awakenings to roots and memory through the singing of folk music; the very music and rhythms they once discovered through *Al-ḥalqa*'s troubadours, entertainers and bohemian storytellers in the streets of their neighborhood in Ḥay Moḥammādi became the quintessential interest of their artistic and theatrical career.

Ahagour Boujemaa

Ghīr khodūnī lilāh, Ghīr khodūnī
ruḥi nhīb lfdākum, ghīr khodūnī
ma'dūm walfī, lilah dalūni
wa maṣābr anā, 'li mshāw anā maṣābr
ṣfāyḥ fi yidīn ḥadād, anā maṣābr
galbī jā bīn yidīn ḥadād, ḥadād mā yḥan mā yshfaq 'lih
inzal ḍarba 'ala ḍarba, wi la brād zād nār 'lih[91]

Just take me for God's sake, and save me
My soul is offered in sacrifice, just save me
Wandering and lost, for god's sake guide me
Can't forget the beloved ones who have left
My heart is the hands of a blacksmith, less pity he takes
Striking blows after blows
Whenever the hitting cools, he stokes fire even more

Whenever Nass el-Ghiwane are mentioned, the generation of the 1960s onward would undoubtedly have the on stage image of a short brown-complexioned young man with a *da'dū'* over his shoulders flaring up in the minds. Boujemia was an exceptional artist who took a short-lived exceptional journey with the group from 1970 to Saturday, October 26, 1974, when he passed away; a death that has been engulfed in mystery and obscurity for years now. Boujemaa Ahagour, did not spend much time with the group but he was instrumental in laying the foundations for a new musical genre in Morocco and influential in his vision as an artist who was able to disseminate his songs and ideas through his writings, his penetratingly high-pitched voice and his *da'dū'*, also called *Al-Ḥarrāz* (medium-sized hand-held clay drum with a large opening and a skinned bottom) which became his companion throughout the period he spent with Nass el-Ghiwane. Boujemia

Ahagour Boujemia, the charismatic leading figure of the group in its beginnings (courtesy Omar Sayed).

was born around 1944 in Ḥay Moḥammādi from a poor family that came from *Tata* in Southern Morocco to settle in the outskirts of a shanty town called *Karyān Lakhlīfa*. Earlier in his age when he was still in the Koranic school, Boujemia showed inclination to music, through the rhythmic instrument called *Ta'rīja* (small-sized hand-held clay drum with a top small opening and a skinned bottom). According to his brother Lahcen Ahagour, "both Boujemia and our mother, Lalla Khdija, were known in the neighborhood for their artistic orientations. They always sing in family ceremonies and gatherings; the mother for the women and Boujemia for the men."[92] In addition to these family events, Boujemia was also involved in the Boy Scouts activities in the late 1950s. He was known in the scouting activities for his singing and drumming abilities. The festive context of independence offered an artistic terrain for Boujemia to keep his drum wherever he was and sing his songs amid gatherings that celebrated the patriotic return of the royal family from exile.

Boujemia started school in 1953 at *Al-ittihad School* in the neighborhood, and then moved to *Al-azhar High School* in 1963 where he would establish a strong friendship with Abou Daoud, a Palestinian activist teacher who influenced him with his patriotic ideas. According to his brother, for personal reasons and in order to help the family withstand life turbulences because the father had to retire, he left school in 1964, though he was highly motivated to complete his studies. He did various humble and low-paying jobs while working in factories around the suburbs of the city. In 1965, he and his family moved to Derb Moulay Cherif where he would soon meet Omar Sayed. Boujemia was also a fan of reading old Arabic stories and during his spare time he would find a retreat in *Al-ḥalqa* performances. He developed a passion for theater and started his theatrical troupe, *Rowād al-khachaba*, made of students and temporary workers from the neighborhood. The idea of starting this theatrical troupe was not fortuitous, as Miloud Oualla, one of the founding members, confirms. At that time, in the 1960s, theater in Morocco

> based its theatrical themes on issues that promoted stereotypical images which further enhanced divisive ideas between various Moroccan ethnic, cultural backgrounds. Shows developed their thematic concerns out of ethnic backgrounds that ridiculed difference in the Moroccan context such *Shelḥ* versus *'aroubi*, *Fāssi* versus *Soussi* and so on ... we thought of dismantling such theatrical mode of denigration and of unproductive satire to create something that talks about real Moroccan issues.[93]

Boujemia wrote and directed a number of plays for his theatrical troupe such as *Filestine* (Palestine), *Lan ya-shība al-ghūrāb* (The Raven Won't Grow Old), *al-miṣmār* (The Nail), *al-Baghlā hadā sh-harhā* (The Mule's Labor Is Due). *Rowād al-khashaba* soon became famous in Casablanca and was a haven for young talented performers in the neighborhood. It also became one of the leading troupes in supplying young theatrical potentialities and nurturing other already established theatrical troupes in the city such as Seddiki's. In 1967, Taeib Seddiki would summon Boujemia to join his professional theatrical troupe that had already been performing in the *Théâter Municipal.* Boujemia performed in Seddiki's theater for three years where he, together with Omar Sayed and Larbi Batma, mostly appeared as vocalists singing pieces from old poetry that Seddiki incorporated in his plays. The *Malḥamat Moulay Ismail, Kadour, Nour o-Ghandour, Zellāqa, Al-Ḥarrāz, Sidi Yāssine f-ṭariq, Diwān Sidi Abderrahman al-majdoub* were all plays where Boujemia and his neighborhood friends appeared. Through these plays, Seddiki's theater attempted to revive *Al-ḥalqa* spectacles. From then on, *Al-ḥalqa* has become widely employed in the modern Moroccan theater as it provides a distinct alternative to the conventional Western stage. In light of this, Khalid Amine who has worked extensively on pre-colonial, colonial and post-colonial Moroccan theatrical forms argues "Seddiki's theater is an exemplary first instance of festive hybridity. After consuming numerous adaptations from the Western theater, he inaugurated a new approach to theater making in Morocco."[94] In fact, Seddiki's theatrical experiences of adaptation and translation from old Moroccan dramatic forms illustrate the example of an avant-gardist festive theatrical enterprise in post-colonial Morocco whose hybridized forms are construed in an 'in-between' space; between western theatrical forms and Moroccan pre-theatrical esthetics. For the first time in the history of Moroccan theater, Saddiki transposed *Al-halqa*, as an esthetic, cultural, and geographical space, into a theater building as the space of the Western Other.

In late 1960s, Seddiki's theatrical troupe left to France. For tough family conditions, poverty and cruel social conditions in Morocco, Boujemia decided to stay in France with his friend Batma as stated earlier in the previous sections. His main objective in the beginning, according to one of his brothers, was to find work in order to help the family; yet, the encounter with Boudia, the Palestinian activist, would change the course of his life itineraries. In addition, Boujemia experienced and witnessed the volatile period of civil unrest in Paris during 1968 which culminated in demonstrations and massive strikes as well as the occupation of universities and factories across France by students. This event left undeniable imprints on the man's rebellious spirit. The experience beyond borders endowed him with reformist ideas and liberatory thoughts that were circulating at that time, and these would later become articulated through the poems he wrote for Nass el-Ghiwane. After a couple of months in France he came back home, and according to Omar Sayed,

> Boujemia who first left with Seddiki's troupe of performers was not the same one who came back later. He was totally different and everybody witnessed the change. He was thought provoking and daring as he talked with more openness on issues that were forbidden to talk about at that time. He showed lots of intrepidity, fearlessness and enthusiasm in talking about Moroccan social and political reality, and about the Palestenian cause as well. The influence of Boudia was noticeable for sure.[95]

Afterwards, when the idea of starting a musical band became mature enough to be set, it was Boujemia who suggested the word "Ghiwane" for the group. According to a family friend called Omar,

> There was a traveling troupe of troubadours from Tata, from Doublane tribes, South Morocco, who left their village and traveled on foot to Casablanca. They used to play Moroccan Ḥassāni /Sahraoui music during the Sunday performances in Ḥay Moḥammādi. The troupe was called "ahl-al-Ghīwān." This band played various musical styles from the Sahara which fascinated Boujemia a lot. He once came to me asking what the word "Ghīwān" meant. Six months later, he showed up again and told me that he was planning to start a musical group and that he was thinking of Nass el-Ghiwane as a name. This Ḥassāni troupe had tremendous effect on the man."[96]

In fact, Nass el-Ghiwane's songs in the beginning borrowed a lot from the *Ṭarab Ḥassāni*. The language used was simple but powerful in meanings. "Nass el-Ghiwane" as a catchphrase is loaded with meanings, metaphors and signifiers which transcend linguistic structures and formal representations to express states of prophecy, vision, revelation, truths, questions, and dreams. It refers to *nāss al-fhāma* "people of knowledge" or *nāss al-ma'nā* "people of meanings" who stretch language utterances further and push understanding beyond the surface implications they purport; people who are inclined to look for meanings in the deep bustle of metaphors and images. Most of these were traveling poets, as was the case with "ahl al-Ghiwane," who were inspired by popular Sufi orders that emerged in Morocco early in the fourteenth century, and led a wandering life of nomadism and dislocation, chanting their ordeals and journeys from a village to another. Among these Moroccan troubadour poets incarnating this traveling spirit and who also influenced Nass el-Ghiwane's writings and musical repertoire are *Sidi Abderrahman al-Majdoub, Boualem al-Jilali, Sidi Kaddour al-Alami, Ibn al-Mouaquit al Morrakochi*.... The *Majdoub* figure in these poets inspired Boujemia and his friends in Nass el-Ghiwane who found bounteous sanctuary in texts and poems they revisited in order to recover the history, spiritual journeys and obscure subjectivities of these traveling minstrels. Boujemia was selective in appropriating the majdoub's spirit and texts and reworked them to suit the social and political situations of the 1970s Morocco at a time when straightforward criticism of authority in the postcolony would lead to imprisonment, torture or even extermination. The appropriation of these texts was soft with overtoned insinuations that are meant to downsize meanings but which would at the same time disseminate powerful messages that are open to various interpretations.

Though Boujemia left earlier, the echoes of his texts and songs are still alive today among Nass el-Ghiwane's fans. Boujemia had a vision for Moroccan arts making, drive and energy for a new esthetics of music that went beyond the mere fact of singing with a group of musical artists. His brother, Abdellah, sums up in meaningful terms the man's illuminating far-sightedness and visibility for the Moroccan society. He contends that Boujemia "wanted certainly to say things and deliver messages about Moroccan issues than just carry his *Da'dū'* to sing with the group."[97] Boujemia's death remains a real mystery to his family and to his fans as well. None of his friends who have been interviewed for Moroccan TV programs believed how his death came in such a quick and sudden way. On Thursday 24th, 1970, the group performed in Ksar el-Kbir in the Northern part of the country. After the show, the band came back to Casablanca. Boujemia was at that time living in *Roches Noires* in a garage where the band used to compose and rehearse their songs. According to his close friend, Mohamed Bouhafa, who was living with him at that time,

> That evening, Boujemia asked for a herbal drink; he asked me to boil water and make Aloysia drink for him. When he got it, he ordered me to close the door and never let anybody to wake him even if it were *Ba Brahim*, his dead father. What made me wake him later was the following: he had agreed with a man to go to Essaouira to get him a piece of a poem from Mlhun, called *Sham'a* (candle). That night, I went home and found out quite by chance that the Moroccan TV was broadcasting the song. I recorded it for him on K7 audio cassette. I came the following day to show him the tape. I shook him and said teasingly "here is the poem you need; and what's more, it's free of charge!," but I found out that he was already dead. I still feel unable to dig it up.[98]

Boujemia's initial lineup with Nass el-Ghiwane did not last for long. His short-lived artistic experience with the group was a rich itinerary both in its human and humane dimensions. His fellow members remember him as a simple, unpretentious open-minded man whose voice would never be forgotten. He was a man of universal values, peace, principles and kind-heartedness. As Batma has put it in his *Al-Raḥīl*, "Boujemaa often said: if you should take my shirt by force, I'll give it to you with much love but when you wear it would you be satisfied in."[99] The obscurity surrounding Boujemia's death remains in fact enigmatic. His brothers assume that he was poisoned given a number of conflicting facts with the official narrative that declares stomach ulcer to be the main cause. One of Boujemia's brothers states that when he went in to see the corpse of his brother he found out that foamy thick white saliva was surrounding his lips, which favors a poisoning plot. Furthermore, a girl was seen with him prior to his death, but she miraculously disappeared forever leaving an unsolved puzzle that still forces questions to be answered. The doctor who examined the corpse refused the burial on the grounds of having an autopsy first, but within few minutes, the events took a different turning point. The same doctor insisted on the burial as soon as possible. The shock of the death did not allow the family to think further.[100] For his close friends, however, Boujemia might have died because of a chronic ulcer he had ignored for long until it was too late. Yet, what is quite evident is that with this tragic ending, Nass el-Ghiwane's story inaugurated temporal beginnings with departures. Some members left willingly to be replaced by others, Mahmoud Esaaadi and Abdelaziz Tahiri; others would later be eclipsed by the specter of death as was the case with Larbi Batma and Abderrahman Paco.

Abderrahman Paco

al-kanz al-makhfī likūm ftaḥtū
o-sar al-ghāmeq likūm fraztū
b-liyām lāghīt
mākfāt fikum kalma, walā ghamzā mn 'yn al ḥāl[101]

I opened your treasures that vanished from sight
I interpreted your propound riddles
The days that I talked about
Neither words nor winks from the eyes of a trance-driven
Would ever suffice to wake you up

Abderrahman Kirouche, also called Paco was an artist whose name has always been associated with *Sentīr* and Gnāwa dances within Nass el-Ghiwane musical band. He was born around 1948 in Essaouira; a rich historical space caught at the crossroads of colonial legacy, neocolonial ventures and postcolonial ambitions, which remains rhetorically powerful in Paco's life narrative. The city has always been a haven and retreat for Gnāwa music and musicians for long; it was also a "contact zone" of intricate "social spaces where disparate cultures meet, clash, and grapple with each other, often in highly asymmetrical relations of domination and subordination."[102] Paco's artistic flair became quite eminent from an early age when he and his friends would secretly, and against the families' will, attend Gnāwa *Līlla* (all-night spirit possession ritual) held in various parts of the city. Paco was deeply enthralled by *Tagnāwit* and its magical powers and revelations, and showed early signs of a *M'alem Gnāwi* (Gnāwa master) when he was eight years old.

Abderrahman Paco during the recording of *Mahmūma*, Eden Hotel, Paris (ca. early 1980s) (courtesy Rachid Batma).

According to Cherif Regraggi, a childhood friend of the 1950s, Paco was intrigued by the world of Gnāwa earlier in his life, "he used to recite school lessons in Gnāwa rhythms white beating with his fingers against his schoolbag. A paragraph from any given lesson for example would be rehearsed in a Gnāwa tune."[103] Paco also showed signs of rebellion against his father who wanted to stump his artistic orientations and complete his studies instead. Yet, he had to drop out in secondary school and became a carpenter apprentice to meet the needs of his father's expectations. Carpentry and the world of the craftsmen would soon turn into a bountiful artistic space that consolidated his musical friendship with many Gnāwa *M'alem(s)* across the city. According to Ahmed Radi, Paco's nephew, "the world of the craftsmen in Essaouira should not be viewed as mere space of manual and physical hard work; it is also an intellectual and artistic terrain wherein craftsmen talk about *Malḥūn* poetry, music, literature and philosophy as well…."[104]

Paco found himself trapped in this rich and fertile field of artistic and cultural practices in their Moroccan traditional forms and styles. Then, he started learning secretly the arts of *Tagnāwit* from other fellow craftsmen. The authority of the father often hampered his artistic inclinations as he wanted him to learn the craft of carpentry for a living; but soon after his death in 1961, and according to Paco's brother Abdelaziz, "Abderrahman stretched out the horizons of his freedom with the death of the father; the once repressed and camouflaged artistic feelings have now become free to emerge because there is nobody to control them anymore."[105] He started learning Gnāwa musical instruments and got the arts of *Tagnāwit* from distinguished and already established Gnāwa masters in the city such as *M'alem* Haddad and *M'alem* Boubker whom he attended the *Līlla* with on a regular basis. When these *M'alem*(s) witnessed his artistic potential at such an early age, they

> took him to Sidna blal *Zawiya* in the city where he had to play his *Sentīr* in the presence of other *Sentīr* masters. The Gnāwa *M'alem(s)* agreed on accepting him as part of their community and assigned him the serpent *mlūk* (a supernatural and powerful entity). The dancers in this *mlūk* ritual dance in serpent-like twists in front of three eggs while being clothed in white.[106]

A new turning point in Paco's life will be witnessed when the Hippie movement was first introduced to Moroccans. According to Larbi Riyad, "Essaouira was an anchorage for global cultures from the Americas, Europe and the Arab world. It was a small capital city for intercultural encounters. Paco soon became part of this amalgamation."[107] The city in late 1960s turned into an established enclave for artistic and cultural contacts. It was a contact zone for Westerners concerned with the quest for new experiences to discover the Other's exotic locales and to fulfill their artistic, sexual and interracial desires in disantant lands. Paco's Essaouira turned into a city of numerous spatial experiences, of global intrigue and cultural transgression[108] to become a liberating space that "holds out opportunities for emancipation from a patriarchal culture and the promise of an engagement with a broader experience of community."[109]

Within this promising space of boundless artistic freedom, Jimi Hendrix, the famous rock musician, visited Essaouira in the summer of 1969. He hit a random encounter with Paco while the latter was playing his *Sentīr* for a troupe of performers. What first amazed Hendrix was Paco's *Sentīr* and how this three-stringed instrument could yield rhythmic, timbral and melodic tunes that are musically balanced, and bring new sonorities that can create a variety of trance states, moods and atmospheres. Both artists became closer friends and played pieces together during rehearsals in the *Diabat* village where Jimi sojourned during his stay in Morocco. Hendrix was accurate in calling him *ṭabīb al-arwāḥ*, the healer of souls. Paco remembers the circumstances that brought that nickname to become attached to him. He said:

> I was playing during one of the *Līlla* that I organized for a huge crowd of Nazarenes and Moroccans. I started around 9.pm and at 8.am I still have not finished the round to demystify all the *mlūk* that need normally to be covered in the Gnāwa *Līlla*. I was so tired and could not feel my fingers anymore. I handed over my *Sentīr* to another Gnawi whom I trusted to keep the same chronological order that is basically inherent in building states of trance in the individual. There was a man in the crowd who had already been taken into trance; but the gnawi unintentionally failed to follow the order prescribed; the man fell down and fainted. I heard knocks on the door and the other *M'alem* came asking to save the situation. I played again until the man taken in trance woke up. Jimi Hendrix was there and was amazed at how the man came into life again. When the *Līlla* was over, he said "you are the healer of souls."[110]

During the same summer, a troupe of traveling artists appeared in the city. These are referred by Abderrahman in the above-cited quotation as the "Nazarenes." It was the "Living Theater" company headed by both Judith Malina and Julian Beck. These nomadic touring artists performed dramatic shows which incorporated music for theatrical effects.[111] When they headed to Morocco, this troupe had previously established a directorial style which was geared towards the exploration of improvisatory and collaboratively musical possibilities with native artists. They soon met with Paco who had already been acquainted with many European and American artists of the time that were fascinated by the chance for exotic vacations and novel artistic encounters and experiences. The "living Theater" produced a new theatrical piece in Essaouira wherein they integrated Gnāwa music with the sound background provided by Paco. The friendship struck with this troupe culminated in a romantic love story that ended in an interracial marriage between Paco and a performer named Christina. Despite the barriers of language between the two, as Paco did not speak English, "the couple communicated most of the time through music, gestures and sometimes through friends who translated the converstaions for both."[112]

Paco also organized *Līlla* for the troupe, something unusual for a Gnāwa master at that time. This was often viewed as a sacrilegious act in Gnāwa circles as they strictly forbid non–Muslims to attend Gnāwa rituals. The encounter with Western musicians in the case of Paco was subversive and provocative as he was the first Gnawi to have freed *Tagnāwit* from its sacred fillings and connotations while orienting it towards western artists and public. *Tagnāwit* is built on the premise of purity and ablution, a cleansing of the body with water basically for religious rituals such as prayers. The Gnāwa community found that allowing the Nazarenes to attend the *Līlla* disturbs if not violates and destroys one of the tenets of *Tagnāwit*. Paco's rebellion over these traditional beliefs strongly perceptible and respected in Gnāwa cultural environment led to various intolerant reactions and condemnation from the

Gnāwa *M'alem(s)* who sued his case and turned it into a legal matter. In fact, Paco was one of the first Moroccans to have brought the art of Gnāwa closer to Western audiences and was highly influential in giving *Tagnāwit* a global dimension it is cherishing nowadays.

Within this historical juncture, Moroccan musical landscape started to witness emerging musical bands which followed the lead of Nass el-Ghiwane; an already established tradition. Jīl Jilāla was in its earlier phases of inception. Its founding member Hamid Zoughi had four members ready for the musical adventure but needed a *Sentīr* player join the group. He went to Marrakech looking for the Baqbou Gnāwa family to get Mustapha, the son. Finding out quite by chance that he was away in Essaouira, they left to bring him. As they did not find him, few city inhabitants convinced them to check out a different local *Sentīr M'alem* (master of the Sentīr) who was involved and excelled in the arts of *Tagnāwit*. They soon hit it off with Paco who left immediately with them to Casablanca. Another artistic and musical itinerary would begin as Paco joined without a slightest hesitation the newly born group of Jīl Jilāla. Within few weeks, they came out with their first album and played in a yet still-to-remember concert in Rabat. The experience did not last much with Jīl Jilāla due to an artistic misunderstanding during a recording session with the other members of the group. According to Hassan Habibi, "the new song that Jīl Jilāla wanted to release did not appeal to Paco; it did not musically and rhythmically stir him enough to be produced for the fans."[113] Paco had to leave the studio, just to continue in other studios but this time with Nass el-Ghiwane whose left-handed *Sentīr* player, Moulay Abdelaziz Tahiri had just, within unclear circumstances, broken up with the group.

Abdderrahmane Paco enriched Nass el-Ghiwane's music by brilliantly incorporating Gnāwa rhythms in meaningful ways. He left an indelible inscription and legacy on Moroccan popular music that quickly turned him into a Gnāwa icon in the Ghiwani tradition. To his fans, he will always remain an unforgettable figure that has sealed his artistic journey with creative musical pieces such as *Narjāk anā, Ghīr khodūnī, Annādī anā, Mahmūma* … etc. On stage, Paco was visible through his melodic groaning and his mournful-like sounds uttered in derisions, disapprovals and desires that characterized the condition of postcolonial Morocco. These melodies that he inherited from a long Gnāwa tradition intersected with the musical rhythms of his *Sentīr* in balanced and harmonious ways. His overloaded sounds would melt in a state of delight as he threw his body and soul into a cataleptic dance by the end of each live performance. Paco left Nass el-Ghiwane when his friend Batma was in hospital, a fact that brought him lots of criticism from the band and from the fans as well. The issue this time was probably about a financial disagreement with the group. Paco left back to Essaouira where he joined his children, also artists, and formed a musical group together and started recording their CDs. But, this experience did not last much because he would soon succumb to his disease and die in October 2012 after a long battle with chronic hypertension that left him paralyzed for over five years, unable to speak or move after a long thriving career as a gnawi musician, as a wandering singer and *Sentīr* player.

Allal Yaala

rāḥt shems al-'shi, rāḥt fi ḥkām al-bārī ta'āla
qāl zīn anā bghīt namshī
waqt larwāḥ hāda māfīh mqāla
liyām dāyza o-denyā raḥāla
rwāḥ awā l-tāwra ramwālef bīha
tshūf al-'azbā mḥanyā o-lkhwātm fidīha
sidī rabī lā tkater shdā 'la'bād
tebqā lblād zāhya al-ghīwān m'a lūlād[114]

Afternoon sun has set, set peacefully by the great God's wisdom
The beautiful ones said they needed to leave,
Time for leaving with no delays,
The days are running by and the world is not eternal.
Let us go to *Tāwra* that you're familiar with
To see the maidens putting *Henné* and wearing rings
God! Do not tighten it up on your believers
The country shall live in peace, and al-Ghiwan plays for the fans

Allal Yaala, or *ba Allal* (father Allal) as his fellow musicians would call him, is another emblematic figure in Nass el-Ghiwane whose life story needs particular consideration as well. Allal is still considered an icon in the Moroccan artistic and musical landscape and an undeniable guarantor for the stability and continuity of the group for over forty years now, though he has recently stopped playing because of health problems. Originally from *Oulād Berhil* in the outskirts of Taroudant, South Morocco, from migrant parents, Allal was born in the early 1940s in *Karyān Jdid* Derb Moulay Cherif, Hay Mohammādi. He grew up in a family environment with rich musical background as his father managed and played with *Howāra* Troupe, from the Houara Tribe; and one of his uncles belonged to a Gnāwa troupe of entertainers. The loss of his brother, Idder, in the 1950s impacted tremendously on him and he had to endure a shocking, traumatic individual experience since his early age. Following this incident, Allal turned to music that became both a genuine relief and a therapeutic retreat ever after. He soon became a talented Luth player and started his early career as musician in orchestra bands of the neighborhood.

Allal was also part of the young dwellers of the shanty neighborhood who endured the specter of poverty, unemployment, and disillusionment after independence, and who aspired for change through music and artistic commitment. He learnt music without instructors and opened a small music classroom to teach music for the children of the neighborhood. He played and mastered various Moroccan musical instruments such as the violon, *al-ghīta* (the pipe), the Luth, Banjo, *Bendīr* ... etc. He has always been referred to as a "walking orchestra," a nickname that was given to him by his fellow Ghiwane members. In the 1960s, he joined Taieb Seddiki's theatrical troupe, not as actor, but as musician who composed background music for theatrical effects. Allal declares that he was the first to join Seddiki's theater even before his friends debuted with the troupe and he was also the first to leave before the others.[115] When Mahmoud Essaadi left Nass el-Ghiwane, as stated before, he was asked to join the group. The choice of Allal by the group was not fortuitous at all since Boujmai and Batma who first sent for him when they wanted to record their *Ṣiniya* knew perfectly well that his multi-instrumentalist talent would serve the new Ghiwani style forever.

Allal Yaala, the maestro of the group (courtesy Omar Sayed).

What is remarkable about Allal is that during live concerts, either broadcast or not, we feel that the man is always keen on inventing tunes on the spur of the moment. Very often Nass el-Ghiwane's recorded songs on audio cassettes are governed by a particular paradigm of rhythms with melodic stops wherever and whenever necessary; but on stage we feel important rhythmic shifts in the arrangement of the song played for and connected with the audience. What I mean is that there are moments of musical tune playing that extend beyond the regular timing imposed by the lyrics. Sometimes he would momentarily escape musically from the rhythm that he breaks and inverses into fragments to follow an opposite rhythmic track that his banjo yields in balanced and meaningful ways without loosing the overall linearity that the song purports. These are of course unplanned melodies and musical twists that Allal excels at delivering through his instrument. I have come to understand these musical twists in Allal's artistic behavior through the facial expressions of the other members of the band. Batma's watchful eyes on stage for example, or Paco's, tell much about these enchanting twists in Allal's improvisations. Whenever such musical escapes occur on stage, Batma shows delight through occasional winks and follows the rhythm balancing his curly hair and swinging his upper body that his *Ṭbilāt* does not hide.

Within this same vein, Hassan Habibi states that "Allal is an artist who has developed a vast knowledge of music over the years, but what characterizes his music is the beats on the strings that yield a rhythm similar to that of a Moroccan percussion instrument such as the *Bendīr.*"[116] If this artistic talent hints to anything, it undoubtedly refers to the fact that Allal takes music first and foremost as personal delight. He has once declared that he is not the kind of musician who would only play to arise the audience's satisfaction, but above all he plays for his own gratification: "On stage, I play to please myself first."[117] Allal is a self-made musician who has learnt the art of music without instructor. He states: "The first music manual I was able to lay hand on was on music theories by Salim Lahlou. I started studying the solos hard and alone; and the result was immediate as if I were in a lebaneese school."[118]

If the role of the mother has been tremendous in shaping the artistic flair of the members of the group, Allal's mother on the other hand was also special in the neighborhood. She was a *Qābla* (midwife in the traditional Moroccan way) who attended to the birth of most children in Ḥay Moḥammādi in the absence of medical care and birthing centers for poorer families of the time. Her job as a traditional birth attendant was done free of charge. What she would always ask for, instead, was a punch of salt from the family of the newly born baby. Though the influence of the mother was not immediate in Allal's artistic career, she was an icon of communal midwifery and a bringer of enjoyment and festivity to families.

Allal recalls an important episode in his life in Ḥay Moḥammādi when he was member of an orchestra of the blind before joining Nass el-Ghiwane. Those blind musicians were often invited to play for women in family ceremonies and gatherings. Allal used to pass for blind by wearing sunglasses and behaving like a disabled musician. At that time, celebrations were gendered as men were not allowed to mix up with women. The common belief among Moroccans of the time supposed that the blind were much safer to leave with women during family celebrations, and were reliable enough to ward off the lascivious gaze of men. The invitation of the orchestra of the blind to play for women was also believed to bring about less threat of seduction and enthrallment in the absence of the husbands and relatives. Allal used to play with the blind, though he is not blind, and in nightclubs and cabarets around Casablanca as musical activity to make a living. Later he would open a small school to teach music in the neighborhood and then joined Nass el-Ghiwane after the departure of Mahmoud Essaadi.

Nass el-Ghiwane and After: Alternative Voices in Moroccan Fusion Music and the Quest for Identity Construction

As argued earlier, late 1960s and early 1970s witnessed the birth of a novel style in Moroccan music in a context of social and political crises that culminated in serious violations of human rights; an interesting juncture in Moroccan contemporary history known as the "years of lead." Nass el-Ghiwane's music then appeared as a loud call and popular reaction that attempted to express individual and group aspirations to defend their rights and freedoms. This protest song advocating change would soon become popular and would establish itself as a cultural medium for identity quest and self-affirmation. Nevertheless, during the first decade of the twenty-first century, and in a context of democratic transition, a new movement of young artists has taken over contestation and protest issues to deal with the country's social and political matters. These young artists have developed a new musical style that aspires for the emergence of a new society wherein the scope of freedoms is much more enlarged than before. This section attempts to read this new movement in its local and global contexts and tries to look at the possible esthetic connections that might exist between the 1970s protest esthetics and that of nowadays. It also attempts to look at the extensions that have been forged within the thematic, esthetic and poetic Ghiwani tradition and which influenced the development of such a genre.

It is, however, interesting to assert that the first decade of the 21st century, witnessed various economic, social and political changes that affected cultural life in Morocco in significant ways and filled up the conditions in which the embryonic youth movement nurtured and reared. At this particular historical juncture, the government started an on-going process of privatizations, including various media outlets such as television, newspapers and radio stations. This process also impacted on the press arena and led to the spreading out of daily magazines and newspapers. Also, the global widespread of

Internet and the virtual booming of web access in Morocco had a tremendous influence on Moroccan social and cultural life as well. This contributed largely in creating a more open atmosphere for cultural expression.

The mid–1990s of the twentieth century witnessed a growing number of Moroccan artistic troupes that started a novel experience of musical production. This musical revolution was defined in the beginning as "underground," and later baptized as "*Nāyḍa*." The term "*Nāyḍa*" derives its meanings from the Moroccan vernacular that literally means "standing up" or "erected," but which metaphorically refers to a process of revival, swing, or rise. "Noud" as a verb has nuanced meanings that denote an action verb, either to stand up, or to wake up. *Nāyḍa* is often used when a boiling situation of misunderstanding between two or more people is uncovered, or when an activity, such as dancing, is in full swing. *Nāyḍa* as an artistic movement emerged from the confines of marginalization and took up the combination of traditional Moroccan musical styles with a variety of transnational genres for its esthetic expression. *Nāyḍa* was first associated with a number of Rock, Rap and Hip Hop Moroccan musical groups that built up their musical rhythms and lyrics while relying heavily on Bob Marley's and Nass el-Ghiwane's legacies. Though the artistic works of these bands were basically a bricolage derived out of a mixture of rhythms and beats from various local and global genres, their orientation was geared towards Moroccanizing their repertoires while essentially emphasizing the use of Moroccan vernacular. Yet, while the efforts of these musicians were geared toward the redefinition of few aspects of Moroccan identity, artists of the new movement have distanced themselves from any political engagement. Their musical endeavors were mainly directed toward a new musical vision and their primary desire was to create a new style of music.

Though these emerging groups had no political orientations and ideological affiliations, they raised issues about corruption, poverty and denounced the unfair and unequal relations of power and systems using a language that would be understood by everybody. Initially, to understand the *Nāyḍa* of young Moroccan artists aspiring for freedom at all levels, it is of urgent need to position the movement in its historical context. Few key days seem illuminating for this discussion.

In 1999, and for the first time in Morocco, the first edition of the "Boulevards des Jeunes Musiciens" took place. This event, initiated by Mohamed Merhari, otherwise known as Momou, and Hicham Bahou, was initially thought to be a competitive venue for the existing Moroccan musical underground bands of the time. Over the years, this event flourished and grew to become a leading reference nationwide. 1999 is of dual importance as well since it witnessed a transition in the political scene with the enthronement of the new king of Morocco, Mohamed VI. This meant a political break with the period known as the "years of lead." In 2003, a turning point revolves around two major incidents that shook the country. Thirteen young Moroccan heavy metal musicians were arrested and jailed on the grounds of being involved in Satanism and for ostensibly disturbing public order; "a case that was assisted by the fundamentalist religious mentality that associates the impersonation of evil traits, however theatrically, with devil worship, a highly punishable crime in Morocco."[119]

The story of these young artists acquired nationwide media coverage and became rich material for filmic production. Ahmed Boulane, for instance, has capitalized on the issue and shot his "les Anges du Satan" [Satanic Angels] in 2007. The film retells the story of the thirteen young artists and targets issues pertaining to the Moroccan context such as freedom of expression. According to El-Maarouf, the filmmaker declares in an interview: "why do not we give freedom to young Moroccans to express themselves, because if we corner them, they fall prey to the dark forces which will firstly contain them and secondly turn them into time bombs."[120] Boulane is undoubtedly alluding to the other incident that shook the country in May 2003, when five simultaneous explosions initiated by a group of suicide bombers from a Casablanca's long-neglected bidonville shook the city and the whole nation, just few weeks after the jailed artists were released. The twelve young who were held responsible for the terrorist attacks came from the same social background, and also from the same neighborhood. These bombings were viewed as an immediate outcome of social deprivation, economic unrest and religious zeal, and as a noticeable potential threat underlying the city's flagrant inequalities.

This traumatic event that was new to Morocco and to Moroccans was vehemently denounced. Civil society, politicians, the government thought it of urgent need to open spaces of expression to young people. The festivals initiated either by civil associations or by the State, soon became an ideal outlet of reconciliatory terrains that would generate consolidated and reunited communities across time and space through themed performances that reiterate the need to live with respect and openness in modern tolerant new Morocco. So, the 2003 incident on the trial of the young artists, followed by the suicide bombings of the same year, generated an unprecedented wave of music festivals across the country. Every region in the country had its own festival, in addition to the already existing ones: "Festival des musiques sacrées, Fez" (2003), "Timitār" of Agadir (2004), "Festival de Casablanca: Théatre et Cultures" (2006), "Festival Méditerranéen d'Al Houceima" (2005), "Festival du Rai d'Oujda" (2005), "Mer et Desert, Dakhla" (2007), "Voix de Femmes, Tetouan" (2008), "Awtār, Ben Guguerir" (2009), and last but not least, "Mawāzin, Rabat" which has become an established musical venue for local artists and others beyond borders since 2008. These special events, which can be defined as temporary occasions of public celebrations, have been created with the goal of fostering community pride and "shaping identity and cultural difference into some form of community and so promote social cohesion and a sense of belonging."[121] They soon became magnets of attraction to young artists.

Yet, whatever the format of these festivals and their cyclicality and despite the fact that they constitute transitory events in the lives of people and places, it is essential to view them primarily as discursive arenas. Today they are not only local sites of "public memory and recall" but global events of overlapping experiences and crisscrossed discourses. They are "site[s] of intensification, with links and connections within and beyond locality"[122] in which they take place. Festivals in Morocco have been restaged and reshaped to serve global concerns. They have become strategical devices implemented to overcome the phobia of terrorism. Living in an age of disproportionate extremisms and violent political, social and cultural reactionary attitudes, festivals held nowadays in Morocco seem to be increasingly conceptualized as vehicles of cultural dialogs and vital means for reaction against terrorism and nightmarish fantasies. Often, festivals would serve as a means of reaffirming and reviving a local culture or a tradition and would offer the communities the chance to celebrate their identities; however, responses, to the possible threats of terrorism have led to a complex and complicated series of associations in the present discursive formations of festivals in Morocco. With the rise of the new global war on terror and with the emergence of the religious zeal motivated by an Islamophobic mindset, festivals seem to be advocating multiculturalist visions and versions of coexistence and tolerance.

The wide range of festivals that sparked in the country was at the genesis of musical revival in Morocco, backed up by the advent of private radio stations all over the country. These media outlets were instrumental both in paving the way to various musical bands to broadcast their music, and in giving new visibility on the Moroccan musical landscape. Radio stations such Aswat, Hit-Radio, Radio 2M, Chada FM, Atlantic Radio became potential partners to festivals, and interviewed artists live from the backstages while broadcasting their music on a regular basis. Soon *Nāyḍa*, as concept and movement, became widespread among Moroccans.

The new musical groups that acquired legitimacy in festivals were also at the genesis of the rise of a blending musical style known as "fusion" which would later turn into a distinct genre with its own supporters and fans among the youth. The most important aspect of these groups is that their musical repertoire draws upon various local, global and cross-cultural musical genres. They primarily draw on Moroccan popular *al-Sha'bī*, Rock and Roll, Blues music, Jazz music, Moroccan festive chants. Yet, for these groups, the Ghiwani song remains one of the most important mediums that furnish ample grounds for an expressive language that makes use of the Moroccan vernacular to celebrate belongingness, authenticity and faithfulness to identity distinctiveness.

Back into the 1970s, mainstream western music and musicians, such as Jimi Hendrix, Santana, Dire Straits and Bob Marley to name but a few, had undeniable musical effects on Moroccan musicians through blended individual or collective performances. Hendrix, for example, was a favorite of Abderrahman Paco of Nass el-Ghiwane, who incorporated *fusion* in Gnāwa musical pieces they played together. Likewise, the influence of French-based fusion developed by immigrant descendants had also largely influenced Moroccan fusion musicians in the late 1980s. The most dominant of these are Orchestre National de Barbès and Gnāwa Diffusion. These French North African fusion players have common concerns with Moroccans not only through musical connections but also through the revival of issues about cultural identity that were geared towards the arousal of cultural awakening in the country.

These historical junctures developed a favorable musical terrain for a number of young musicians to start embryonic fusion movement towards a distinct musical genre in the Moroccan society. The early 1990s as stated before was decisive in fostering fusion rhythms and lyrics among musicians. The most significant of these were those who initiated "Gnāwa fusion style." Inspired by the Gnāwa tradition, Hamid el Kasri and Abdelmajid Bekkas started musical collaboration with the already existing artists involved in "Moroccan Jazz" music and led to their recording of tapes on *Gnāwa jazz fusion*. Gnāwa and Jazz-Moroccan style became immediately of great appeal to fans as both styles share innumerable rhythmic and melodic elements. Ted Swedenburg captured the effect of such blending in a description during the 1998 Gnāwa Festival of Essaouira. He states that Saha Koyo is the result of collaboration between Gnāwa musician Hamid el Kasri, who sings and plays guembri, and producer and jazz keyboard player Issam-Issam. He confirms that

> The result is a kind indigenous Gnāwa jazz. Unlike most of the collaborations with Western jazz or rock players, here the fit between the playing of the guimbri and the jazz keyboards is just perfect. The keyboard work is faithful to the spirit of the Gnāwa, and yet turns it into something new. Issam-Issam's playing on the organ and the Rhodes piano not only meshes, but also manages to capture the mood of the Gnāwa songs, which are sometimes joyful, sometimes redolent with dread. The spirits (known as *mlūk*) the songs are meant to propitiate are capricious, neither wholly good nor evil, and they can bring blessings, or harm.[123]

It is interesting to state, however, that all the musical groups of the early *Nāyḍa* style, then fusion as a label shortly after, claim certain definite inspirational affiliation to Nass el-Ghiwane. In fact, the affiliative interconnections between Nass el-Ghiwane and the other musical groups that grew and flourished in the *Nāyḍa* stages of festivals and elsewhere is complex. The social, textual and musical discourses inherent in the new song pioneered by these artists reveal important multifaceted aspects that are worth reading. In fact, these groups often emphasize the innovative aspect of their artistic movement and highlight it as a social phenomenon. These young artists speak an unvarnished Moroccan language to lay bare the unbearable reality of the country, but with a sense of rhythm and musical effort that share a basic approach to music making, and which in turn, outweighs the desire to revolt. Like their ancestors, Nass el-Ghiwane, but in varied degrees of musical esthetics, who were able to disseminate encrypted messages which revolted against inequality and absence of freedom, these groups attempted to follow the lead of the Ghiwani voice that represented people in times of repression, political unrest and social confusion.

One of the main essential components of the fusion music is the blending of Moroccan and non–Moroccan genres. Many bands are almost highly inclined to combine their music with other transnational genres, such as Jazz, Salsa, Reggae, Rai and Rock, the latter being the non–Moroccan element that clearly influences their performance style. This approach is clearly noticeable among different groups such as "Hoba Hoba Spirit," with its punk influences and tendencies, Barry's band and its hardcore-driven style, the Gnāwa rock of Darga, and the jazz-inflected singer-songwriter style of Askouri. However, there is one commonly agreed component that these groups cherish and apprize. In their use of Moroccan music, they rely heavily on the multifaceted and rich rhythmic resources that can be extracted from the various genres of Moroccan music. Their music, hence, becomes transgressive in obscuring the boundaries of transnational music styles. Still, the influence of early fusion bands that developed their musical styles beyond borders, in France and elsewhere, cannot by any means be overlooked.

The musical works of early fusionists, a label that traveled from France, such as Gnāwa Diffusion and Orchestre National de Barbés are undeniable. These bands, led by musicians of Algerian and Moroccan descent who lived on the margins of French society, blend North African musical genres with other genres in a manner that highlights their shared origins, affiliations and belonging. Moroccan fusionists to come into existence shortly after found a haven of inspiration in these bands which articulated musical discourses about identity assertion, cultural integrity and musical affiliation. Moroccan fusionists became acquainted with their expatriate musicians through recordings and invitations to Moroccan festivals, especially the Gnāwa Festival of Essaouira which soon turned into one of the main venues of performance opportunities to these young Moroccan artists.

The widespread reputation of the Gnāwa Festival of Essaouria founded in late 1990s became an attractive space to young Moroccan musicians as it has gradually emphasized the fusion genre as a basic constituent of its festive programs. The Essaouira Festival has been very influential in initiating musical blendings between performers from various parts inside the country and beyond borders as well. It has also been influential in creating an audience for fusion as a distinct genre in Moroccan musical landscape. The involvement of fusion music in Essaouira Festival soon led to the widespread of this genre in other festive venues. It soon became an integral part of festival programs initiated by governmental and non-governmental organizations and associations on a yearly basis. Another important aspect of the Gnāwa Festival in Essaouira, besides being a sanctuary of attraction to researchers and academic scholars worldwide working on Gnāwa music, is its revitalization of Gnāwa *M'alem*(s) (masters) and their musical legacy among Moroccans who used to associate them and their performances with negative epithets. Now, audiences could see Gnāwa *M'alem(s)* onstage performing with musicians from Europe, Africa and America, presenting a global music in their collaboration with renowned and well-established musical icons of jazz music and other pluralistic musics. Young Moroccan artists, together with other North African fusionists, have extensively drawn from Gnāwa music and have prominently deployed it in their musical repertoires.

The reception and recognition of fusion music and fusionist musicians was established through festivals in Morocco. The popularity of such music among young Moroccans is undeniable because they conceive of it as contemporary popular music that combines electrical instruments and harmonies with mainstream Moroccan popular music. Such appeal is derived from the fact that Moroccan music with a Western touch, visible enough in fusion music, can produce rhythmic effects that stir emotions and send messages about the real issues plaguing Moroccan society and politics. For fans, fusion is not only about the sounds of the music, but also the link fusionists create between the traditional musics of the country and the instruments they use. Such music, according to fans, is capable of generating transic states and experiences, just as it was the case with the Ghiwani tradition. Fusion performances, accordingly, can turn into a spiritual musical practice eminent in popular religious brotherhoods if the Gnāwa, Hmadcha and '*Aisāwa* chants are incorporated in meaningful ways.

Fusion music in Morocco has become part and parcel of an established tradition in Moroccan musical landscape and has contributed to the making of a new style in Moroccan music. Its main aspect is that it has enabled the young Moroccan musicians to get acquainted with various musical genres across the country, and use that repertoire in their musical productions. Its orientation as a cultural expression is clearly tied up with cultural roots basically through the use of Moroccan vernacular and through the

Moroccanization of western musical instruments. Inspiration and connections to traditional forms and practices of Moroccan music has turned it into an appealing form of expression for the youth who came from various classes of Moroccan society. If this alternative music genre has witnessed an increasing popularity in the past few years, it is undoubtedly because of the enabling spaces festivals allow and also, to a larger extent, because of media support and encouragement. Newspapers and magazine reporters, television-broadcast shows, and radio stations, have been very instrumental in creating greater visibility and festival visitability for fusion music and performances, and in redefining the tenets of contemporary Moroccan music.

The "*Nāyḍa*" or fusion movement of young musicians in Morocco is an urban occurrence and singularity in the discursive practices it purports. It has turned into one of the most greatly consumed forms of artistic practice among young Moroccan generation. Because of its enormous appeal among the youth, it has been deployed by musicians, fans and audiences as a means of expressing a wide range of ideas, feelings and emotions. For years now, the movement has been criticized for creating associations and specific strands that range from gangsterism to vandalism and inclination towards disturbing the foundations upon which Moroccan tradition is constructed. This genre's thematic signification does not need to be reduced into a mere transitory phenomenon. It is a new form of oppositional culture that articulates discourses of resistance about social injustice and political dislocation in the country.

This movement is also to be approached as discourse and to be viewed as counter culture within the new global cultural transformations of religious violence and current responses to the war on terror. It is a heterogeneous space of various forms of identity and cultural influences in circulation that are meant to reshape the local. In fact, academic efforts to disengage the discursive underpinnings and put to task the implicatures that go into the making of the movement will be an insightful endeavor. Obviously, one of the main concerns of this cultural movement is to celebrate the culture and identity of the people staging events where these young artists appear massively. This objective is geared towards establishing a distinct national identity through the promotion of social cohesion and a sense of belonging. Yet, processes of global commodification have been blamed for weakening local distinctiveness and for the loss of identity, authenticity and meaning.[124] For Stuart Hall,

> Global mass culture is dominated by the modern means of cultural production, dominated by the image which crosses and re-crosses linguistic frontiers much more rapidly and more easily, and which speaks across languages in a much more immediate way.[125]

The spread of global cultures, visible enough in *Nāyḍa*/fusion musical movement in Morocco, tends to diminish the sense of place, produce hybridized identities and manufacture cultural authenticity for global consumption. The global dissemination of cultural forms and ideas has been conceived of as an explicit threat to the existence of local cultures and traditions, also noticeable in the heavily consumed western art in the bands' musical repertoires. Certainly, this youth movement has led to the emergence of new subjectivities and subjects, new regions, and new communities that have previously been excluded from the major forms of cultural representation. The marginal and the local in this musical genre have ben able to acquire voice and speak for themselves in meaningful ways through artistic regeneration of old and new, traditional and modern musical practices. An esthetic approach to this movement would certainly be very limited for it fails to politicize identities and fails to see into the *Nāyda* music as a site of identity articulation whereby the global and the local, the postmodern and the postcolonial are engaged in a perpetual struggle over representation and power. The movement, in fact, is not just an artistic occurrence, but also a cultural space where identities are performed and constructed through texts, music and body performance on the basis of such parameters as nation, class, gender, place and belonging. So important also is that this artistic movement about the experience of "New" Moroccan music turns into a political site where the global postmodern tends to appropriate the local, while this latter is inclined to resist and articulate its marginality in a perpetual quest for representation and power. Such resistance is bound up with the creative efforts of musicians to assert a distinctly Moroccan identity through a strategical blending of Moroccan and non–Moroccan musics to ensure freedom of artistic expression.

Of critical importance also is the view geared towards enhancing an interesting connection between the cultural transformations that occurred in Morocco in the 1960s and in the early 1990s. Unlike Nass el-Ghiwane who drew heavily from Moroccan folklore and various established musical genres in the country, *Nāyḍa* musicians relied profoundly, if not worryingly, on Western musical influences which they locally tamed and appropriated in order to serve as expressive mediums of expression that outvoice their grievances and dissatisfactions. Still, what is worth also considering is that both movements can be viewed as legitimate offsprings of street culture. As stated by Oamar Boum, these street movements

> can be a potential site of symbolic struggle and empowerment. At the same time, these musical modes of contention are challenged by the state. What we see through [these] cultural experiences [...] are sites of contestation where struggles for and against hegemony are exhibited.[126]

In his insightful research paper on Moroccan youth, Aomar Boom refers to Bennani Chraibi, who in turn has elaborated on the concept of *siba* (dissidence and non-conformism) to describe how Moroccan young musicians were able to challenge the state's authority and free themselves from the patriarchal discourse of society[127]; and how, by the same token, these young artists have dismantled the inherited rules of conduct visible enough in the respectful fear that characterized the previous generations. As Rémy Leveau argues, these young artists

> reject any model which is too definite, starting with that of their parents or the official discourse model [...] Moroccan youths no longer believe in the founding myths of power, and when they look for a collective meaning which would give more content to their indicidual quests, it is more likely to be within the small groups and communities that they create in [...] the neighborhood that the discourse rejecting the society in which they are living is elaborated.[128]

These young musicians' adoption of a westernized mode of expression can initially be viewed as a revolting discourse against society through the reproduction of novel musical genres that are appropriated to fit within the social and cultural realities of the country. One of the main positive achievements of these bands in *Nāyḍa* /fusion music genre is that they have managed to raise the youth's awareness about the social constraints and economic challenges that the country is facing.

Conclusion

This work has been concerned with Nass el-Ghiwane's music in general and with Larbi Batma in particular as one of the founding members of the group. During the course of this book, I examined the socio-cultural factors that gave rise to the post-independence culture and the influence of this culture on the esthetic patterns and musical tastes that shaped the collective awareness of postcolonial Moroccans. I have attempted to show how popular music, during the post-independence period was instrumental in shaping and forging identity construction and people's self-awareness as distinctive sensibilities of style and taste that led to the emergence and promotion of an alternative music genre during the last decades of the 1960s and early decades of the 1970s in the twentieth century.

Nass el-Ghiwane as a musical group was formed in the 1970s by four young men from Ḥay Moḥammādi, a working-class shanty district in Casablanca, who voiced the most common concerns of average Moroccans of the time. Even now, more than forty years later, the group is still viewed as one of the pillars of Moroccan music and culture. If Moroccans needed to musically record and document what is now politically referred to as the "years of lead" in Post-colonial Morocco, a large proportion of this musical archiving would be encompassed in the group's songs, poems and musical itinerary. Nass el-Ghiwane has initiated a musical legacy that is still alive, and their poems that are loaded with rebellious discourses provide invaluable insights into postcolonial Moroccan society, taking a daring musical journey while dipping into some of the thorniest and subversive issues in society in a musical adventure geared towards representing people's frustrations and giving voice to their aspirations. Nass el-Ghiwane's music, as has been argued, is concerned with new ways of redefining and expanding musical horizons in cultural discourse; new openings and venues that interrogate the social coercive forms of knowledge and configurations of power relations within the postcolony.

The social, political and cultural upheavals in postcolonial Morocco have been musically and artistically translated by the Ghiwani movement and experience to question the very nature of how artistic change through music was interpreted, and how official forms of knowledge, as a reflection of the interests of dominant groups rather than the masses or ordinary citizens, have been dismantled and criticized. It has been argued in this work that the changes that occurred in late 1960s and early 1970s-Morocco ushered in a new musical esthetics with intensity and density of meanings that eventually reoriented musical tastes into a novel cultural production that celebrated memory and cultural heritage to break away from intruding musical styles of the time.

This work makes use of postcolonial approach to read Nass el-Ghiwane. This approach seems to be more pertinent to draw attention to the voices and histories that neocolonial ideological conceptions have attempted to silence. The choice of this approach is not an individual or a fortuitous decision which is inspired by the relevance of a specific and ready-made method to test and prove the relevance and validity of some definite critical categories; it is rather a discursive and critical intervention on a paradigmatic consciousness which addresses marginality and unfolds peripheral discourses to emphasize inconsistencies and contradictions embedded in mainstream narratives of national affiliations.

The critical attitude defining this consciousness is marked by a discursive attempt to demonstrate that Nass el-Ghiwane's musical registers inscribe cultural discourses that could be used to illuminate history beyond official and ordinary binary oppositions. It is also inspired by a two-way process of reading that takes locality, power and history into consideration to disorient and dismantle neocolonial hegemonic practices. Therefore, such a qualification as postcolonial becomes intelligible enough as a critical category and discursive position to empower the reading of these voices from the precincts of the neocolonial setting.

Rereading the experience of Nass el-Ghiwane is not inspired simply by the fact that it is an artistic movement that enacted temporary musical delights scheduled for audiences, but rather stimulated by the interrogation of its discursive affiliations with the political, social, cultural, and artistic formations in Morocco that kept informing each other in such a highly complex juncture as the 1970s-Morocco. In fact, this reading endeavor has attempted to look for substantial grounds upon which epistemological connections between musical performance and socio-cultural discourses could be disclosed and illuminated.

This work has also attempted to read Larbi Batma's autobiographical account from a postcolonially-inflected consciousness to disengage issues pertaining to the state of fluctuation between history's afflictions and individual desires in the postcolony. The dialogic interplay of narration and memory in Batma's narrative has revealed complex discourses about individual formation and national construction of identity in postcolonial Morocco. As autobiographical writing is inextricably bound up with memory, Batma's *Al-raḥīl* attempts to recreate and reconstitute a floating and unstable self through the act of reminiscing that allows the past to be internalized in the form of what Paul Ricoeur calls "meditative memory," a phenomenon marked by activity in memory which strives to make the past reactivated and relived.[1] Batma takes his readers to meditate issues that have plagued post-independence Morocco. He offers an interesting corrosive account of what it really means to live in the underground arenas of transitory moments where space and time intersect to produce complex configurations of the politics of inclusion and exclusion in a postcolonial society.

Batma's account combines the narration of his life story with a gradual critique of its sociopolitical reality. In his *Forgotten Voices*, Ali Ahmida reflects on literary works as instrumental in the study of society and political life in the Middle East. He states that "arab poets and novelists have been active in political and social challenges of postcolonial society and are taken very seriously by the public."[2] In the postcolony, as Ahmida argues, writers themselves are valuable resources through which neocolonial concerns are conveyed, and their works need to be read against the background of social and political commentary. *Al-raḥīl* in this work is taken as a faithful commentary on socioeconomic disparities instigated through the perpetuation of colonial legacy in the neocolonial order. Batma offers a subversive account as it sheds light on the hidden parts of society by mirroring the collective life experience of subaltern groups caught in cultural schizophrenia, hypocrite realities, social injustice, political corruption and brutal psychological frustrations that characterized post-independence Moroccan society. Batma's autobiographical text questions postcolonial Morocco and its overbearing patriarchal government that emerged from the confines of the colonizing practices to give voice to marginality. In other words, it engages in a counter-discourse that reflects what Khatibi calls a *pensée-autre*, an-other way of thinking about otherness that furnish marginal sites of narration and creativity. The confessional style of this text incites readers to think about the "uncharted areas of the writer's imagined community" wherein the narrative mode is oriented towards making a deliberate choice to describe individual confrontations with the norm, and to overturn controversial realms that characterize Moroccan society.[3]

Batma, and through his individual experience, explores the lives of the marginalized who, unwilling to fit into the roles and boundaries laid down for them by society and history, inadvertently bring about their own version of narrating history. Regardless of being a life story that revolves around the loss of dreams, hopes and lives, Batma's *Al-raḥīl* deploys the workings of evocative memory to juxtapose individual experiences with collective ones in order to construct a narrative of and about the transgressions of the marginalized who do not surrender to the social constraints but defy and reject the historic ideals imposed by a colonizing mindset whose political, cultural and ideological imprints are still perpetuated in the postcolony. This is an important aspect that needs to be taken into consideration while reading Moroccan postcolonial narratives in general.

Another issue that Batma's work has successfully raised is the way the postcolonial has been defined in the narrative. Batma's work has managed to offer an exceptional version of the postcolonial condition as a historical moment and continuing process, and as discourse about postcolonial subjectivities and individual experiences within the postcolony. These two dimensions are brought by the narrative in the way they overlap and intersect with one another. The postcolonial in Batma's text has turned into a paradigm that enables the understanding of the postcolony as locality that is being grounded in individual experience that, in turn, moves across various contexts and places to translate a deep-seated malaise in the neocolonial order.

Also, in *Al-Alam*, the second part of his autobiography published posthumously, Batma raises important questions in Moroccan autobiographical writing; questions that are fraught with depth of meditation than only meeting and discovering the narrating "I" throughout a journey into life. These issues are linked with writing about death as the author is coming closer to an ultimate end, not the end of his narration about the self, but of the narration of his tragic end. This remains in certain sense very strange to autobiographical writing in the Moroccan context. Death in this part of his autobiography acquires much authority and becomes one of the most influential protagonists of the narrative. Influential in the sense that it orients, disorients and reorients the feelings of the author in various directions across the narrative divide. As time runs out for the dying narrator, readers from time to time get stunned by a powerful voice that surfaces depths of despair to express its celebration of life and existence. This unfathomable but daring attitude of the author is what makes narration in *al-Alam* exceptional because the voice persists on documenting with minute details the complexities of an inner self torn out between moments of being and becoming, between life and death, existence and demise, desire and agony. It is quite interesting to see how he transcends the borders of narration to process the very event of illness, loss and death, and narrate what is almost impossible to relate. Batma wrote the last chapter of his life to resist death and to resist the "little death that ending an autobiography represents as well."[4] These conflictual moments become apparent in how the author plays with the concepts of life and death in his work to add an interesting dimension to the overall effect of the narrative.

Talking about Batma does not by any mean scale back the importance of the other members of the group. The section on "Stories from the Margin: Nass el-Ghiwane Narrate History and Memory through individual Representations of the Past" has attempted to shed light on early members of the group who formed the initial lineup in the Ghiwani tradition and whose names were closely associated with Nass el-Ghiwane as legacy. This section is compiled through the reading of a set of oral testimonies about life experiences that are collected from various interviews conducted with the members of Nass el-Ghiwane on various occasions by media reporters for local TV shows. The main objective of this reading is to draw attention to oral testimonies and their relevance both in the process of historical documentation, and in the reconstruction of the past in the absence of written records about the events lived and experienced, as is the case with the members of the group. These oral testimonies have revealed how each individual's experiences contributed in shaping a new musical style and in sealing the group with a distinct musical identity.

The last part of this work has attempted to offer a discussion on the impact of Nass el-Ghiwane on other musical styles that emerged in Morocco in the 1990s within the global economy of performance and music circulation. In a new context marked by political, economic and social transition, a new movement of young artists emerged in Moroccan musical and cultural landscapes. These young artists have started a new musical style that celebrates global musical genres for artistic expression within a new society wherein the scope of freedoms is much more enlarged than before. This new movement is read in its local and global contexts with an attempt geared towards looking at the possible artistic connections that have existed between the 1970s protest in musical esthetics and today's artistic manifestations characterizing youth culture. Such connections reveal that the extensions that have been forged within the thematic, esthetic and poetic Ghiwani concerns have largely influenced the development of the 1990s youth musical genre in the country. Various musical groups have adopted a western musical style wherein Moroccan dialects and rhythms are conveyed through the Moroccanization of western musical instruments. These young musicians attempt to follow the lead of the Ghiwani tradition to musically represent the country's controversial issues about society, politics and culture. Their musical efforts are geared towards revolting against unequal power relations and absence of freedom. These young artists speak a straightforward language to lay bare the intricacies of Moroccan social and political realities.

This book does not pretend to be an all-inclusive reading of the Moroccan cultural and musical landscape, it has only tried to shed light on few aspects of a musical experience by means of reading available material and sources on Nass el-Ghiwane and its members, with a heavy focus on one of the leaders of the group through his autobiographical text. The scarcity of documents on Nass el-Ghiwane has made it a challenging endeavor in the course of this study, and I believe there still exist issues to be raised in looking at the experiences of not only Nass el-Ghiwane but also of other musical groups that appeared later and became vital to Moroccan music and arts. Lamshāhab, Jīl Jilāla, Tagadda, al-sihām, Izenzāren have largely been influential in forging new musical esthetics in postcolonial Morocco. These groups and those which emerged in the 1990s within the *Nāyḍa* movement of fusion music, and which purported to follow the lead of Nass el-Ghiwane, engage a multifarious experience of music and performance pertaining to social identity and cultural subjectivity. Certainly, reading and writing about the life and musical experiences of these groups, as discourse about continuous negotiation of culture which bridges the gaps between music and society, will add an interesting dimension both to the understanding of the complexities involved in the production, hybridization and mobilization of Moroccan identity, and to how alternative musical genres have shaped the construction of identity and nation within the fraught neocolonial cultural dynamics in Morocco.

Nass el-Ghiwane with Tunisian fans at Carthage Theater, Tunisia, 1978 (courtesy Omar Sayed).

Though this book has attempted to look at few songs from Nass el-Ghiwane's musical repertoire, it does not claim to have given an all-encompassing reading of the Ghiwanian poetry, for this is very demanding and time consuming and needs another work that I am planning to start soon. This new perspective of investigation and research in Nass el-ghiwane's musical experience will attempt to translate and read their poems against the background of postcolonial issues wherein culture, history and music coalesce together to shed light on the sites of contradictions and ambivalences in discourses about nation, class, religion, ethnicity characterizing postcolonial Morocco.

As I conclude this study, I would like to state that a new phenomenon in dealing with Nass el-Ghiwane's songs has started to be visible in the past few years. Generation of young artists from Batma's family and from other fans, as emergent artists, have adopted a new musical style in reproducing Nass el-Ghiwane's songs and poems; a new musical style that blends western instruments and rhythms with the Ghiwani songs with various changes brought to the original rhythms of the songs. These young artists, whether they have the rights to rework Nass el-Ghiwane's repertoire or not, threaten in a certain sense the transformation and even the distortion of the complete musical heritage that belongs not only to Batma family, but to Moroccans as well. My fear is that if there should be no willingness to archive the old repertoires of the group, the next generations of Moroccans would lose track of an important historical archive in Moroccan popular music.

Discography

Moulay Abdelaziz Tahiri: Sentīr, Vocals (1970–1974).
Abderrahman Kirouche (Paco): Sentīr, Vocals (1973–1993).
Allal Yaala: Banjo, Vocals (since 1970).
Boujemaa Ahagour: Da'dū,' Vocals (1970–1974).
Larbi Batma: Ṭbilāt, Vocals (1970–1997).
Omar Sayed: Bendīr, Vocals (since 1970).

Ṣiniya (Golden Disc)

Morocco. LP, Album: Polydor (2944 007), 1973.
Morocco. LP, CDr, Album, RE: Ouhmane Cassette (OCD 1013), 2002.
France. LP, CDr, Album, RE: Suiphone (SUD 33007), Unknown.
Morocco. LP, CDr, Album, RE: Ouhmane Cassette (OCD 1013), Unknown.
Al-Māḍī Fāt / Ṣiniya / Allah Yā Mūlāna / Yā Banī Insān / Yāmna / Fīn Ghādi Biya Khūya / Wāsh Ḥnā Hūma Ḥnā.

Al-Ḥaṣādā

France. LP, CDr, Album, RE: Suiphone (SUD 223), 1973.
Al-Ḥaṣādā/ Jūdi brdāk.

Ghīr Khodūni

Morocco. Vinyl LP, Album: Polydor (2.944 008), 1974.
Lahmāmī / Mzīne M'Dīḥek / Yūm Malqāk / Al-Ḥaṣādā / Ghīr Khodūni.

Wannādī Anā

France. LP, Album: Disques Espérances (ESP 1704),1975.
Prance. LP, Album: Cléopatre, Plein Soleil (CLEO 376-315),1975.
Wannādī Anā/ Erraghāyā.

Ghīr Khodūni

France. Vinyl LP, Album: Cléopatre (CLE 1975 111), 1975.
France. LP, Album: Disques Espérances (ESP 1718), 1975.
Mzīne M'Dīḥek / Jūdi brdāk / Ghīr Khodūni / Hamūdā.

Hommage à Boujemia

Morocco. LP: Cléopatre (CLE 1975–110), 1975.
France. LP, Vol. II: Cléopatre (CLE 1975–110), 1975.
Yāṣāḥ / Ahyā wīn / Al-Ḥaṣādā / Lahmāmī.

Ṣobḥan Allah

France. LP, Album: Cléopatre (CLE 376 316), 1976.
Morocco. LP, Album: Cléopatre, Plein Soleil (CLE 376 316), 1976.
Māhamūni / Ḥān O-shfāq / Hawlūni / Ṣobḥan Allah.

Shams Eṭāl'a

France. LP, Album: Cléopatre (CLE 377 150), 1977.
France. LP, Album: Disques Espérances (ESP 1705), 1977.
Narjāk Anā / Shams Eṭāl'a / Ḍāy'īn.

Tāghūnja

France. LP: Cléopatre (CLE 379 152), 1979.
France. LP, Album: Disques Espérances (ESP 1709), unknown.
Tāghūnja / Labṭāna.

Zād al-ham

France. LP: Editions Hassania (3390), 1981.
Morocco. Cassette: Editions Hassania (EH 2013), 1981.
Zād al-ham / Sif al-baṭar / Al-qasam.

Ahmed El Maanouni

Nass el-Ghiwane Transe. Distributed By—SFP (Société Française de Productions Phonographiques) (Background music).
France. Vinyl, LP: Spalax music (SPX 6835), 1981.
Ḍāy'īn / Ghīr Khodūni / Hanta gulū / Zād al-ham.

Mahmūma

France. Vinyl LP: Azwaw (AZW 140), 1983.
Magwāni / Al-Ma'nā / Mahmūma / Ṣabra O-shatīlā.

Oulād al-'ālam

France. LP, Album: Triomphe Musique (TM 870), 1987.
France. CDr, Album, RE: intermede (CTM018), 1988.
Laghrīb / Oulād al-'ālam / al-ūma / Yā-Sāyel.

A-Ṣamṭa

Morocco. LP, Album: Sonya Disc (TK7–1289), 1992.
A-Ṣamṭa / Mūlā nūba / Shāb rāssi / Lasskām.

Nass el-Ghiwane

France. CD, Album, Reissue: Cléopatre (EC 1041), 1998.
Wannādī Anā / Erraghāyā / Narjāk Anā / Shams Eṭāl'a.

Hommage à Boujemaa

France. CD, Album: Aladin le Musicien (AM2049, AM2409-C6B), 2000.
Morocco. CDr, Album: Ouhmane Cassette (OCD 1011), 2002.
Yāṣāḥ / Ahyā wīn / Al-Ḥaṣādā / Lahmāmī / Mzīn M'Dīḥek /Jūdi brdāk / Ghīr Khodūni / Hamūdā.
A reissue of two LPs (CLE 1975 110) and (CLE 1975 111) in one release.

Live Concert of Eternal Songs, Vol. I

Morocco. CDr, Album, Reissue: Disques Gam (G.B 1–87 CD), 2002.
First part of a live recording of Boujmia's early concerts. Recorded live in 1973 at Cinema Vox in Casablanca, and Mohamed V Theater in Rabat.
Ṣiniya / Qiṭatī / Shams Eṭāl'a / Yā Khyī / Kholkhīl / 'awīsha / al-Ḥarrāz.

Live Concert of Eternal Songs, Vol. II

Morocco. CDr, Album, Reissue: Disques Gam (G.B 2–87 CD), 2002.
Allah Yā Mūlāna / Mā-hamūnī / Ḥallāb / Fīn Ghādi Biya Khūya / Yāṣāḥ / Ghīr Khodūni.
Second part of a live recording of Boujmia's first concerts. Recorded live in 1973 at Cinema Vox and Mohamed 5th Theater in Rabat.

Live Concert of Eternal Songs Vol. III

Morocco. CD, Album, Reissue: Disques Gam (G.B 3–87 CD), 2002.
Banī Insān / Yāmna / Ahyā wīn / Arfak Yā Mālkī / Wāsh Ḥnā Hūma Ḥnā / Al-Mādī Fāt.
The third and last part of a live recording of Boujmia's first concerts. Recorded live in 1973 at Cinema Vox in Casablanca, and Mohamed V Theater in Rabat.

'Alī O-Khallī

Original release from Etoile Verte and Sonya Disques, Morocco (AM2473-C5A P&C), 1995.
France. CDr, Album, Reissue: Aladin le Musicien (AM 2473), January 2004.
Yā Men Jānā / f-Rḥāb M'ālīk / Yā Dam Sāyel / Khadra yā blādi / Ghādī F'ḥalī / Lahmūm Ḥraftī.

La Légende Vol. 3

Morocco. CD, Album: Platinum Music 3 (33–33–05), 2006.
A-Ṣamṭa / Lasqām / Yā Dem Sāyel / Khadra yā blādi / Ghādī F'ḥalī / Lahmūm Ḥraftī / 'Alī O-Khallī / Yā Men Jānā / f-Rḥāb M'ālīk.
2005 Platinum Music Company (2006 on back cover).

Ghīr Khodūni

Belgium. CD, Album: Platinum Records (AMD—5425019292317), 2006.
Sif al-Baṭār / Ghīr Khodūni / Liyām Tlāghi / Yūm Malqāk.

Nass el-Ghiwane (Untitled)

Morocco. CDr, Album, Reissue: Sawt al-Atlas (CD 12/2000), 2006.
Intifāẓa / Mardūma / Dallāl / al-Karāma (Lyrics by Ali Kilani).

Omar Sayed: Bendīr, Vocals (since 1970).
Allal Yaala: Banjo, Vocals (since 1970).
Rachid Batma: Ṭbilāt, Vocals (since 1993).
Redoune Raifq: Sentīr, Vocals (1993–2004).
Hamid Batma: Sentīr, Vocals (since 2004).

A-naḥla Shāma

Belgium. CD, Album: EMI Music Arabia (0946 396080 2 7), 2007.
Yā Shalāl / Al-qiāma / A-Ṣamṭ / Lātsālūni / Al Jirāḥ / Jārī / La'shāb / Al-rāḍa / Jīlī / Mūwāl Zerwāl.
A-naḥla Shāma is a poem written by El Haj Thami Lamdaghri (?–1856), a well-known Moroccan writer and composer of *Malḥūn* songs. This song is about a conversation between a sultan and the queen of the bees.

Nass el-Ghiwane—La Légende

Belgium. CD, Album, Limited edition: EMI Music Arabia (0946 389274 2 6), 2007.
Ṣobḥān Allah / Ṣiniya / Al-Ḥaṣādā / Shams Eṭāl'a / Erraghāyā / Ḍāy'īne / Yūm Malqāk / Wannādī Anā / Narjāk Anā.

All the tracks are some re-recorded versions of previously released songs. Produced by Platinum Music Company. Copyright of this sound recording is owned by Platinum Music Company, under exclusive license to EMI Music Arabia.

Maydūm Ḥāl

Morocco. Cassette: Sawt al-Atlas (V/A 1055), 1999.
Maydūm Ḥāl / T'āla / Khallīni / Ḥyāt Laḥzāne / Aḍar al Wā'r / 'Allūla / 'Allām Laqbīla / Dūga / Qallāt.

Ḥawḍ Ana'nā'

Morocco. CD, Album: Sawt al-Atlas, 2007.
Ḥawḍ Ana'nā' / Shīkhī f-al-Ḥāl / Zūrnā Yā maḥbūb al-qalb / ḥbīb arūḥ / Samḥūni / Klamnā Yā Shīkh al-blād / Yā Khātem a-rṣūl / Rabī mūlay / t'ālā t'ālā / Al-Ghāba.

Al-bāraka

Morocco. CD, Album: Maroc Cultures and Platinium Music, 2014.
Al-bāraka / Al-māl / Tamaguīt / Ḥarrārz 'wīsha / al-mdāmen / Mūja / tānrjāk / Hājūj o-mājūj / kūb atāy.
For the first time, Nass el-Ghiwane's musical repertoire includes a song in Tamazīght (Tamaguīt, meaning identity).

Chapter Notes

Preface

1. Hassan Nejmi talking during an interview about Nass el-Ghiwane in Laila Chafik and Omar Kamili Ben Hamou, "Nass el-Ghiwane," Al-Jazeera documentary (2012).

Introduction

1. Ifeyinwa A. Mbakogu, "Is There Really a Relationship between Culture and Development?" *Anthropologist* 6, no.1 (2004), 37.
2. Stuart Hall, "Notes on Deconstructing 'the Popular,'" *People's History and Socialist Theory*, ed. Raphael Samuel (London: Routledge & Kegan Paul, 1981), 228.
3. John Pierre Entelis, *Culture and Counterculture in Moroccan Politics* (Boston: University Press of America, 1996), 25.
4. Abbass al-Jirari, "Moroccan Culture: its Origins and Particularities," (a paper given at a conference organized by Allal al-Fassi Institute, Rabat, 1999), 159.
5. *Ibid.*
6. Tarik Sabry, "Migration as Popular Culture," 2. Retrieved June 2013 from http://www.portalcomunicacion.com/bcn2002/n_eng/programme/prog_ind/papers/s/pdf/s007_sabry.pdf . See also the same article published in *European Journal of Cultural Studies* (SAGE Publications) 8, no.1 (2005), 5–22.
7. *Ibid.*
8. Abdassamad Belkbir, "On the Meaning of Popular Culture" in *Athaqāfa a-sha'biya, Ihdā Rakāiz Wahdat al-Maghrib al-Arabī*, 17 (1991), 15–27. Paper presented at the Conference of Nadour, Morocco, quoted in Tarik Sabry's "Migration as Popular Culture," 3.
9. Tarik Sabry, "Migration as Popular Culture," 3.
10. Roy Shuker, *Understanding Popular Music*, 2nd edition (London and New York: Routledge, 1994). 1. Shuker's insightful work is a comprehensive introduction to the history and meaning of popular music. It starts with a critical analysis of the various ways in which popular music has been studied and the debates which surround the analysis of popular culture and popular music in general. Drawing on recent critical works about popular music, Roy Shuker explores key issues about music industry, including production, fans, audiences and subcultures, music journalism, and the reception and consumption of popular music.
11. Vincent Crapanzano, "Reflections on Hope as a Category of Social and Psychological Analysis," *Cultural Anthropology* 18, no. 1 (2003), 9.
12. Omar Sayed, *Klām al-Ghīwan* (Casablanca: Najah al-Jadida, 2010), 15–18. The translations from this book are mine unless stated elsewhere. The transliterations I have adopted are from the *Index Translationum* of UNESCO (Organization des Nations Unis pour l'Education, la Science et la Culture).
13. Hassan Nejmi, "Forword," in Omar Sayed's *Klām al-Ghīwan* (Casablanca: Najah al-Jadida, 2010), 5–12.
14. Fatima Sadiqi, "Gender Perception in Moroccan Culture," http://www.cmiesi.ma/acmiesi/file/notes/fatima-sadiqi_2.pdf (accessed Oct. 2014), 169–170.
15. Salah Cherki, *Musique Marocaine* (Mohammedia: Impr. Fedala, 1981), 212.
16. Omar Sayed, *Klām al-Ghīwan*, 26.
17. Philipe Lejeune, *On Autobiography*.

Trans. Katherine Leary (Minneapolis: Univ. of Minnesota Press, 1989), 4.

18. Frantz Fanon, *the Wretched of the Earth*, trans. C. Farrington (New York: Grove Press. 1963), 241.

19. *Ibid.*, 243.

Chapter I

1. See Ibrahim El-Khatib, "La literature Marocaine: L'appropriation du Réel," *Oriente Moderno* 16, no. 77 (1997), 257–262.

2. Abdellah Guenoun, *Ahādith fi Al-Adab Al-Maghrebī Al-Hadīth* [Issues on Contemporary Moroccan Literature] (Cairo: Arab Literary Center, 1964), 17. The translations from this book are mine, unless stated elsewhere.

3. See Ahmed Almadini's *Al-Kitāba a-Sardiya fi Al-Adab Al-Maghrebī Al-Hadīth* [Narrativization in Modern Moroccan Literature] (Rabat: Dar al-maarif al-Jadida, 2000), 67–71.

4. Tetz Rooke, "Moroccan Autobiography as National Allegory," *Oriente Moderno, Nuova serie* 77, no. 2/3 (1997), 289–305. This article gives a succinct discussion of Moroccan autobiographical novels and mentions Larbi Batma's *Al-raḥīl* in an insightful section on collective imagination as national allegory in writing individual experiences.

5. *Ibid.*, 289.

6. Fredric Jameson, "Third-World Literature in the Era of Multinational Capitalism," Social Text 15 (Fall 1986), 65–88.

7. *Ibid.*, 66.

8. *Ibid.*, 69.

9. Benedict Anderson, *Imagined Communities. Reflections on the Origin and Spread of Nationalism* (London and New York: Verso, 1991).

10. *Ibid.* 205.

11. Gonzalo Fernandez Parrilla, "Breaking the Canon: Zafzaf, Laroui and the Moroccan novel," in From New Values to New Esthetics. Turning Points in Modern Arabic Literature: Postmodernism and Thereafter, eds. Stephan Guth and Gail Ramsay (Wiesbaden: Verlag, 2011), 75–85.

12. Abdelhamid Aqqar, "Taṭawur a-naqd al-adabī fī al-Maghrib" [the Development of Literary Criticism in Morocco], *Fikr wa Naqd* (1998), 6.

13. Abdelkabir Khatibi, *Le Roman M*aghebin (Paris : Editions F. Maspero, 1979), 27–30. Quoted in Driss Maghraoui, ed. *Revisiting the Colonial Past in Morocco* (London: Routeledge, 2013), 226.

14. Hamid Lahmidani, *Al-Riwāya al-Maghribiya wa-Ru'yat al-Wāqiʿ al-Ijtimʿī* (Cairo: Dar al-Thaqafa, 1985), 255.

15. Franz Fanon, *the Wretched of the Earth* (New York: Grove Press, 1963), 152–153.

16. Bill Ashcroft, Gareth Griffiths, Helen Tiffin, *The Empire Writes Back: Theory and Practice in Post-colonial Literatures.* 2nd edition (London and New York: Routledge, 2002), 102.

17. *Ibid.* 222.

18. Tetz Rooke, "From Self-made Man to Man-made Self: A Story about Changing Identities," in Annette van Beugen's and Gonzalo Fernández Parrilla's (Coordinators) *Remembering for Tomorrow,* European Cultural Foundation and Escuela de Traductores de Toledo, 24.

19. *Ibid.*

Chapter II

1. For further discussion of Al-ḥalqa, see Khalid Amine and Marvin Carlson's "Al-ḥalqa in Arabic Theatre: An Emerging Site of Hybridity," Theatre Journal 60, no. 1 (Mar., 2008), 71–85.

2. See for example Ghafour Dahchour, "Fi-adhākira: Larbi Batma" [In Memory: Larbi Batma,] TV show produced by the Moroccan Television RTM, and directed by Samir Kass (2008), retrieved from https://www.youtube.com/watch?v=lnOYEEAC0Eo (accessed Feb. 2015).

3. Short interview with Naima Bouchrita where she talks about Batma's writing rituals in Ghafour Dahchour's "Fi-adhākira: Larbi Batma" [In Memory: Larbi Batma,] TV show produced by the Moroccan Television RTM, and directed by Samir Kass (2008).

4. *Ibid.*

5. "Al-hāl," translated as Transe, is a documentary film tracing the lives of the members of the musical band Nass el-Ghiwane, produced by Izza Genini and directed by Ahmed al-Maanouni in 1981. Like many concert-based documentaries, there is much footage from the group's musical tours, intercut with interviews about moments with each of the band's four members. The group discusses without pretension the nature of Nass el-Ghiwane's music

and the members' immersion into its mystic complexities. The film also offers various moments about the hypnotic effect their style of chanted singing with incessant rhythm has on the audiences. The film is not called *Transe* by accident as the title is derived from one of the songs the group has composed. All of their music is tinged by spiritual and religious beliefs and stress the importance of freedom in an environment of oppression and social injustice.

6. Interview with Othmane Benalila in Rachid Nini's "Nostalgia: Larbi Batma," TV show produced by the Moroccan TV Channel 2M, and directed by Abdellatif Talbi (2004), http://www.dailymotion.com/video/x3uscq_nostalgia-batma (accessed February 2015).

7. Larbi Batma, *Al-Alam* (Casablanca: Dar Toubkal, 1998), 6.

8. Talal Asad, "The Concept of Cultural Translation in British Social Anthropology," in *Writing Culture: The Poetics and Politics of Ethnography*, ed. James Clifford and George E. Marcus (Berkeley: University of California Press, 1986), 141–164.

9. Ismaïl El-Outmani, "Prolegomena to the Study of the "Other" Moroccan Literature," *Research in African Literatures* 28, no. 3, Arabic Writing in Africa (autumn, 1997): 116.

10. Salah Moukhlis, "Localized Identity, Universal Experience: Celebrating Mohamed Choukri as a Moroccan Writer," in Khalid Amine, Andrew Hussey and Barry Tharaud, eds. *Writing Tangier: Conference Proceedings* (Tanger: Imprimerie Altopress, 2005), 76.

11. *Ibid.*

12. Khalid Amine, "Tangiers' Eyes and the Anxiety of Writing Exile," in *Margins of Theories and Theories of Margins*, Colloquia Series, ed., A. Akbib, K. Amine and A. Mars (Tetouan: Abdelmalek Essaadi University), 159.

13. Khalid Amine, "Tangier and Site-Specificity," in *Performong / Picturing Tangier*, ed., Khalid Amine et al. (Tanger: Altopress, 2007), 63.

14. Paul Carter, "Naming places," in *The Postcolonial Studies Reader, ed.* Bill Ashcroft et al. (London and New York: Routledge, 1995), 405.

15. Stephen Daniels and Simon Rycroft, "Mapping the Modern City," *Transactions of the Institute of British Geographers*, New Series 18, no. 4 (1993), 460.

16. Timothy Oakes, "Place and the Paradox of Modernity," *Annals of the Association of American Geographers* 87, no. 3 (1997), 510.

17. David Richards, "Framing identities," in *A Concise Companion to Postcolonial Literature*, ed. Shirley Chew and David Richards (Blackwell Publishing Ltd., 2010), 23.

18. Prakash, Gyan. "Writing Post-Orientalist Histories of the Third World: Perspectives from Indian Historiography," in *Mapping Subaltern Studies and the Postcolonial*, ed., Vinayak Chaturvedi's (London: Verso, 2000), 180.

19. Mikhail Bakhtin, *Rabelais and His World*, Trans. Hélène Iswolsky (Indiana: Indiana University Press, 1984), 49.

20. Ismaïl El-Outmani, "Prolegomena to the Study of the "Other" Moroccan Literature," Research in African Literatures 28, no. 3, Arabic Writing in Africa (Autumn, 1997), 115.

21. *Ibid.*, 115–116.

22. Jesus Lopez-Pelaez Casellas, "Forms of Exile in the Narrative of Mohamed Choukri," in *Borderlands: Negotiating Boundaries in Post-colonial Writing, ed.*, Monika Reif-Hulser (Amsterdam: Rodopi B.V, 1999), 209.

23. David Richards, "Framing Identities," in *A Concise Companion to Postcolonial Literature, ed.* Shirley Chew and David Richards (Blackwell Publishing Ltd., 2010), 22.

24. Graham Huggan, *the Postcolonial Exotic: Marketing the Margins* (London: Routledge, 2001), 20.

25. Franz Fanon, *the Wretched of the Earth* (New York: Grove Press, 1963), 11.

26. Larbi Batma, *Al-raḥīl* (Casablanca: Dar Toubkal, 5th edition, 2009).

27. *Ibid.*, 7–8.

28. Nirvana Tanoukhi, "Rewriting Political Commitment for an International Canon: Paul Bowles's *For Bread Alone* as Translation for Choukri's *Al-Khubz Al-Ḥāfī*," Research in African Literatures 34, no. 2 (2003), 152.

29. Ferial Ghazoul and Barbara Harlow, *The View From Within* (Cairo: American University of Cairo Press, 1994), 220.

30. Walter Benjamin, "The Work of Art in the Age of Mechanical Reproduction." Illuminations, ed. Hannah Ardent (New York: Schocken, 1985), 232, quoted in Nirvana Tanoukhi's Rewriting Political Commitment for an International Canon: Paul Bowles's

For Bread Alone as Translation for Choukri's *Al-Khubz Al-Hāfi, Research in African Literatures* 34, no. 2 (2003), 152.

31. Stephen Ellis, "Writing Histories of Contemporary Africa," *the Journal of African History* 43, no. 1 (2002), 4.

32. Ato Quayson, *Postcolonialism: Theory, Practice, or Process* (Blackwell Publishers Ltd., 2000), 48.

33. In the Moroccan context, postcolonial readers such as Khalid Bekkaoui, Jamaleddine Benhayoun, Sadik Rddad, Mohammed Laamiri, to name but a few, have, albeit in other registers dealt with Moroccan culture as they attempted to look at history from below and theorize for new historiographical writing.

34. Larbi Batma, *Al-raḥīl*, 76.

35. *Ibid.*

36. *Ibid.* 24–25.

37. Terry Eagleton's After Theory (New York: Basic, 2003), 61.

38. Batma, *Al-raḥīl*, 92.

39. In the early 1950s, Morocco was invaded by locusts, also called *Dociostaurus maroccanus*. These are chewing insects that damage wheat and other crops. They are reddish yellow with dark spots and red on their hind legs.

40. Batma, *Al-raḥīl*, 8.

41. *Ibid.*, 43.

42. Batma, *Al-raḥīl*, 44.

43. See Batma's descriptive mode of Uncle Hammou in his autobiography, 46–47.

44. *Ibid.*

45. *Ibid.*

46. Batma, *Al-raḥīl* , 9.

47. *Ibid.*, 8–10.

48. Batma. *Al-raḥīl*, 47.

49. *Ibid.*

50. Batma. *Al-raḥīl*, 48.

51. *Ibid.*, 29.

52. *Ibid.*, 57.

53. *Ibid.*, 71–72.

54. *Ibid.*, 58–59.

55. Batma, *Al-raḥīl*, 12. It is worth noting that Batma's autobiography is not a mere individual experience, but rather a political statement about the whole era of post-independence Morocco.

56. *Ibid.*, 14.

57. *Ibid.*, 22.

58. *Ibid.*, 89.

59. Mohammed Zahiri, "La Figure du Pere Dans Le Roman Marocain," Presence Francophone: Revue Internationale de Langue et de Litterature 34 (1987), 107–127.

60. Mohamed Choukri, *For Bread Alone*, tr. Paul Bowles (London: Peter Owen, 1973).

61. Sellam Chahidi, *Hijra ilā ardi al-aḥlām* [Migration to the Land of Dreams] (Tanger: Infoprint, 1999).

62. Sellam Chahidi, *Hijra ilā ardi al-aḥlām*, 10.

63. *Ibid.*, 8, 12, 14.

64. See for example *la Nuit Sacrée* (Paris: Seuil, 1987), *Harrouda* (Paris: Denoel, 1973), *Les Yeux Baissés* (Paris: Seuil, 1991), *La reclusion solitaire* (Paris: Denoel, 1976) where the figure of the father takes multidimensional perspectives. As Tahar Benjelloun himself has asserted, "le pére n'etait pas tout a fait absent de mon oeuvre, mais il était là plutôt comme une ombre en négatif" [The father was not totally absent from my work, but was rather like a negative shadow] (Denise Brahimi, "Conversation avec Tahar Ben Jelloun." *Notre Libraire* 103 (1990), 41.

65. Larbi Batma, *Al-raḥīl*, 78.

66. Sue Prideaux, *Edvard Munch: Behind the Scream* (New Haven, Yale University, 2005), 2.

67. Batma, *Al-raḥīl*, 15.

68. *Ibid.*, 11–12.

69. *Ibid.*, 123.

70. *Ibid.*, 43.

71. *Ibid.* 21

72. *Ibid.*, 30.

73. Batma, *Al-raḥīl*, 108–110

74. See my reading of Sellam Chahidi's work, "The Postcolonial in Motion: *Hijra ilā ardi al-aḥlām* and the Construction of Postcolonial Counterdiscourse," *Middle East Journal of Culture and Communication* 3 (2010), 289–311.

75. Salah Moukhlis, "Deconstructing Home and Exile: The Subversive Politics of Ben Jelloun's *With Downcast Eyes,*" Postcolonial Text 2, no. 2 (2006). http://journals.sfu.ca/pocol/index.php/pct/article/view/442/199. (Accessed 13 Sept. 2010).

76. Lisa Lowe, "Literary Nomadics in Francophone Allegories of Postcolonialism," *Yale French Studies* 1, no. 82 (1993), 45.

77. Thomas G. Couser, "The Shape of Death in American Autobiography," *The Hudson Review* 31, no. 1 (Spring, 1978), 53.

78. Barrett John Mandel, "Basting the Image with a Certain Liquor: Death in Autobiography," *Soundings: An Interdisciplinary Journal* 57, no. 2 (Summer 1974), 179.

79. Larbi Batma, *Al-alam* (Casablanca: Dar Toubkal, 1998), 9.

80. *Ibid.* 70.

Chapter III

1. See Andy Bennett, Cultures of Popular Music (Bukingham: Open University Press, 2001). Bennett's *Cultures of Popular Music* "explores popular music styles in relation to their audiences, from 1950s rock and roll to contemporary dance music. Beginning with an overview of the socioeconomic circumstances that gave rise to the development of the postwar youth market, the discussion promptly proceeds to identify several key technological innovations that revolutionized the music industry in countries like Britain and the USA. At the same time, youth 'counter-culture' movements, especially in the 1960s, are similarly shown to have had a lasting influence on the formation of certain styles of popular music."

2. *Ibid.*, 1

3. Hassan Nejmi, "Aghāni al-Ghīwane: Aswātun Ḥaya min dākhili al-raḥim al-Sha'bī" [The Ghiwani Songs: Live Voices from the Popular Womb], in Omar Sayed, *Klām al-Ghīwan* (Casablanca: Najah al-Jadida, 2010), 5.

4. Omar Sayed, *Klām al-Ghīwan* (Casablanca: Najah al-Jadida, 2010), 8–9.

5. Farid Al-Zahi, *Al-Ḥikāya wa al-Mutakhayal* [Narrative and the Imaginary] (Casablanca: Afriqiyya al-Sharq, 1991):137–140. Translated by Tahia Khalid Abdel Nasser as "The "Possessed" or the Symbolic Body," *Alif: Journal of Comparative Poetics* 15, Arab Cinematics: Toward the New and the Alternative (1995):267.

6. *Ibid.*, 268.

7. "Ghiwane" or "ghiwani" refers to affection, adoration, love and good-humored spirit. Nass el-Ghiwane stands for the "people of love" or "people of temptation." The whole interviews with the members of the group would refer to Nass el-Ghiwane's aspirations for a world of love, peace and social reconciliation beyond the injustices of class disparities.

8. Carolyn Landau, "My own Little Morocco at Home: a Biographical Account of Migration, Mediation and Music Consumption," in *Migrating Music*, ed. Jason Toynbee's and Byron Dueck (Oxen: Routledge, 2011), 42.

9. Simon Frith, "Towards an Aesthetic of Popular Music," in *Music and Society: The Politics of Composition, Performance and Reception*, ed. Richard Leppert and Susan McClary (Cambridge: Cambridge University Press, 1987), 136.

10. Ibrahim Ait Ho, *Idaʾāt Hawla al-Ūghniya Al Maghribiya*(Tangiers: Shiraa, 1999):12.

11. *Ibid.*, 12.

12. Elias Muhanna, "Folk the Kasbah: A Conversation with Omar Sayed, leader of Nass el-Ghiwane," *Transition* 12, no. 4 (2003), 140.

13. Mbarek Hanoun, *Al-Ūghniya Sha'biya Al-Jadīda: Ẓāhirat Nāss el-Ghīwane* (Casablanca: Ouyoune, 1987), 52.

14. Ibrahim Ait Ho, *Idaāt Hawla al-Ūughniya Al Maghribiya* (Tangiers, Shiraa, 1999), 13.

15. Jonathan H. Shannon, "Performing al-Andalus, Remembering al-Andalus: Mediterranean Soundings from Mashriq to Maghrib," *The Journal of American Folklore*, 120, no. 477 (Summer, 2007):321.

16. *Ibid.*

17. *Ibid.* 322.

18. John Storey, *an Introduction Guide to Cultural Theory and Popular Culture* (Hertfordshire: Prentice Hall / Harvester Wheat Sheaf, 1993), 25. It is worth- noting that it was Mathew Arnold who launched the view of culture as a canonized tradition, a perspective that totally ignores popular culture and associates it with anarchy, the underlying implication of such association is the subordination of culture to the established social order, which cannot be maintained if leadership is not given to what he calls the "sound minority."

19. Raymond Williams, *Keywords: A Vocabulary of Culture and Society* (London: Fontana, 1983), 90.

20. See for example Mohamed Bouhmid, "Innahum yurīdūn Al-'ayṭaka-ḍajīj li-jamī ' al-ḥushūd" [They are planning to turn *Al-'ayṭa*into noisy spectacle for the crowds] *al-Ittiḥad al-Ishtiraki* (15 April1995), 6; Deborah Kapchan, *Gender on the Market: Moroccan Women and the Revoicing of Tradition* (Philadelphia: university of Pennsylvania Press, 1996); Hassan Bahraoui, *Fan Al-'ayṭafi al-Maghrib: Musāhama li-al ta'rīf* (Rabat: Ittiḥad Kottab al-Maghrib, 2002); Hassan Nejmi, *Ghinā' Al-'ayṭa: Al-shi'r Al-*

shafawī wa al-Mūsīka al-Taqlīdiya fi al-Maghrib (Casablanca: Dar Toubqal li-Annashr, 2007); Alessandra Ciucci, "Embodying the Countryside in Aiṭa Ḥaṣbawiya (Morocco)," *Yearbook for Traditional Music* 44 (2012).

21. Deborah A. Kapchan, "Moroccan Female Performers: Defining the Social Body," *The Journal of American Folklore* 107, no. 423 (1994):82.

22. Alessandra Ciucci, "Embodying the Countryside in *Aiṭa Ḥaṣbawiya* (Morocco)," *Yearbook for Traditional Music* 44 (2012), 110.

23. See Kapchan's *Gender on the Market: Moroccan Women and the Revoicing of Tradition* (Philadelphia: University of Pennsylvania Press, 1996) and "Moroccan Female Performers: Defining the Social Body," *The Journal of American Folklore*107, no. 423 (1994).

24. Hassan Nejmi, *Ghinā' Al-'ayṭa: Al-shi'r Al-shafawī wa al-Mūsīka al-Taqlīdiya fi al-Maghrib* [Singing Al-'ayṭa: Oral Poetry and Traditional Music in Morocco] (Casablanca: Dar Toubkal, Vol. I, 2007):110.

25. *Ibid.* 157.

26. Abdellatif Laabi, "Réalités et dilemmes de la culture nationale (I)." *Anfās /Soufles* 4 (1966). http://www.seattleu.edu/soufles/s04/2_1.htm. Quoted in Alessandra Ciucci's "Embodying the Countryside in Aiṭa Ḥaṣbawiya (Morocco)," 119.

27. Ahmed Al Maanouni, *Al-hāl* (Transe), documentary film about Nass el-Ghiwane that was released in 1981.

28. Batma, *Al-raḥīl*, 109.

29. In his Belated Modernity and Aesthetic Culture: Inventing National Culture (Minneapolis: University of Minnesota Press, 1991), Gregory Jusdanis Traces literature's function in the formation of the nation-state through the "belated" emergence of national aesthetic culture. In paraphrasing Ngugi Wa Thiongo, he states that "Art for Art's sake has no meaning in Africa. The African situation necessitates not an esthetic, but a political understanding of writing," 7.

30. Batma, *Al-raḥīl*, 76.

31. Said Graiouid, "Post-colonial Literature in Morocco: Nation, Identity and Resistance Esthetics," in *Revisiting the Colonial Past in Morocco*, ed., Driss Maghraoui (London: Routeledge, 2013), 222. This insightful book explores the concept of 'Colonial Cultures' and aims at uncovering some aspects of Moroccan culture in its popular orientations while overviewing more complex and nuanced understanding of Moroccan colonial history.

32. *Ibid.*

33. Hassan Bahraoui, "Al-Ghīwān: Al-aṣl wa Al-ma-āl," [Al-Ghiwane: Roots and Destiny], in *Al-Ūghinya al-Iḥtijājiya bi al-Maghrib: Mawrūt Majmū'at Nāss Al-Ghīwāne* [Protest Song in Morocco: The Legacy of Nass el-Ghiwane], ed., Allal Reggoug et al. (Rabat: Publications de L'institut Universitaire, 2013), 12–13.

34. Omar Sayed, *Klām al-Ghīwan*, 19.

35. Batma, *Al-raḥīl*, 109.

36. Omar Sayed talking about Larbi Batma in Rachid Nini's *Nostagia* produced for the Moroccan TV Channel 2M in 2004.

37. *Ibid.*

38. Hind Semlali and Mathias Chaillot, "Omar Sayed: Avec Nass el-Ghiwane nous étions des faibles, et c'était notre force" [Omar Sayed: With Nass el-Ghiwane we were weak and that's where our strength came out] (June 3rd, 2011). https://casablanca.madeinmedina.com/fr/article-omar-sayed-avec-nass-el-ghiwane-nous-etions-des-faibles-et-cetait-notre-force-271.html. (Accessed March 2015).

39. Batma, *Al-raḥīl*, 112.

40. Hassan Bahraoui, Al-Ghīwān: Al-aṣl wa Al-ma-āl," [Al-Ghiwane: Roots and Destiny], in *Al-ūghinya al-Iḥtijājiya bi al-Maghrib: Mawrūt Majmū'at Nāss Al-Ghīwāne* [Protest Song in Morocco: The Legacy of Nass el-Ghiwane], ed., Allal Reggoug et al. (Rabat: Publications de L'institut Universitaire, 2013), 11.

41. Larbi Batma, *Al-raḥīl*, 120.

42. Omar Sayed, *Klām al-Ghīwan*, 56.

43. Jonathan Porter Berkey, *The Formation of Islam: Religion and Society in the Near East, 600–1800* (New York: Cambridge University Press, 2003), 237.

44. Dale F. Eickelman, *Moroccan Islam: Tradition and Society in a Pilgrimage Center* (Austin: University of Texas Press, 1976), 25.

45. Clifford Geertz, *Islam Observed: Religious Development in Morocco and Indonesia* (Chicago: University of Chicago Press. 1968), 44.

46. Jane E. Goodman, "Singers, Saints, and the Construction of Postcolonial Subjectivities in Algeria," *Ethos* 26, no. 2 (June 1998), 204–228

47. According to Clifford Geertz in his

Islam Observed, a *Zawiya* literally means a "retreat for the pious to gather in and carry out various sorts of spiritual exercises (it derives from a root meaning 'corner' or 'nook,' the term is also applied to the voluntary religious organization, the brotherhood of which the particular lodge is, in general way, sort of affiliate," 51.

48. Omar Sayed, *Omar Sayed raconte Nass el-Ghiwane*, Martin Scorsese's preface (Casablanca: Sirocco, 2011).

49. Gueertz, *Islam Observed.*

50. Arjun Appadurai, *Modernity at Large: Cultural Dimensions of Globalization* (Minnesota: University of Minnesota Press, 1996).

51. Jonathan H. Shannon "Emotion, Performance, and Temporality in Arab Music: Reflections on *Ṭarab*," *Cultural Anthropology* 18, no. 1 (Feb., 2003), 74.

52. *Ibid.*, 81.

53. Hanoun Mbarek, *Ẓāhirat Nāss el-Ghīwane: Tajribat Tahdīth al-Ūughniya al-Sha'biya* [Nass el-Ghiwane phenomenon: Towards a Modernization of the Popular Song] (Rabat: Dar al-Amane, 2nd edition, 2007), 11. Hanoun is one the earlier Moroccan readers who first studied Nass el-Ghiwane as a musical phenomenon. His study appeared as a monograph in 1975 for the completion of his BA degree in the Department of Arabic Studies affiliated to Sidi Mohamed Ben Abdellah University, Fez. Hanoun has also published his *Al-Ūghniya Sha'biya al-Jadīda: Ẓāhirat Nāss el-Ghīwane* [The New Popular Song: Nass el-Ghiwane Phenomenon] (Casablanca: Manchourat Oyoune, 1987). This study is based on semiotics in the analysis of Nass el-Ghiwane's poetry as theorized by Charles Sanders Pierce, Rossi-Landi, Julia Kristeva and Umerto Eco.

54. *Ibid.*, 13.

55. *Ibid.*

56. See for example Fatima al-Ifriqui's interview with Batma in *Al-majala al-faniya* [Arts Magazine] produced by the Moroccan Television Channel, https://www.youtube.com/watch?v=E4k0aaxe5q0 (accessed December 2014).

57. Mohammed Guettat, Musique Arabo-Andalouse (Paris: Editions Fleurs Sociales, 2000), 223.

58. David Goodman, "The Space of Africanness: Gnāwa Music and Slave Culture in North Africa." *Journal of Cultural Studies* 5, no. 1 (2003), 38.

59. Deborah Kapchan, *Traveling Spirit Masters: Moroccan Gnāwa Trance and Music in the Global Marketplace* (Middletown: Wesleyan University Press, 2007).

60. Ziad Bentahar, "The Visibility of African Identity in Moroccan Music," *Wasafiri* 25, no. 1 (2010), 42.

61. Larbi Batma, *Al-raḥīl*, 115.

62. *Ibid.*, 122.

63. Abdelhai Sadiq, *Protest Song Marocain* (Marrakech: Al Watanya, 2006), 38.

64. Tim Abdellah Fuson, "Musical Imagining in Morocco: The Voice of the Gnāwa in the Music of Nas al-Ghiwan," Paper read at the Annual meeting of Middle Eastern Studies Association, San Francisco, CA (November 1997), 4.

65. Omar Sayed, *Klām al-Ghīwan*, 84.

66. Van Djik, *A Hand book of Discourse Analysis* (London: Academic Press , 1985). It is important to note that Gunther Kress in his ideological Structures in Discourse stresses the fact that the relationship between text and discourse is one of realization, and not of equation .

67. Aomar Boum, "Youth, Political Activism and the Festivalization of Hip-Hop Music in Morocco" in *Contemporary Morocco: State, Politics and Society under Mohammed VI*, ed., Bruce Maddy-Weitzman and Daniel Zisenwine (Oxon and New York : Routledge, 2013), 166.

68. Omar Sayed, *Klām al-Ghīwan*, 115.

69. Elias Muhanna, "Folk the Kasbah: A Conversation with Omar Sayyed, leader of Nass el-Ghiwane," *Transition* 12. 4 (2003), 64. It is worth-noticing that the translation of Nass el-Ghiwane's songs is not only difficult, but also demanding as their language is deeply immersed in Moroccan oral tradition.

70. Elias Muhanna, "Folk the Kasbah: A Conversation with Omar Sayyed, leader of Nass el-Ghiwane," *Transition* 12. 4 (2003), 62. Quoted in Aomar Boum's "Youth, Political Activism and the Festivalization of Hip-Hop Music in Morocco" in *Contemporary Morocco: State, Politics and Society under Mohammed VI*, ed., Bruce Maddy-Weitzman and Daniel Zisenwine(Oxon and New York : Routledge, 2013):166–167.

71. Omar Sayed, *Klām al-Ghīwan*, 50–52.

72. The original members of Jīl Jilāla were Hamid Zougghi, Mohmoud Saâdi, Mohamed Darham, Moulay Tahar Asbahani, and Sakina Safadi, female voice in the group. Over the years, the band had numer-

ous line changes and later members included, Moulay Abdelaziz Tahiri who came from Nass el-Ghiwane, Abderrahman Paco, who became member of Nass el-Ghiwane, Abdel Karim al-Kasbaji, Hassan Meftah (who died recently) and Mustapha Baqbou who left the band to start up his own in Gnāwa style in the 1990s.

73. One of their socially committed songs that created a controversy in 1973 was "*Liyām tnādi*," which spoke out against political repression. It included the line: "*la'shāb nābta f-blādi*" ("bad herbs have invaded my country").

74. Most scholars have characterized *Malḥūn* as a "semi-classical" genre as opposed to the "classical" Andalusian genres (see for example, Schuyler 1974). Jīl Jilāla is regarded as successfully working on *Malḥūn* songs that were faithful to this genre.

75. Ḥannoun Mbarek, *Dāhirat Nās al-Ghīwān: Tajribat taḥdīth al-ughniyya al-sha'biya* [The Phenomenon of Nass el-Ghiwane: The Experience of Modernizing the Folksong] (Rabat: Dar al-Aman, 2007), 12.

76. *Ibid*., 12–13.

77. Mohamed Jibril, "Les Nass Al Ghiwane vus par Ahmed. Maanouni," *Lamalif* 125 (1981), 38.

78. Sidi Abder-rahman al-majdub is one of Morocco's most renowned sixteenth-century popular wandering poet. He was a dedicated Sufi who traveled all over Morocco to preach. According to Khalid Amine and Marvin Carlson in their article on "Al-ḥalqa in Arabic Theatre: An Emerging Site of Hybridity," al-Majdub originated from a small village, Tit, on the plains of Azemmour north of Al-jadida, and then moved to Meknes. His poetry occupies a significant position in Morocco's orality. *Tayeb Saddiki* is the first Moroccan to transpose it to literature, and then to theatrical production.

79. Omar Sayed, Klām al-Ghīwan, 81.

80. Omar Sayed, Klām al-Ghīwan, 31.

81. Omar Sayed, *Klām al-Ghīwan*, 109.

82. Danile Feldman, "Poetry in Question: The Interrogative Lyric of Yeats's Major Poems," Journal of Literature and the History of Ideas 12, no. 1 (January 2014), 91.

83. The opening of a *Malḥūn*-based poem titled *Ḥan wa-shfaq* (Take Pity and Care) by Sidi Qaddur al-'Alamī (1742–1850) as mentioned previously. This piece was reworked by the band and sung by Omar in an extraordinary way.

84. Laila Chafik and Omar Kamili Ben Hamou, interview with Hassan Habibi, in "Nass el-Ghiwane," 2012 Al-Jazeera documentary. Directed by Omar Kamili Ben Hamou. Retrieved from https://www.youtube.com/watch?v=X16qOn1NGmk

85. *Ibid*.

86. *Ibid*.

87. *Ibid*.

88. Laila Chafik and Omar Kamili Ben Hamou, interview with Hassan Habibi, in "Nass el-Ghiwane," 2012 Al-Jazeera documentary. Directed by Omar Kamili Ben Hamou. Retrieved from https://www.youtube.com/watch?v=X16qOn1NGmk

89. See a random conversation between Omar Sayed and Larbi Batma in Maanouni's documentary film *Al-hāl*.

90. See Siham Ghazouli, Hassna Boufalja, *Fi-adhākira: Omar Sayed* [In Memory: Omar Sayed]. Directed by Samir Kass (2009). Retrieved from http://www.dailymotion.com/video/x9xv8v_omar-sayed-nass-al-ghiwane-fi-dakir_music

91. Omar Sayed, *Klām al-Ghīwan*, 48.

92. See *Boujemia Fi-adhākira* [Boujemia In Memory]. Produced by the Moroccan TV Channel 1 (2010), Retrieved from https://www.youtube.com/watch?v=8t9qwvj0k_4

93. Miloud Oualla talking about Boujemia in Rachid Nini's *Nostalgia*. Retrieved from https://www.youtube.com/watch?v=KQVT8R3wU4o

94. See Khalid Amine, *Moroccan Theatre Between East and West* (Le Club du Livre de la Faculté des Lettres et des sciences Humaines de Tétouan, 2000), 113. For further readings on Al-ḥalqa performance and its adaptation and dramatization in the Moroccan context, see Khalid Amine and Marvin Carlson, "Al-ḥalqa in Arabic Theatre: An Emerging Site of Hubridity" in *Theatre Journal*, Volume 60, Number 1, March 2008, pp., 71–85. Hassan Habibi, *Tayeb Saddiki: Ḥayāto Maṣraḥ* [Tayeb Saddiki: A Theater's Life] (Casablanca: Matbaàt Dar al-Nashr, 2011). Khalid Amine, "Crossing Borders: Al-ḥalqa Performance in Morocco from the open Space to the Theatre Building" in *The Drama Review* 45: 2 (Summer 2001), pp. 55–69. Hassan Mniai, *Al-Maṣraḥ al-Iḥtifāli min at-Ta'sīs ilā Ṣinā'at al-Furja* [Festive Theater: from Construction to the Making of Spectacle] (Fes: Publications de la Faculté des Lettres, 1994).

95. Rachid Nini's Nostalgia. Retrieved

from https://www.youtube.com/watch?v=KQVT8R3wU4o

96. See *Fi-adhākira* [In Memory]. Produced by the Moroccan TV Channel 1 (2010), Retrieved from https://www.youtube.com/watch?v=8t9qwvj0k_4

97. See Rachid Nini's *Nostalgia*, a Television program produced by Moroccan TV 2M (2005). Retrieved from https://www.youtube.com/watch?v=KQVT8R3wU4o

98. Mohamed Bouhafa talking about Boujemia in Rachid Nini's *Nostalgia* (2005).

99. Larbi Batma, *Al-raḥīl*, 95.

100. Abdellah Ahagour and Lahcen Ahagour talking about Boujemia in Nini's *Nostalgia* (2005).

101. Opening of a song, titled *zād-al ham* [more worries] by Nass el-Ghiwane sung by Paco.

102. Mary Louise Pratt, *Imperial Eyes: Travel Writing and Transculturation* (London: Routledge, 1992).

103. See Interview with Cherif Rggragui talking about Paco in Imane Taddaout's and Jihane Nouaoui's *Fi-adhākira: Abderrahman Paco* [In Memory: Abderrahman Paco], a TV program produced in 2004. Retrieved from https://www.youtube.com/watch?v=baiKFOW3kF4

104. See Ahmed Radi talking about Paco in *Fi-adhākira* [In Memory].

105. See Abdelaziz Kirouche talking about his brother Paco in *Fi-adhākira* [In Memory].

106. See Ahmed Radi talking about Paco in *Fi-adhākira* [In Memory]. *Zawiya Sidna Blal* is the Gnāwa sanctuary in the city where Gnāwa would meet to initiate new maallems, and to celebrate their *Līlla* as well. It has been erected in Essaouira in honor to Sidna Bilal, the prophet Mohammed's caller for prayers. It has is a special sacred space managed by Gnāwa community whose members possess real Gnāwa lineage. Canonical festive Gnāwa rituals are held during Islamic calendar months of *Sha'bān* and *al-Milūd* (the Prophet's birthday). Outside of these canonical days Gnāwa masters organize *Līlla* at the request of their devotees, primarily for therapy, and also to gain *baraka* (blessings) during life eventful celebrations such as birthdays and weddings, and during other special occasions. These are often smaller scale occasions that last a single evening. Gnāwa also hold a special celebration called *Gassaa* in the *Zawiya* in order to initiate new maallems. During this event the new would-be master needs to perform a complete *Līlla* in the presence of invited Gnāwa masters.

107. See Larbi Riyad talking about Paco in *Fi-adhākira* [In Memory].

108. Brian T. Edwards, *Morocco Bound: Disorienting America's Maghreb, From Casablanca to Marrakech Express* (Durham and London: Duke University Press, 2005).

109. See Abdellatif Khayati, "Picturing the Urban homeless in Casablanca, Moving Worlds: Postcolonial Cities, Africa" 5, no. 1 (2005), 31–32. Quoted in Lhoussain Simour's "Postcolonial Fluid Zones of Possibilities in Mohammed Mrabet's Look and Move On: Retrieving Subalternity and Negotiating Sexuality," *Middle East Critique* 21, no. 1 (Spring 2012), 117–133

110. Rachid Nini, *Nostalgia: Abderrahman Paco*, TV show produced by 2M (June 2003). Retrieved from http://www.dailymotion.com/video/xaud4b_part-2-nostalgia-rend-hommage-a-abd_music

111. The "Living Theatre" Company emerged as one of the most radical groups in theater that directed its artistic performances towards a revolutionary social function. The troupe built its theatrical vision of social, cultural, economic, and historical transformation on a dialectical premise of performance that addressed situated issues of social concerns. In the 1960s, the troupe became an emblematic embodiment of countercultural challenge and aimed at unsettling theatrical boundaries that drew lines of demarcation between actor and character, cast and audience, art and politics. The troupe evolved into a collective ensemble, living and performing together toward the reinvention of a new form of theatrical esthetics founded on the actor's political and physical engagement with theater as means for promoting social change. *Mysteries, The Connection, Antigone, Frankenstein, Paradise Now, the Legacy of Cain*, to cite but a few, are among the works of the troupe.

112. See Larbi Riyad talking about Paco in *Fi-adhākira* [In Memory].

113. See Hassan Habibi talking about Paco in *Fi-adhākira* [In Memory].

114. Extract from *al-homāmi*, a solo sung by Allal at the end of each live concert.

115. Nini, Rachid. "Nostalgia: Allal Yaala," TV show produced by the Moroccan TV

Channel 2M, directed by Abdellatif Talbi (2004). Retrieved from http://www.popscreen.com/v/7x1sI/nostalgia-Allal-3

116. *Ibid.*

117. *Ibid.*

118. *Ibid.*

119. Moulay Driss El-Maarouf, "Local Arts versus Global Terrorism: The Manifestations of Trauma and Modes of Reconciliation in Moroccan Music Festivals," 70. In Lizelle Bisschoff and Stefanie Van de Peer (eds.), *Art and Trauma in Africa: Representations of Reconciliation in Music, Visual Arts, Literature and Film* (London: I. B Tauris & Co. Ltd., 2013), 69–90. *Art and Trauma in Africa* reflects on the various ways of analyzing the ethical responsibility at the heart of an artist's decision to tackle such controversial and painful subjects as global terror, religious fundamentalism and artistic expression. In adopting a multidisciplinary approach to culture, the volume examines a diverse range of art forms such as hip hop, performance, dance, filmic representations and literature.

120. *Ibid.*

121. Michelle Duffy, "Performing identity within a multicultural framework," in *Social and Cultural Geography*, Vol. 6, No. 5, 680 (October 2005), 677–692.

122. Michelle Duffy, "Lines of Drift: Festival Participation and Performing a Sense of Place," in *Popular Music*, Vol. 9, Issue 1, 52 (January 2000), 51–64.

123. Ted Swedenburg, "Hamid El Gnawi/Saha Koyo," (January 15th, 200), retrieved from *http://www.popmatters.com/review/elgnawihamid-saha/*, edited by PopMatters (1999–2014).

124. Monserrat C. Vallbona et al., "The meaning of cultural festivals: Stakeholders perspectives," in *International Journal of Cultural Policy*, Vol. 13, Issue 1 (February 2007):103–122.

125. Stuart Hall, "The Local and the Global: Globalization and Ethnicity," 27, in Anthony D. King (ed.) *Culture, Globalization and the World-System: Contemporary Conditions for the Representation of Identity* (Minnesota: University of Minnesota Press, 1997), 19–39.

126. Aomar Boum, "Youth, Political Activism and the Festivalization of Hip-Hop Music in Morocco." In Bruce Maddy-Weitzman and Daniel Zisenwine (Eds.) *Contemporary Morocco: State, Politics and Society under Mohammed V*, 167 (Oxon and New York: Routledge, 2013), 161–177.

127. *Ibid.*, 169.

128. Rémy Leveau, "Youth Culture and Islamism in the Middle East." In Laura Guazzone (ed.) *The Islamist Dilemma: The Political Role of Islamist Movements in The Contemporary Arab World* (Berkshire: Ithaca Press, 1995), 272.

Conclusion

1. Paul Ricoeur, *Memory, History, Forgetting*, Trans. by Cathleen Blamey and David Pellauer (Chicago and London: University Chicago Press, 2004), 38–39;

2. Ali Abdullatif Ahmida, *Forgotten Voices: Power and Agency in Colonial and Postcolonial Libya* (New York: Taylor & Francis Publishing, 2005), 56.

3. Valerie K. Orlando, *Francophone Voices of the "New" Morocco in Film and Print* (New York: Palgrave Macmillan, 2009), 111.

4. Leigh Gilmore, *The Limits of Autobiography: Trauma and Testimony* (Ithaca NY: Cornell University Press, 2001), 97. This insightful work on autobiographical writing, according to Lynn Domina, aims to examine the nature of autobiography by analyzing several specific texts that lie, as some would say, outside its boundaries or, as Gilmore would say, at its "limits." Gilmore explores the distinctions between autobiography and fiction, autobiography and biography, and autobiography and history. Her goal, however, is not to reinforce these generic distinctions but rather to arrive at a fuller understanding of autobiography by analyzing how other kinds of texts treat the concerns of autobiography (the construction of the self, the nature of memory, the social position of the subject, etc.) within narratives that somehow permit a writer to speak what cannot be spoken in a conventional autobiography. The theme that links the texts under consideration is trauma, which Gilmore links in her introduction to violence.

Bibliography

Primary sources

Batma, Larbi. *Al-raḥīl*. Casablanca: Dar Toubkal, 5th edition, 2009.
Batma, Larbi. *Al-alam*. Casablanca: Dar Toubkal, 1998.
Sayed, Omar. *Klām al-Ghīwan*. Casablanca: Najah al-Jadida, 2010.

Secondary Sources

Ahmida, Ali Abdullatif. *Forgotten Voices: Power and Agency in Colonial and Postcolonial Libya*. New York: Taylor & Francis, 2005.

Ait Ho, Ibrahim. *Idaāt Hawla al-ūughniya Al Maghribiya* [Few Enlightening Aspects of Moroccan Music]. Tangiers: Shiraa, 1999.

Al Maanouni, Ahmed. *Al-hāl* (Transe), 1981, documentary film.

Al-Ifriqui, Fatima. "Al-majala al-faniya" [Artistic Magazine], produced by the Moroccan Television Channel1, retrieved from https://www.youtube.com/watch?v=E4k0aaxe5q0.

Al-Jirari, Abbass. *Moroccan Culture: its Origins and Particularities* (a paper given at a conference organized by Allal al-Fassi Institute, Rabat, 1999.

Al-Madini, Ahmed. *Al-Kitāba a-Sardiya fi Al-Adab Al-Maghribī Al-Ḥadīth* [Narrativization in Modern Moroccan Literature]. Rabat: Dar al-maarif al-Jadida, 2000: 67–71.

Al-Zahi, Farid. *Al-Ḥikāya wa al-Mutakhayal* [Narrative and the Imaginary] (Casablanca: Afriqiyya al-Sharq, 1991): 137–140. Translated by Tahia Khalid Abdel Nasser as "The "Possessed" or the Symbolic Body," *Alif: Journal of Comparative Poetics* 15, Arab Cinematics: Toward the New and the Alternative (1995): 267–271.

Amine, Khalid and Marvin Carlson. "Al-ḥalqa in Arabic Theater: An Emerging Site of Hybridity," *Theater Journal*, 60, no. 1 (Mar., 2008): 71–85.

Amine, Khalid. "Tangier and Site-Specificity." In Khalid Amine et al. (eds.) *Performong / Picturing Tangier*. Tanger: Altopress, 2007: 63–73.

Amine, Khalid. "Tangiers' Eyes and the Anxiety of Writing Exile." In A. Akbib, K. Amine and A. Mars (eds), *Margins of Theories and Theories of Margins*, Colloquia Series. Tetouan: Abdelmalek Essaadi University, 2003: 159–163.

Amine, Khalid. "Crossing Borders: Al-ḥalqa Performance in Morocco from the open Space to the Theater Building" *The Drama Review* 45. 2 (Summer 2001): 55–69.

Amine, Khalid. *Moroccan Theater between East and West*. Tétouan: Club du Livre de la Faculté des Lettres et des sciences Humaines, 2000.

Anderson, Benedict. *Imagined Communities: Reflections on the Origin and Spread of Nationalism*. London: Verso, 1991.
Andy Bennett, *Cultures of Popular Music*. Bukingham: Open University Press, 2001.
Appadirai, Arjun. *Modernity at Large: Cultural Dimensions of Globalization*. Minnesota: University of Minnesota Press, 1996.
Aqqar, Abdelhamid. "Taṭawur a-Naqd al-Adabī fi al-Maghrib" [the Development of Literary Criticism in Morocco], *Fikr wa Naqd* (1998).
Asad, Talal. "The Concept of Cultural Translation in British Social Anthropology." In *Writing Culture. The Poetics and Politics of Ethnography*, ed. James Clifford and George E. Marcus. Berkeley: University of California Press, 1986: 141–164.
Bahraoui, Hassan. "Al-Ghīwān: Al-aṣl wa Al-ma-āl" [Al-Ghiwane: Roots and Destiny.] In Allal Reggoug et al. (eds.) *Al-ūghinya al-Iḥtijājiya bi al-Maghrib: Mawrūt Majmū'at Nāss Al-Ghīwāne* [Protest Song in Morocco: The Legacy of Nass el-Ghiwane]. Rabat: Publications de L'institut Universitaire, 2013: 7–19.
Bahraoui, Hassan. *Fan Al-'ayṭa fi al-Maghrib: Musāhama li-al ta'rīf.* [Al-'ayṭa music in Morocco: Contribution for Definitions]. Rabat: Ittiḥad Kottab al-Maghrib, 2002.
Bakhtin, Mikhail. *Rabelais and His World*, Trans. Hélène Iswolsky. Indiana: Indiana University Press, 1984.
Belkbir, Abdassamad. "On the Meaning of Popular Culture' (in Arabic)," *Athaqāfa a-sha'biya, Ihdā Rakāiz Wahdat al-Maghrib al-Arabī* (1991), paper presented at the Conference of Nadour, Morocco: pp. 15–27.
Ben Jelloun, Tahar. *Harrouda*. Paris: Denoel, 1973.
Ben Jelloun, Tahar. *la Nuit Sacrée*. Paris: Seuil, 1987.
Ben Jelloun, Tahar. *La reclusion solitaire*. Paris: Denoel, 1976.
Ben Jelloun, Tahar. *Les Yeux Baissés*. Paris: Seuil, 1991.
Benjamin, Walter. "The Work of Art in the Age of Mechanical Reproduction." *Illuminations*. Ed. Hannah Ardent. New York: Schocken, 1985: 217–51.
Bentahar, Ziad. "The Visibility of African Identity in Moroccan Music," *Wasafiri* 25. 1 (2010): 41–48.
Berkey, Jonathan Porter. *The Formation of Islam: Religion and Society in the Near East, 600–1800*. New York: Cambridge University Press, 2003.
Bouhmid, Mohamed. "Innahum yurīdūn Al-'ayṭa ka-ḍajīj li-jamī' al-ḥushūd" [They are planning to turn *Al-'ayṭa* into noisy spectacle for the crowds] *al-Ittiḥad al-Ishtiraki* (15 April 1995).
Boum, Aomar. "Youth, Political Activism and the Festivalization of Hip-Hop Music in Morocco." In Bruce Maddy-Weutzman, Daniel Zisenwine (eds.) *Contemporary Morocco: State, Politics and Society under Mohammmed VI*. Oxon: Routledge, 2013: 161–177.
Brahimi, Denise. "Conversation avec Tahar Ben Jelloun." *Notre Libraire* 103 (1990).
Carter, Paul. "Naming Places." In Bill Ashcroft et al. (eds.) *The Postcolonial Studies Reader*. London: Routledge, 1995: 402–406.
Chafik, Laila and Omar Kamili Ben Hamou. "Nass el-Ghiwane," Al-Jazeera documentary. Directed by Omar Kamili Ben Hamou. 2012. Retrieved from https://www.youtube.com/watch?v=X16qOn1NGmk
Chahidi, Sellam. *Hijra ilā ardi al-aḥlām* [Migration to the Land of Dreams]. Tanger: Infoprint, 1999.
Cherki, Salah. *Musique Marocaine*. Mohammedia: Impr. Fedala, 1981.
Choukri, Mohamed. *For Bread Alone*. Trans. Paul Bowles. London: Peter Owen, 1973.
Ciucci, Alessandra. "Embodying the Countryside in *Aiṭa Ḥaṣbawiya* (Morocco)," *Yearbook for Traditional Music* 44 (2012): 109–128.

Couser, G. Thomas. "The Shape of Death in American Autobiography," *The Hudson Review* 31.1 (Spring, 1978): 53–66.

Crapanzano, Vincent. "Reflections on Hope as a Category of Social and Psychological Analysis," *Cultural Anthropology* 18. 1 (2003): 3–32.

Dahchour, Ghafour. "Fi ad-dakira: Larbi Batma" [In Memory: Larbi Batma,] TV show produced by the Moroccan Television RTM, and directed by Samir Kass (2008), retrieved from https://www.youtube.com/watch?v=lnOYEEAC0Eo.

Dahchour, Ghafour. "Fi-adhākira: Omar Sayed" [In Memory: Omar Sayed]," TV show produced by the Moroccan RTM, and directed by Samir Kass. Retrieved from https://www.youtube.com/watch?v=hUS2hFgPlIk.

Daniels, Stephen and Simon Rycroft. "Mapping the Modern City," *Transactions of the Institute of British Geographers, New Series* 18. 4 (1993): 460–480.

Djik, Van. *A Hand book of Discourse Analysis*. London: Academic Press, 1985.

Duffy, Michelle. "Lines of Drift: Festival Participation and Performing a Sense of Place," *Popular Music* 9. 1 (January 2000): 51–64.

Duffy, Michelle. "Performing identity within a multicultural framework" *Social and Cultural Geography* 6. 5 (October 2005): 677–692.

Eagleton, Terry. *After Theory*. New York: Basic, 2003.

Edwards, Brian T. *Morocco Bound: Disorienting America's Maghreb, From Casablanca to Marrakech Express*. Durham: Duke University Press, 2005.

Eickelman, Dale F. *Moroccan Islam: Tradition and Society in a Pilgrimage Center*. Austin: University of Texas Press, 1976.

El-Khatib, Ibrahim. "La literature Marocaine: L'appropriation du Réel" *Oriente Moderno* 16. 77 (1997): 257–262.

Ellis, Stephen. "Writing Histories of Contemporary Africa," *the Journal of African History* 43. 1 (2002). 1–26.

El-Maarouf, Moulay Driss. "Local Arts versus Global Terrorism: The Manifestations of Trauma and Modes of Reconciliation in Moroccan Music Festivals." In Lizelle Bisschoff and Stefanie Van de Peer (eds.), *Art and Trauma in Africa: Representations of Reconciliation in Music, Visual Arts, Literature and Film*. London: I. B Tauris & Co. Ltd., 2013: 69–90.

El-Outmani, Ismaïl. "Prolegomena to the Study of the "Other" Moroccan Literature," *Research in African Literatures* 28. 3, Arabic Writing in Africa (autumn, 1997): 110–121.

Entelis, John Pierre. *Culture and Counter-culture in Moroccan Politics*. Boston: University Press of America, 1996.

Fanon, Frantz. *The Wretched of the Earth*, trans. C. Farrington. New York: Grove Press. 1963.

Feldman, Danile. "Poetry in Question: The Interrogative Lyric of Yeats's Major Poems," *Journal of Literature and the History of Ideas* 12. 1 (January 2014): 87–105.

Fernandez Parrilla, Gonzalo. "Breaking the Canon: Zafzaf, Laroui and the Moroccan novel" in *From New Values to New Esthetics. Turning Points in Modern Arabic Literature: Postmodernism and Thereafter*, edited by Stephan Guth and Gail Ramsay. Wiesbaden: Verlag, 2011: 75–85.

Fuson, Tim Abdellah. "Musical Imaginging in Morocco: The Voice of the Gnāwa in the Music of Nas al-Ghiwan," Paper read at the Annual meeting of Middle Eastern Studies Association, San Francisco, CA (November 1997).

Geertz, Clifford. *Islam Observed: Religious Development in Morocco and Indonesia*. Chicago: University of Chicago Press. 1968.

Ghazoul, Ferial and Barbara Harlow. (eds.) *The View From Within* (Cairo: American University of Cairo Press, 1994).

Ghazouli, Siham, and Hassna Boufalja, *Fi-adākira: Omar Sayed* [In Memory: Omar Sayed]. Directed by Samir Kass. 2009. Retrieved from http://www.dailymotion.com/video/x9xv8v_omar-sayed-nass-al-ghiwane-fi-dakir_music.

Gilmore, Leigh. *The Limits of Autobiography: Trauma and Testimony*. Ithaca, NY: Cornell Uinveristy Press, 2001.

Goodman, David. "The Space of Africanness: Gnāwa Music and Slave Culture in North Africa." *Journal of Cultural Studies* 5.1 (2003): 35–6.

Goodman, Jane E. "Singers, Saints, and the Construction of Postcolonial Subjectivities in Algeria," *Ethos* 26. 2 (June 1998): 204–228.

Graiouid, Said. "Post-colonial Literature in Morocco: Nation, Identity and Resistance Esthetics." In Driss Maghraoui (ed.) *Revisiting the Colonial Past in Morocco*. London: Routledge, 2013: 220–233.

Guennoun, Abdellah. *Aḥādith 'an al-Adab al-Maghribī al-Ḥadīth* [Issues on Contemporary Moroccan Literature]. Cairo: Arab Literary Center, 1964.

Guettat, Mohammed. *Musique Arabo-Andalouse*. Paris: Editions Fleurs Sociales, 2000.

Habibi, Hassan. *Tayeb Saddiki: Ḥayāto Maṣraḥ* [Tayeb Saddiki: A Theater's life Narrative]. Casablanca: Matba'at Dar al-Nashr, 2011.

Hall, Stuart. "Notes on Deconstructing 'the Popular.'" In *People's History and Socialist Theory*, ed. by Raphael Samuel. London: Routledge & Kegan Paul, 1981: 227–40.

Hall, Stuart. "The Local and the Global: Globalization and Ethnicity." In Anthony D. King (ed.) *Culture, Globalization and the World-System: Contemporary Conditions for the Representation of Identity*. Minnesota: University of Minnesota Press, 1997: 19–39.

Hanoun, Mbarek. *Al-ūghniya Sha'biya Al-Jadīda: Ẓāhirat Nāss el-Ghīwane* [The New Popular Song: Nass el-Ghiwane Phenomenon]. Casablanca: Manchourat Oyoune, 1987.

Hanoun, Mbarek. *āhirat Nāss el-Ghīwān: Tajribat Tahdīth al-ūghniya al-Sha'biya* [Nass el-Ghiwane phenomenon: Towards a Modernization of the Popular Song]. Rabat: Dar al-Amane, 2nd edition, 2007.

Huggan, Graham. *The Postcolonial Exotic: Marketing the Margins* (London: Routledge, 2001).

Jameson, Fredric. "Third-World Literature in the Era of Multinational Capitalism," *Social Text* 15 (Fall 1986): 65–88.

Jibril, Mohamed. "Les Nass Al Ghiwane vus par Ahmed Maanouni," *Lamalif (*1981).

Jusdanis, Gregory. *Belated Modernity and Esthetic Culture: Inventing National Culture*. Minneapolis: University of Minnesota Press, 1991.

Kadawt, Imane. "Fi-adhākira: Boujemaa Ahagour" [In Mmemory: Boujemaa Ahagour]. Produced by the Moroccan TV Channel RTM (2010), Retrieved from https://www.youtube.com/watch?v=8t9qwvj0k_4.

Kapchan, A. Deborah. "Moroccan Female Performers: Defining the Social Body," *The Journal of American Folklore* 107. 423 (1994): 82–105.

Kapchan, A. Deborah. *Gender on the Market: Moroccan Women and the Revoicing of Tradition*. Philadelphia: University of Pennsylvania Press, 1996.

Kapchan, Deborah A. *Traveling Spirit Masters: Moroccan Gnāwa Trance and Music in the Global Marketplace*. Middletown: Wesleyan University Press, 2007.

Khatibi, Abdelkabir. *Le Roman Maghebin*. Paris : Editions F. Maspero, 1979: 27–30. Quoted in Driss Maghraoui, ed. *Revisiting the Colonial Past in Morocco*. London: Routeledge, 2013.

Khayati, Abdellatif. Picturing the Urban homeless in Casablanca, Moving Worlds: Post-colonial Cities, Africa 5. 1 (2005): 31–32. Quoted in Lhoussain Simour's "Postcolonial Fluid Zones of Possibilities in Mohammed Mrabet's Look and Move On: Retrieving Subalternity and Negotiating Sexuality," *Middle East Critique* 21. 1 (Spring 2012): 117–133.

Laâbi, Abdellatif. "Réalités et dilemmes de la culture nationale (I)." *Anfās/Soufles* 4 (1966). Quoted in Alessandra Ciucci's "Embodying the Countryside in *Aiṭa Ḥaṣbawiya* (Morocco)," *Yearbook for Traditional Music* 44 (2012): 109- 128.

Lahmidani, Hamid. *Al-Riwāya al-Maghribiya wa-Ru'yat al-Wāqi' al-Ijtim'ī*. Cairo: Dar al-Thaqafa, 1985.

Laila Chafik and Omar Kamili Ben Hamou, interview with Omar Sayed, in "Nass el-Ghiwane," 2012, Al-Jazeera documentary. Directed by Omar Kamili Ben Hamou. Retrieved from https://www.youtube.com/watch?v=X16qOnlNGmk.

Landau, Carolyn. "My own Little Morocco at Home: a Biographical Account of Migration, Mediation and Music Consumption." In Jason Toynbee's and Byron Dueck's (eds.) *Migrating Music*. Oxen: Routledge, 2011: 38–45,

Lejeune, Philipe. *On Autobiography*. Trans. Katherine Leary. Minneapolis: University of Minnesota Press, 1989.

Leveau, Rémy. "Youth Culture and Islamism in the Middle East." In Laura Guazzone (ed.) *The Islamist Dilema: The Political Role of Islamist Movements in The Contemporary Arab World*. Berkshire: Ithaca Press, 1995: 265–287.

Lopez-Pelaez Casellas, Jesus. "Forms of Exile in the Narrative of Mohamed Choukri." In Monika Reif-Hulser (ed.) *Borderlands: Negotiating boundaries in post-colonial writing*. Amsterdam: Rodopi B.V, 1999: 205–214.

Lowe, Lisa. "Literary Nomadics in Francophone Allegories of Postcolonialism," *Yale French Studies* 1. 82 (1993): 43–61.

Mandel, Barrett John. "Basting the Image with a Certain Liquor: Death in Autobiography," *Soundings: An Interdisciplinary Journal* 57. 2 (Summer 1974): 175–188.

Mbakogu, Ifeyinwa A. "Is There Really a Relationship between Culture and Development?" *Anthropologist*, 6. 1 (2004): 37–43.

Mniai, Hassan. *Al-Maṣraḥ al-Iḥtifāli min at-Ta'sīs ilā Ṣinā'at al-Furja* [Festive Theater: from Construction to the Making of Spectacle]. Fes: Publications de la Faculté des Lettres, 1994.

Moukhlis, Salah. "Deconstructing Home and Exile: The Subversive Politics of Ben Jelloun's *With Downcast Eyes*," *Postcolonial Text* 2. 2 (2006). Accessed 13 Sept. 2010 http://journals.sfu.ca/pocol/index.php/pct/article/view/442/199.

Moukhlis, Salah. "Localized Identity, Universal Experience: Celebrating Mohamed Choukri as a Moroccan Writer." In Khalid Amine, Andrew Hussey and Barry Tharaud (eds.) *Writing Tangier: Conference Proceedings*. Tanger: Imprimerie Altopress, 2005: 73–81.

Muhanna, Elias; "Folk the Kasbah: A Conversation with Omar Sayyed, leader of Nass el-Ghiwane," *Transition* 12. 4 (2003): 132–149.

Nejmi, Hassan. "Aghāni al-Ghīwane: Aswātun Ḥaya min dākhili al-raḥim al-Sha'bī" [The Ghiwani Songs: Live Voices from the Popular Womb]. In Omar Sayed's *Klām al-Ghīwan*. Casablanca: Najah al-Jadida, 2010.

Nejmi, Hassan. *Ghinā' Al-'ayṭa: Al-shi'r Al-shafawī wa al-Mūsīka al-Taqlīdiya fi al-Maghrib* [Singing Al-'ayṭa: Oral Poetry and Traditional Music in Morocco]. Casablanca: Dar Toubkal, Vol. II, 2007.

Nejmi, Hassan. *Ghinā' Al-'ayṭa: Al-shi'r Al-shafawī wa al-Mūsīka al-Taqlīdiya fi al-Maghrib* [Singing Al-'ayṭa: Oral Poetry and Traditional Music in Morocco]. Casablanca: Dar Toubkal, Vol. I, 2007.

Nini, Rachid. "Nostalgia: Abderrahman Paco," TV show produced by the Moroccan TV Channel 2M, and directed by Abdellatif Talbi (June 2003). Retrieved from http://

www.dailymotion.com/video/xaud4b_part-2-nostalgia-rend-hommage-a-abd_music.

Nini, Rachid. "Nostalgia: Allal Yaala," TV show produced by the Moroccan TV Channel 2M, directed by Abdellatif Talbi (2004). Retrieved from http://www.popscreen.com/v/7x1sI/nostalgia-Allal-3.

Nini, Rachid. "Nostalgia: Boujemaa Ahagour," TV show produced by the Moroccan TV Channel 2M, and directed by Abdellatif Talbi (2005). Retrieved from https://www.youtube.com/watch?v=KQVT8R3wU4o.

Oakes, Timothy. "Place and the Paradox of Modernity," *Annals of the Association of American Geographers* 87. 3 (1997): 509–531.

Orlando, Valerie K. *Francophone Voices of the "New" Morocco in Film and Print.* New York: Palgrave Macmillan, 2009.

Prakash, Gyan. "Writing Post-Orientalist Histories of the Third World: Perspectives from Indian Historiography." In Vinayak Chaturvedi's (ed.) *Mapping subaltern studies and the postcolonial.* London: Verso, 2000: 163–190.

Pratt, Mary Louise. *Imperial Eyes: Travel Writing and Transculturation.* London: Routledge, 1992.

Prideaux, Sue. *Edvard Munch: Behind the Scream* (New Haven, Yale University, 2005).

Quayson, Ato. *Postcolonialism: Theory, Practice, or Process.* Blackwell Publishers Ltd., 2000.

Reggoug, Allal et al. (eds.), "Al-Ghīwān: Al-aṣl wa Al-ma-āl," [Al-Ghiwane: Roots and Destiny], in *Al-Ūghinya al-Iḥtijājiya bi al-Maghrib: Mawrūt Majmū'at Nāss Al-Ghīwāne* [Protest Song in Morocco: The Legacy of Nass el-Ghiwane]. Rabat: Publications de L'institut Universitaire, 2013: 7–19.

Richards, David. "Framing identities" in Shirley Chew's and David Richards' (eds.) *A Concise Companion to Postcolonial Literature.* Blackwell Publishing Ltd., 2010: 9–28.

Ricoeur, Paul. *Memory, History, Forgetting,* Trans. by Cathleen Blamey and David Pellauer. Chicago: University Chicago Press, 2004.

Rooke, Tetz. "From Self-made Man to Man-made Self: A Story about Changing Identities." In Annette van Beugen's and Gonzalo Fernández Parrilla's (Coordinators) *Remembering for Tomorrow (*European Cultural Foundation and Escuela de Traductores de Toledo): 19–24

Rooke, Tetz. "Moroccan Autobiography as National Allegory," *Oriente Moderno, Nuova serie* 77. 2/3 (1997): 289–305.

Sabry, Tarik. "Migration as Popular Culture," *European Journal of Cultural Studies* SAGE Publications 8.1 (2005): 5–22.

Sadiq, Abdelhai. *Protest Song Marocain.* Marrakech: Al Watanya, 2006.

Sadiqi, Fatima. "Gender Perception in Moroccan Culture," pp. 169–170 (retrieved from http://www.cmiesi.ma/acmiesi/file/notes/fatima-sadiqi_2.pdf).

Sayed, Omar. *Omar Sayed Raconte Nass el-Ghiwane.* Casablanca: Sirocco, 2011.

Semlali, Hind and Mathias Chaillot. "Omar Sayed: Avec Nass el-Ghiwane nous étions des faibles, et c'était notre force" [Omar Sayed: With Nass el-Ghiwane we were weak and that's where our strenght came out] (June 3rd, 2011). Retrieved from https://casablanca.madeinmedina.com/fr/article-omar-sayed-avec-nass-el-ghiwane-nous-etions-des-faibles-et-cetait-notre-force-271.html.

Shannon, Jonathan H. "Emotion, Performance, and Temporality in Arab Music: Reflections on *Ṭarab,*" Cultural Anthropology 18. 1 (Feb., 2003): 72–98.

Shannon, Jonathan H. "Performing al-Andalus, Remembering al-Andalus: Mediterranean Soundings from Mashriq to Maghrib," *The Journal of American Folklore* 120. 477 (Summer, 2007): 308–334.

Shuker, Roy. *Understanding Popular Music*, 2nd edition. London: Routledge, 1994.
Simon, Frith. "Towards and Esthetic of Pupular Music." In Richard Leppert and McClary, Susan (ed.) *Music and Society: The Politics of Composition, Performance and Reception*. Cambridge: Cambridge University Press, 1987: 133–150.
Simour, Lhoussain. "The Postcolonial in Motion: *Hijra ilā ardi al-ahlām* and the Construction of Postcolonial Counterdiscourse," *Middle East Journal of Culture and Communication* 3 (2010): 289–311.
Storey, John. *An Introduction Guide to Cultural Theory and Popular Culture*. Georgia: Grorgia University Press. 1993.
Swedenburg, Ted. "Hamid El Gnawi/Saha Koyo," (January 15th, 200), retrieved from http://www.popmatters.com/review/elgnawihamid-saha/, edited by Pop Matters (1999–2014).
Taddaout, Imane and Nouaoui, Jihane. *Fi a-dākira: Abderrahman Paco* [In Memory: Abderrahman Paco], a TV program produced in 2004. Retrieved from https://www.youtube.com/watch?v=baiKFOW3kF4.
Tanoukhi, Nirvana. "Rewriting Political Commitment for an International Canon: Paul Bowles's *For Bread Alone* as Translation for Choukri's *Al-Khubz Al-Hāfi*," *Research in African Literatures* 34. 2 (2003): 127–144.
Vallbona, Monserrat C. et al. "The meaning of cultural festivals: Stakeholders perspectives," *International Journal of Cultural Policy* 13. 1 (February 2007): 103–122.
Williams, Raymond. *Keywords: A Vocabulary of Culture and Society*. London: Fontana, 1983.
Zahiri, Mohammed. "La Figure du Pére Dans Le Roman Marocain." *Revue Internationale de Langue et de Litterature* 34 (1987): 107–127.

Index

Abdelaziz Tahiri, Moulay Abdelaziz 98, 111, 118, 128, 138, 159, 163, 185
Abderrahman Kirouche, Paco 3, 114, 115, 118, 120, 128, 138, 148, 150, 159, 160, 161, 162, 171, 185
Ahagour Boujemaa, Boujemia 3, 115, 117, 118, 119, 128, 150, 153, 154, 155, 156, 157, 158, 159, 185
'Aisāwa 97, 122, 129, 173
Al-Alam 4, 40, 84, 85, 86, 87, 88, 90, 91, 180
Al-'ayṭa 17, 106, 107, 109, 115
Al-Harrāz 117, 122, 137, 138, 154, 156, 187
Al-Khubz Al-Hāfi 54, 55
Allah Yā Mūlāna 112, 137, 185, 187
Allal Yaala 3, 5, 111, 114, 115, 118, 120, 121, 148, 150, 164, 165, 166, 167, 185, 188
Al-Mādī Fāt 135, 185, 187
Al-raḥīl 4, 11, 13, 15, 35, 36, 40, 41, 42, 43, 44, 45, 47, 48, 49, 50, 51, 52, 53, 54, 55, 57, 58, 59, 60, 63, 64, 65, 66, 67, 79, 81, 84, 90, 92, 110, 159, 179
al-Ṣaḍma 129
alternative music 3, 13, 20, 99, 132, 174, 177, 182
al-Ūghniya 13, 118
Amazīgh, Tamazīght 8, 9, 10, 12, 14, 16, 97, 104, 109, 115, 116, 140, 151, 153, 189
artists 1, 2, 3, 5, 17, 20, 21, 36, 38, 40, 43, 44, 46, 55, 57, 58, 66, 67, 69, 71, 75, 79, 80, 86, 89, 90, 91, 94, 95, 97, 102, 105, 106, 109, 110, 111, 112, 115, 116, 117, 118, 132, 136, 138, 153, 154, 158, 159, 161, 162, 163, 166, 167, 168, 169, 170, 171, 172, 173, 174, 176, 181, 183
a-Ṣamṭa, Samta 142, 187, 188
audience(s) 12, 96, 107, 109, 110, 112, 117, 118, 123, 128, 138, 139, 146, 147, 153, 163, 165, 166, 173, 174, 178
authority 2, 19, 25, 28, 33, 52, 55, 63, 65, 71, 72, 87, 100, 101, 102, 103, 113, 114, 134, 136, 149, 151, 158, 161, 176, 180

Banjo 62, 121, 165, 166, 185, 188
Batma, Larbi, Rachid and Mohamed 2, 3, 4, 5, 11, 13, 15, 18, 19, 34, 35, 36, 37, 38, 39, 40, 41, 42, 43, 44, 45, 46, 47, 48, 49, 50, 51, 52, 53, 54, 55, 56, 57, 58, 59, 60, 61, 62, 63, 64, 65, 66, 67, 68, 69, 70, 71, 72, 73, 74, 75, 76, 77, 78, 79, 80, 81, 82, 83, 84, 85, 86, 87, 88, 89, 90, 91, 92, 94, 96, 94, 98, 109, 110, 111, 113, 114, 115, 116, 117, 118, 120, 125, 128, 147, 148, 150, 154, 156, 157, 159, 163, 165, 166, 177, 178, 179, 180, 181, 183, 185, 188
Beatles 16, 100, 101, 110
bendīr 58, 109, 121, 122, 129, 165, 166, 185, 188

cancer 13, 40, 58, 69, 87, 88
canonical, non-canonical 21, 26, 28, 32, 104
Casablanca 2, 3, 4, 19, 35, 36, 43, 46, 48, 49, 50, 51, 52, 60, 66, 67, 70, 76, 86, 88, 101, 108, 112, 113, 114, 117, 118, 135, 138, 148, 150, 152, 156, 157, 158, 163, 167, 169, 177, 187
colonialism 23, 28, 31, 52, 70, 82, 86, 100, 114
culture(s) 1, 2, 4, 7, 8, 9, 10, 11, 12, 15, 18, 20, 23, 26, 27, 30, 31, 39, 41, 48, 55, 56, 58, 62, 65, 72, 81, 82, 83, 84, 93, 97, 99, 100, 101, 102, 103, 104, 105, 107, 108, 109, 112, 115, 116, 122, 123, 124, 125, 126, 134, 136, 139, 149, 160, 161, 169, 170, 174, 175, 177, 181, 182, 183, 189

dārija 7, 10, 14, 58, 106, 109, 123, 124, 128, 135, 139, 153
discourse 4, 11, 12, 18, 20, 23, 24, 25, 26,

27, 31, 32, 33, 41, 44, 46, 47, 48, 49, 51, 54, 55, 56, 60, 65, 71, 75, 76, 77, 78, 80, 83, 86, 92, 95, 97, 100, 106, 108, 125, 130, 131, 135, 138, 140, 141, 144, 145, 149, 150, 170, 172, 174, 176, 177, 178, 179, 180, 192, 183
Dowār 35, 36, 60, 62, 64

Essaada 61, 62, 68, 153

family 4, 5, 14, 27, 29, 35, 37, 43, 46, 48, 49, 54, 61, 62, 63, 64, 65, 67, 69, 70, 72, 74, 112, 113, 115, 116, 119, 134, 151, 152, 153, 156, 157, 158, 159, 163, 164, 166, 167, 183
Fīn Ghādi Biya Khūya 146, 185, 187
folk, folklore 13, 15, 20, 53, 58, 75, 95, 96, 97, 105, 109, 110, 116, 121, 124, 126, 129, 136, 139, 140, 154, 175
fusion music 167, 171, 172, 173, 174, 176, 182

Ghīr Khodūni 154, 163, 185, 186, 187, 188
global 11, 12, 16, 20, 27, 49, 100, 101, 102, 139, 161, 163, 167, 168, 170, 173, 174, 175, 181
Gnāwa 1, 97, 109, 115, 121, 126, 127, 128, 129, 130, 159, 160, 161, 162, 163, 164, 171, 172, 173

Ḥamādsha 97, 122, 129
Hannoun Mbarek 124
Hassan Bahraoui 110, 118
Hassan Nejmi 3, 4, 15, 94, 95, 107
Ḥay Moḥammādi 3, 5, 35, 38, 69, 70, 95, 113, 114, 115, 116, 117, 148, 151, 152, 154, 155, 157, 164, 166, 177
Hendrix, Jimi 162

independence, post-independence 3, 11, 18, 21, 23, 24, 27, 28, 29, 30, 31, 32, 40, 41, 44, 48, 52, 53, 57, 69, 70, 80, 81, 92, 79, 99, 101, 102, 103, 104, 105, 108, 110, 112, 113, 114, 115, 116, 131, 132, 133, 134, 140, 143, 144, 145, 149, 151, 155, 165, 177, 179
Islam 8, 9, 12, 21, 23, 28, 91, 102, 105, 119, 120, 122

Jīl Jilāla 1, 109, 118, 132, 137, 138, 163, 182

Klām al-Ghīwān 15, 16, 38, 94

Lamshāhab 36, 109, 132, 182
lyrics 3, 11, 13, 15, 17, 18, 43, 74, 80, 83, 94, 95, 99, 103, 106, 107, 109, 110, 112, 114, 117, 118, 119, 124, 125, 126, 127, 128, 129, 130, 133, 135, 136, 138, 139, 141, 146, 166, 168, 171, 188

Mā-hamūnī 109, 110, 117, 186
malḥūn 1, 10, 97, 109, 119, 136, 137, 138, 160, 188
Maṣrah Ennās 117
melody 11, 14, 17, 20, 97, 103, 108, 109, 112, 119, 120, 121, 122, 125, 126, 128, 129, 136, 139, 141, 147, 148, 153, 161, 163, 165, 166, 171
memory 12, 13, 14, 16, 27, 30, 33, 40, 44, 45, 47, 48, 50, 52, 55, 56, 59, 65, 70, 72, 74, 76, 78, 80, 83, 86, 87, 90, 91, 92, 99, 102, 108, 110, 111, 115, 116, 121, 126, 136, 137, 148, 149, 150, 154, 170, 178, 179, 180, 181
Mohamed Choukri 21, 40, 42, 47, 54, 55, 56, 59, 63, 71
Mohamed Zafzaf 21, 32, 40, 42, 47, 56, 59, 60
mother 14, 16, 58, 59, 61, 63, 64, 71, 72, 76, 79, 91, 116, 125, 143, 151, 152, 153, 155, 166
musical bands 19, 40, 74, 84, 100, 157, 159, 163, 170
musical genre 10, 99, 174, 176, 177
musical instruments 17, 99, 106, 120, 128, 161, 165, 174, 181
musical styles 3, 12, 20, 37, 94, 95, 100, 105, 106, 109, 136, 138, 157, 167, 168, 170, 172, 178, 181, 183
musicians 3, 12, 20, 35, 43, 46, 66, 105, 109, 126, 127, 128, 130, 138, 149, 160, 161, 162, 164, 165, 166, 168, 169, 171, 172, 173, 174, 175, 176, 181

Nāyḍa 20, 168, 170, 171, 174, 175, 176, 182
neighborhood 2, 5, 17, 35, 38, 39, 68, 69, 70, 72, 74, 86, 95, 112, 113, 114, 115, 116, 139, 151, 152, 153, 154, 155, 156, 164, 165, 166, 167, 169, 176

Omar Sayed 3, 5, 15, 38, 58, 68, 73, 94, 98, 101, 108, 111, 113, 114, 115, 117, 118, 120, 121, 134, 147, 148, 150, 151, 152, 153, 155, 156, 157, 165, 182, 185, 188
Oulād al-Masnawi 35
Oulād Bouziri 36, 59, 63, 72, 74, 76

performance(s) 11, 12, 20, 37, 49, 50, 51, 57, 67, 79, 81, 84, 95, 96, 97, 103, 105, 107, 109, 117, 118, 119, 121, 122, 123, 125, 127, 137, 138, 153, 155, 157, 163, 169, 171, 172, 173, 174, 175, 178, 181, 182
poetry 1, 2, 6, 10, 13, 15, 19, 20, 24, 36, 37,

38, 39, 43, 54, 57, 59, 75, 80, 83, 84, 85, 86, 88, 91, 96, 97, 105, 106, 107, 109, 110, 111, 113, 116, 119, 121, 124, 125, 128, 136, 137, 138, 139, 140, 141, 143, 144, 145, 146, 147, 156, 157, 158, 160, 177, 183, 188
politics 1, 3, 8, 9, 12, 13, 17, 18, 19, 20, 21, 23, 24, 25, 26, 30, 31, 32, 33, 34, 37, 41, 44, 45, 46, 48, 53, 54, 55, 56, 57, 80, 69, 70, 71, 74, 77, 80, 83, 84, 86, 92, 97, 99, 100, 101, 102, 103, 104, 107, 109, 110, 111, 113, 114, 115, 117, 121, 125, 126, 131, 132, 133, 134, 135, 136, 138, 140, 141, 142, 143, 144, 145, 146, 147, 149, 157, 158, 167, 168, 170, 172, 174, 175, 177, 178, 179, 180, 181
postcolonialism 3, 4, 10, 13, 16, 17, 18, 19, 20, 21, 24, 26, 30, 31, 33, 34, 37, 39, 40, 41, 42, 43, 44, 45, 47, 48, 49, 50, 53, 54, 55, 56, 57, 58, 60, 65, 77, 78, 79, 80, 82, 83, 84, 86, 89, 101, 103, 108, 110, 113, 125, 126, 130, 131, 132, 133, 134, 135, 136, 140, 141, 143, 145, 146, 147, 149, 150, 156, 159, 163, 175, 177, 178, 179, 180, 182, 183
post-independence 3, 11, 18, 21, 24, 31, 32, 40, 44, 48, 52, 57, 81, 103, 108, 115, 116, 131, 132, 133, 134, 140, 144, 177, 179

religion 1, 8, 9, 18, 23, 31, 32, 54, 55, 63, 64, 65, 97, 112, 119, 121, 122, 125, 126, 129, 134, 139, 140, 141, 162, 169, 170, 173, 174, 183
rhythm(s) 3, 10, 11, 14, 17, 18, 20, 38, 74, 93, 95, 97, 99, 105, 106, 107, 108, 109, 115, 116, 119, 120, 121, 122, 123, 125, 126, 127, 128, 129, 133, 148, 153, 154, 155, 160, 161, 163, 165, 166, 168, 171, 172, 173, 181, 183
Rolling Stones 4, 16, 100, 101
Rowād al-khashaba 70, 153, 156
rural 2, 8, 13, 14, 17, 37, 38, 42, 44, 45, 46, 59, 60, 62, 65, 67, 106, 108, 115, 116, 120, 125, 128, 148

Saint 35, 61, 121, 127
Sentīr 78, 109, 121, 128, 129, 130, 159, 161, 162, 163, 164, 185, 188
Ṣiniya 6, 14, 112, 117, 118, 165, 158, 187, 188

tagnāwit 5, 126, 160, 161, 162, 163
Tayeb Saddiki 96, 117, 118, 137, 154, 156
ṭbal 127, 153
ṭbilāt 109, 129, 166, 185, 188
text, textual 11, 13, 15, 16, 17, 18, 19, 20, 22, 23, 25, 26, 27, 28, 29, 30, 31, 32, 33, 34, 39, 40, 41, 42, 43, 44, 45, 64, 48, 49, 50, 51, 52, 53, 55, 56, 58, 59, 60, 63, 64, 65, 67, 71, 72, 74, 75, 76, 77, 78, 79, 81, 82, 83, 86, 87, 89, 95, 104, 105, 106, 107, 109, 110, 111, 115, 123, 131, 134, 136, 137, 138, 140, 149, 158, 172, 175, 179, 180, 182
theater 2, 38, 61, 62, 68, 70, 74, 75, 116, 117, 138, 149, 153, 154, 156, 162, 165, 182, 187
translation 6, 42, 58, 124, 144, 156
traveling 5, 30, 52, 58, 65, 67, 74, 76, 81, 84, 89, 103, 122, 157, 158, 162, 172
tribes 59, 63, 115, 157, 164
troubadours 67, 95, 124, 127, 140, 154, 157, 158

underground 4, 10, 13, 19, 32, 33, 42, 46, 48, 49, 50, 51, 52, 53, 168, 179
urban 1, 8, 19, 42, 44, 45, 46, 59, 97, 100, 104, 106, 113, 116, 129, 152, 174

vernacular, Moroccan 1, 2, 7, 10, 16, 36, 42, 58, 92, 106, 107, 123, 124, 135, 139, 140, 143, 168, 171, 173

Wāsh Ḥnā Hūma Ḥnā 17, 185, 187

Yā Banī Insān 117, 185

Zajal, Zajal poetry 36, 39, 62, 75, 84, 92, 119

www.ingramcontent.com/pod-product-compliance
Lightning Source LLC
Chambersburg PA
CBHW032055300426
44116CB00007B/757
* 9 7 8 1 4 7 6 6 6 4 1 4 9 *